MW00343633

Revenue Management for Hospitality and Tourism

Patrick Legohérel, Elisabeth Poutier

and Alan Fyall

 **Goodfellow Publishers Ltd**

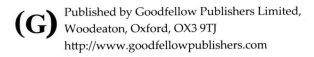

Published by Goodfellow Publishers Limited,
Woodeaton, Oxford, OX3 9TJ
http://www.goodfellowpublishers.com

British Library Cataloguing in Publication Data: a catalogue record for this
title is available from the British Library.

Library of Congress Catalog Card Number: on file.

ISBN: 978-1-908999-49-8

Copyright © Patrick Legohérel, Elisabeth Poutier and Alan Fyall, 2013

All rights reserved. The text of this publication, or any part thereof, may not
be reproduced or transmitted in any form or by any means, electronic or
mechanical, including photocopying, recording, storage in an information
retrieval system, or otherwise, without prior permission of the publisher or
under licence from the Copyright Licensing Agency Limited. Further details
of such licences (for reprographic reproduction) may be obtained from the
Copyright Licensing Agency Limited, of Saffron House, 6–10 Kirby Street,
London EC1N 8TS.

All trademarks used herein are the property of their repective owners, The
use of trademarks or brand names in this text does not imply any affiliation
with or endorsement of this book by such owners.

 Design and typesetting by P.K. McBride, www.macbride.org.uk

Printed by Marston Book Services, www.marston.co.uk

Cover design by Cylinder, www.cylindermedia.com

Contents

Boxes

Figures

Tables

Preface

This book provides hospitality and tourism professionals and students with a primer in the application of revenue management techniques. This is a welcome addition to the learning resources in hospitality and tourism. With our customers making more informed choices and our industry becoming more competitive, revenue management is becoming an increasingly important topic in the hospitality and tourism industry.

Prices continue to fluctuate up and down; something that remains a mystery and a source of great confusion to most consumers. Hospitality and tourism companies are carefully managing the 'game' of revenue management in order to sustain the growth of revenue and profit. Part 1 of this book provides the reader with a thorough overview of the concepts and techniques underlying revenue management implementation in the hospitality and tourism industry.

Part 2, meanwhile, includes many contributions from revenue managers, consultants and academics from around the world, with both experience in and a passion for revenue management. Together, these contributions provide the reader with a comprehensive and contemporary review of revenue management issues in a series of sectoral settings. These include forecasting, customer relationship management and revenue management practices in the cruising, car rental, restaurant, heritage attraction, and theme park sectors of hospitality and tourism, in a number of regions and countries around the world. One such example relates to the exponential growth of the hotel industry in China and the implied need for hotel groups and independent hotels to implement revenue management processes and tools to improve their efficiency and performance. Key performance indicators (including REVPAR and others) are being watched carefully on a daily basis (and almost every minute!) by hotel chain managers and local entrepreneurs.

To survive and prosper in hospitality and tourism, students and professionals must be: (1) aware of the basic concepts of revenue management; (2) suitably qualified to implement revenue management tools and techniques; and (3) kept updated in order to keep improving the efficiency and performance of their business.

I want to congratulate the contributing authors for having produced such an important piece of work, which without doubt will be welcomed by students and professionals in equal measure.

Kaye Chon, Ph.D.
Dean, School of Hotel & Tourism Management
The Hong Kong Polytechnic University

Acknowledgements

We are grateful to the many academics and practitioners who helped to make *Revenue Management for Hospitality and Tourism* a reality. In particular, we would like to thank Tim Goodfellow and Sally North of Goodfellow Publishers Limited for their support and to Professor Kaye Chon who kindly contributed the preface to the book. *Revenue Management for Hospitality and Tourism* also benefited from the generous contributions of those listed below who were willing to share their expertise and who took their valuable time to provide us with such high quality contributions to the book. Our gratitude is most sincere, thank you.

Jad Aboukhater, Carlton Hotel, Cannes, France

Julie Adam, America & Caribbean - Corsairfly, Paris, France

François Albenque, CDiscount, France

David Cretin, Europcar, France

Stephane Gauthier, Best Western, France

Olivier Glasberg, Kuoni Travel, France

Amy Gregory, Rosen College of Hospitality Management, University of Central Florida, USA

Huimin Gu, School of Tourism Management, Beijing International Studies University, China

Cindy Heo, Hong Kong Polytechnic University, SAR China

Christophe Imbert, Sabre Airline Solutions, France

Kelly Kaak, Rosen College of Hospitality Management, University of Central Florida, USA

Sarah Kamensky, Oxford Brookes University, UK

Anna Leask, Edinburgh Napier University, UK

Ady Milman, Rosen College of Hospitality Management, University of Central Florida, USA

Pascal Niffoi, Revenue Management Expert, Apex Conseil, France

SS Padhi, Swiss Federal Institute of Technology, Zurich, Switzerland

Emmanuel Scuto, WeYield Consulting, France

David Selby, Independent Cruise Consultant, UK

Frederic Specklin, Air France, France

Frederic Toitot, ACCOR Hospitality, France

Kate Varini, Oxford Brookes University, UK

Xuan (Lorna) Wang, Middlesex University, UK

Paul Whitelaw, Victoria University, Australia

Larry Yu, School of Business, The George Washington University, USA

Introduction

Through our experiences as consumers, each one of us has faced the phenomenon of price multiplicity and variation: when we enquire about the cost of a hotel room or air ticket, the prices that we are offered seem to be constantly and erratically changing. Many people have, in an aircraft or a train, discovered that the passenger to the right had paid half as much for the ticket as they had paid themselves ... while at the same time, the passenger on the left had paid almost double, and all this for a service which appears to be exactly the same! The consumers (passengers) are astonished and simply do not understand how this situation could have arisen. Is there a pilot (manager) in this plane (company)? Yes, of course there is, and these manoeuvres (sales and pricing decisions) are carried out with increasing skill and precision. New pilots have appeared throughout hospitality and tourism: they are called yield managers or revenue managers.

Let us go beyond the consumer's (understandable) view that prices are fluctuating and consider the complex mechanism of commercial decision making and the revenue management function, which brings together various aspects of marketing management (segmentation, pricing, distribution, etc.) and other issues (turnover optimization, capacity and sales volume management, budget analysis, etc.).

The purpose of this book is to examine the revenue management function and to explain the mechanism of commercial decision making, from the definition of segmentation grids and pricing policy to the final decision to accept or refuse to sell a service at a given price on a given date. The revenue management function, always viewed as integrated to the marketing field, is central to hospitality and tourism companies and, from an operational point of view, reports more often than not to senior management.

The book incorporates many contributions from practitioners, academics, and revenue management experts from across the hospitality and tourism industry, including contributions that cover transport, accommodation, tour operations and car rentals. It has deliberately been written in a very engaging, accessible and student-friendly manner to facilitate learning, with a rich supply of contemporary case material included throughout the book. The case material has been carefully selected to provide the reader with an overview, as up-to-date as possible, of what is really going on in each sector, as well as providing a strong international coverage with case material originating from the USA, Europe and Asia.

The first chapter in Part I presents the foundations of yield/revenue management: its origins, principles, and the evolution of the revenue management function. Chapter 2 deals with the components of revenue management, from marketing fundamentals (customer analysis, segmentation, definition of the pricing policy, etc.) to the more specific elements (performance indicators and optimization levers). Chapter 3, meanwhile, presents the revenue management function: its place in the company and interactions with other functions, the revenue manager's missions, the required skills set, and the function profile. Chapter 4 then details the revenue manager's operational approach: data management, forecasting, and decision making regarding capacity allocation and optimization, while Chapter 5 focuses on presenting the revenue management system and its implementation in the company.

Thereafter, Part 2 provides several examples of the application of revenue management systems in various sectors and types of companies across the wider hospitality and tourism industry. The book concludes with a short synthesis of those issues of particular significance for the future management of revenue in the dynamic industry that is hospitality and tourism.

Patrick Legohérel and Elisabeth Poutier, Angers, France

Alan Fyall, Orlando, USA

February 2013

About the editors

Patrick Legohérel is Professor at the School of Hotel and Tourism Management (ESTHUA – UFR ITBS), and member of the GRANEM Research Department, University of Angers, France. His work has appeared in academic journals such as the *European Journal of Marketing, Journal of Retailing and Consumer Services, Journal of Global Marketing, Journal of Travel and Tourism Marketing, International Journal of Hospitality Management* and *Journal of Hospitality and Tourism Research*. He is Co-Guest Editor of the *Journal of Travel and Tourism Marketing* Special Issue on Revenue Management (2004 & 2014). He also serves on the editorial boards of *Journal of Travel and Tourism Marketing, Journal of Global Marketing, Journal of Vacation Marketing, Journal of Destination Marketing and Management*, and *Journal of China Tourism Research*, while he reviews regularly for other academic journal such as *Tourism Management*.

Elisabeth Poutier is Professor of Marketing at ESSCA School of Management, France, where she is co-director of a dual Master's Degree in Revenue Management and Service Marketing awarded by ESSCA and the State University of Angers. She holds her PhD degree in Management from the Conservatoire National des Arts & Métiers (CNAM) in Paris. In addition to her research in the fields of service marketing and revenue management, she also has a keen interest in corporate social responsibility, ethics and fair trade, and is a member of the ESSCA Research Centre in Social and Solidarity-Based Economy (CeRESS).

Alan Fyall is Professor at Rosen College of Hospitality Management, University of Central Florida, USA. He has published widely in his fields of expertise and is the author of over 100 articles, book chapters and conference papers as well as 14 books. He is Co-Editor of Elsevier's *Journal of Destination Marketing & Management* and Co-Editor of *Contemporary Cases Online*, while he also serves on the editorial boards of *Annals of Tourism Research, Journal of Heritage Tourism, International Journal of Tourism Research, Anatolia* and *Regional Statistics*.

Part I

Revenue Management Concepts and Techniques

1 The Emergence of Yield Management

Patrick Legohérel, Elisabeth Poutier and Alan Fyall

Learning outcomes

After reading this chapter, you should be able to:

■ Understand the historical development of yield/revenue management since its origins in the 1980s.

■ Define revenue management and explain its underlying principles.

■ Understand how revenue management techniques have greatly expanded and affected various application sectors.

■ Appreciate the concepts of Total Revenue Management and Revenue Integrity, which are representative of the evolution of revenue management towards a more general business management (pricing, client relationship, distribution etc.) of hospitality and tourism.

■ The origin of yield management

The foundations of yield/revenue management were laid during the 1980s, whether viewed from an academic or managerial perspective. The first studies, including those of Littlewood (1972), introduced the notion of revenue maximization for a given capacity rather than the maximization of the occupancy rates of an aircraft (i.e. number of passengers).

From a managerial perspective, the emergence of yield management is associated with the evolution of the airline industry in the United States at the end of the 1970s. Deregulation in the sector brought in by the Airline Deregulation Act of 1978 led to the development of numerous companies, thus creating a situation of strong competition. In this context, players tend to launch price wars. Price cutting, the weapon most rapidly set in motion, enables companies to recapture or keep their market share points. This tactic, however, tends to be followed by an identical action from competitors. A price war is then set in motion. The short-term, life-saving solution proves to be destructive in the medium and long term for most of the players. In this context, yield management contributes to avoiding a price war completely or partially. Massive price-cutting exercises are then replaced by finely tuned price variations which are better adapted to the clients' profiles, sales time periods, and product types. These thoughts then led to the emergence of yield management during the air transport crisis in the United States. Operators went progressively from the logic of optimization of occupancy rates to that of optimization of the revenue generated by the sales made, without trying to fill the plane 'at any cost'.

The development of Global Distribution Systems (GDSs) during the same period facilitated the application of yield management techniques and contributed to their spread. Thus, American Airlines is presented as the company which used the first yield management methods, taking advantage of Sabre, its computerized distribution system.

■ Principles of yield management

☐ Principles

Yield/revenue management rests on the principle of strong price variation adapted to the market context (i.e. demand intensity, demand type, competitors' practices). It contributes to the protection of high-contributing clients, while enabling access at more attractive prices in off-peak periods or for bookings made long before the booking date (early booking). The system presupposes a thorough client segmentation, which integrates the value given by the client to the service ('target valuing') and the consumers' sensitivity to price and quality.

A more finely-tuned selection level related to the practices of yield management consists of giving priority to high-contributing clients who will accept higher prices, rather than trying to serve all clients. It thus marks the end of the 'first come, first served' system. Henceforth, clients are selected according to their profile and their potential contribution, and the door is always kept open for the best clients. In this context, and in order to enable a genuine consumer price reaction, service fares are fixed in line with the demand analysis.

In addition, revenue management as a decision-making tool contributes to a partial reduction of the risk inherent in any business decision, as it is based on the accumulation of data (past, present, and future). The role and business skills of the revenue manager or of the sales personnel remain essential, and complement the real support provided by the computerized decision-making tools.

☐ Definition

Yield/revenue management is a sophisticated type of supply-and-demand management which acts simultaneously on prices and available capacity. It is the process whereby the best service is allocated to the best client at the best price and the best time (Smith, Leimkuhler, Darrow & Samules, 1992). This specific approach to dynamic pricing management enables a better management of capacity in order to maximise the overall proceeds, or yield. It defines yield/revenue management as a set of techniques which serve one principle: capacity management leading to a service company's revenue maximization.

☐ Yield management or revenue management

The term *yield* implies a return for effort or investment. In the air transport sector, where yield management originated, the term corresponds to the management techniques that enable the maximization of proceeds per passenger and kilometre (passenger-kilometre). In practice, the terms *yield management* and *revenue management* appear to be used without any real distinction between the terms.

Revenue management resides on the margins of various disciplines such as marketing, information technology, finance, or the sales function. Traditionally, it is found in the marketing and sales domains. The integration of what can be called the 'yield spirit' and the choices made regarding the practice of yield management initially concern the company's strategic orientation. Yield management is not a strategy in itself; rather, it is integrated within the marketing strategy of which it constitutes a major element. Hence, the major orientations regarding revenue management originate in decisions taken at senior management levels, whether in a medium-size company or a large group. Revenue managers are usually found in a chain of command that links them directly to executive management, to whom they report.

■ Service specifications and fixed-capacity management

The development of revenue management techniques rests on a preliminary observation: service companies face the double constraint brought by service specificity (intangibles) and the obligation to sell a number of products which is defined by company capacity (fixed capacity) rather than by market-stated demand.

☐ ## Service intangibility

Service activities are characterised by one major feature: the partial or total intangibility of the service. The service may not be stored. Its value becomes null if it is not commercialised or sold the day the service is realised: an empty seat as a plane takes off or a billboard free of advertising at a particular moment, or time taken, are wasted products. Service sales constraints are thus inscribed within issues regarding mastery of the space-and-timing pair. Any service element (whether billboard square meters, seconds of advertising on TV or radio, aircraft seats, hotel rooms, rental cars available at a precise moment) simply must be sold when the sale is realised. The service cannot be stored or postponed.

☐ ## Fixed capacity (inventory)

Service providers must face yet another constraint: the set of sales units, called capacity or inventory, is fixed. This lack of flexibility is more or less evident: for example, in the air transport or hotel business sectors, you may neither remove an empty seat at take-off, nor make extra passengers travel standing up, nor add seats if demand is strong. Capacity may be more flexible though, for instance when renting space for offices or reception rooms. In all cases, unsold units or unsatisfied demand because of insufficient capacity constitute lost revenue for the company. The sales effort thus has to be placed, for each service realisation, on a given number of units for sale (seats on a plane, rooms in a hotel, etc.) and neither more nor less.

Furthermore, certain sectors, such as air transport or the hotel business, share the characteristic of high fixed costs and lower variable costs which will have to be covered by ensuring minimum occupancy rates. This orientation is appropriate during thin trading periods requiring boosting, but needs to be well balanced, in terms of the relationship between efforts towards occupancy and the sale price level, during more sustained periods.

☐ ## Sales decision making and revenue dilution risk

The notions of perishable service and fixed capacity sales constraints lead to the mention of yet another issue: accepting or refusing the client's booking and the risk of price dilution. A 'logical' argument would be to assert that any new booking which is accepted will generate new revenue. Strictly speaking, there is indeed revenue increase, but in certain cases, this increase may prove to be lower than that which would have been obtained through another sales decision (for instance, selling to another client, selling at another time ... and higher price). The revenue thus generated, but which is lower than the performance one might have attained, is therefore regarded as revenue loss; also called 'price dilution'.

Price dilution may also result from consumers using pricing which does not correspond to their profile.

Box 1.1: Price dilution in the air transport sector

Price dilution is the phenomenon whereby clients use, of their own initiative, prices which are lower than those corresponding to their profile. For example, Air France has set up a new specific fare to enable non-business clients to access its Business Class when they are interested in enjoying its service quality for a price increase which they consider acceptable compared to the Economy Class fare. When setting up this new offer, the challenge was to lay down specific conditions that would ensure that business people, the usual Business Class travellers, do not massively benefit from the attractive fares. A thorough statistical analysis of the traditional Business Class clientele showed that only 6% of business people remained longer than 7 days at their destination and made their reservation 42 days ahead of time. These two conditions thus control access to that specific Business Class fare. Creating the fare brought in a 6% dilution but at the same time enabled Air France to reach 85% of the Leisure clients. The extra revenue this fare generated represents several dozen million Euros.

Source: Bruno Matheu, Deputy Managing Director, Air France, in Information Report n°1161, Hervé Mariton, Finance Commission, French National Assembly, October 2008.

Dilution is a risk which is managed and controlled at the level of business decision analysis. Thus, a reservation or sale request made on the day of the service demanded (for example, a walk-in, that is, a client who arrives at a hotel at the last minute with no reservation) will be accepted, and an available remaining sale unit sold. However, if that unit is sold to a client benefiting from a special promotion or negotiated fare, and another client arrives immediately afterwards, who would have accepted a higher price, the unit could have generated additional revenue - hence, there is revenue dilution. In summary, the commercial constraint consists in selling the highest number of units at the best price in order to avoid revenue dilution.

☐ Application of revenue management: activity sectors and types of businesses

Revenue management is well established in the big companies of the following sectors: air transport (both passenger and cargo), shipping (ferries and cruises), and railway transport (both passenger and goods); the hotel business and, increasingly often, the banquet and seminar services offered by many hotels; car rentals; media agencies (advertising space management); convention centres and venue and office rentals. Revenue management has currently gained attention in other companies such as tour operators, theatres (show venues), healthcare providers, and the telecommunications, energy, and other sectors.

In practice, the integration of revenue management principles varies depending on the sectors:

- Progressive integration: tour operators have long limited the application of revenue management to certain specific services, such as flights only. All products (including packages) are currently being examined. Another example is found in the cultural sector (i.e. opera, museums) where there have been recent attempts to adapt revenue management practices. Applications have already been implemented or are being developed.

- A process that affects parts only of a sector: in the healthcare sector, for example, only private centres, less rule-bound than public centres from an administrative perspective, can apply revenue management practices to some of their services.

- A process which is facing constraints: the catering industry, for example, could, under certain conditions, partly apply revenue management approaches. These, however, are constrained by practical and cultural issues. For example, one cannot ask diners to leave their table at a specific time, in order to optimise the product-time equation, or to go and eat in another restaurant when there are no free tables left; these actions are, however, possible in the hotel or air transport industries.

Generally speaking, companies which are potentially involved in the application of revenue management approaches are those which share the following features:

- Fixed capacity.
- Fluctuating demand.
- A perishable product.
- A product which can be sold in advance.
- The possibility of price segmentation for price-sensitive consumers.
- The possibility of product segmentation (for instance, an extra service justifies a higher price).

Revenue management is mainly used by big companies handling large sales volumes such as hotels of between 100 and 1,000 rooms. Satisfactory experiments have, however, been carried out in smaller companies such as in hotels with around 50 rooms. Very small businesses, such as an independent hotel of 10 or 20 rooms, may integrate revenue management principles (particularly the issue of client value and segmentation) but will not exploit fully the techniques and tools of revenue management. However, if the hotel is part of a network (whether freely or in a franchise), or if it collaborates with other establishments in its market segment, the sharing of resources (joint management of fixed capacity, grouping of the distribution/sales tools, etc.) enables a collective implementation of revenue management techniques.

Box 1.2: Revenue management and tour operating

To improve their revenue and market competitiveness, French tour operators are more and more oriented towards dynamic pricing. Static prices fixed in brochures for a season or more are becoming less normal. Indeed competition, more especially (pure players) and online travel agencies are varying prices dynamically. Consequently, tour operator prices are less and less fixed. It obviously depends on types of products but mainly concerns hotel packages. Products such as escorted tours or private tours are less affected by online competitors and are still based on fixed prices (for legal reasons, anyway, it is still difficult to have varying prices on escorted tours).

Despite tour operators trying to match and launch promotions regularly, it gives inconsistent price signals to customers. In addition, increasingly customers are booking later and later, with many waiting for promotions, as tour operators often used to launch them when their market position is weakest. Consequently, to maintain on the one hand their market shares and to keep and increase their profitability on the other hand, they have no other choice than to use dynamic pricing.

Dynamic pricing is just one element of revenue management. It has been widely agreed that capacity management is also a part of this concept. Pricing determines the price vector which assigns prices to all products and all sales channels. In this case, dynamic pricing actively modulates this initial pricing vector over the booking period, which is primarily subject to projected demand and competitor actions. At the same time, capacity management assigns the volume vector of capacities available for all products given the pricing vector. Both approaches are strongly interdependent and are usually aligned to get the best possible optimization.

Revenue management in the French tour operations industry has a number of different components:

1 **Yield departments are now operational and regularly analyse the following curves:**
   - Sales rhythm over the last 2-3 years per type of product.
   - Margin curves per season.
   - Regular benchmarking regarding hotels, resorts and tours towards selected main competitors.

- Regular benchmarking about selected main competitors' sales prices and in addition to that, teams try to determine the margin rate used by competition.

2   To be more efficient, new curves are now taken into consideration:

In Kuoni in France for instance they now try to analyse: when do they sell what? And, when do they sell what to whom? Then, they can get revenue management in one 'shot': shift the booking curve towards customers' highest willingness to pay. Thanks to this new research, it may help tour operators to:

- Increase their market penetration.

- Upsell on mix in order to maximise their profit.

- Try changing booking habits with target groups; it offers the ability to compose the best possible marketing mix.

- Sell pro-actively. By integrating CRM and customer profile, it allows the definition of specific demand pattern over customer life time cycle.

3   As per benchmarking, new 2.0 tools are now in process.

Benchmarking is now done automatically to incorporate competitors' price curve strategies. Competitors have been identified and loaded in the system. In addition to that, they pre-define packages by selected airlines, hotels and resorts, room types, and departure periods. Thanks to this new tool, one tour operator such as Kuoni gets a weekly snapshot of its benchmark. Best market available rate per departure date and type of product is now known regularly.

4   For some major operators such as Kuoni, one department devoted to these activities has been created, and has been named 'Lates department'.

Meanwhile revenue management in some tour operators works on a 'first minute's activities' basis. This mainly involves key tourism industry players such as TUI or Thomas Cook Group. Indeed, their business models are based on asset-heavy items (planes and hotels) while they also have a heavy reliance on chartering. This said, 'lates' activities remain the most important approach whereby daily tasks consist of observing competition and anticipating market trends and needs, and the regular launching of offers through marketing campaigns with hoteliers and destinations. At the same time, their goal is to also match air capacity (more especially on charters) with land offers

Detailed booking trends are analysed for tour operators at major destinations. Analysis is primarily focused on hotels, resorts and room types. Market trends analysis is prepared in the same way and one continuous price competitive analysis is also carefully studied. Dedicated 'late' contractors have been appointed to permanently collect natural offers from hoteliers on the one hand and to negotiate offers or renegotiate rates for selected hotels on the other. They conduct this on behalf of the yield and pricing team and mainly on their request. Finally, pricing which is also conducted there reflects the competitive environment that they find themselves in, and yield optimization. Availability is also checked to prioritise offers on websites. Those offers are also proposed through Business-to-Consumer and Business-to-Business channels within a short timeline. Thereafter, offline marketing tools (such as flyers) and online marketing campaigns (supported by e-newsletters for instance) support best value offers which have been previously negotiated.

5   **To support their revenue management strategy, tour operators such as Kuoni in France have launched a new technological tool named 2.0 Sales Dynamic Calendar.**

This tool serves to attract final clients more effectively or to convince distributors to sell their product as a priority. Indeed, every night the data system is able to automatically check available airline seats and hotel rooms and calculate prices accordingly. Thereafter, packages are automatically updated and best value offers are easily identified by final clients (Business –to-Consumer) or by retail travel agents (Business-to-Business website). Thanks to this dynamic calendar, it is now very easy to select best available price by destination, hotels, departure date. It is also easier to compare prices for one month and beyond.

Source: Olivier Glasberg, Kuoni France, November 2012

■   Toward total revenue management

The concept of 'simple' revenue management is currently being replaced by that of total revenue management which corresponds to a broader approach to a company's revenue optimization. Revenue optimization is similar to the search for commercial performance, which has long-term and all-embracing characteristics.

To perform well does not mean to 'conduct a coup' with limited scope. This point may be illustrated via an endurance race analogy: in the 24 Hours Le Mans race, winning drivers are certainly fast (they are successful), but they do not necessarily realise the best lap performance, in other words, a short-lived performance that would not reflect the overall performance. Winners are also those who avoid wasting precious time in the pit. By the same token, the commercial performance of a hotel needs to combine a regular high turnover with a successful fight against revenue losses. Indeed, the contribution of coupons received to the overall performance may prove to be low if, at the same time, revenue losses are recorded. The total revenue management approach is here closely linked to the new emergent practice of revenue integrity.

Box 1.3: Expert opinion - revenue integrity

Revenue integrity is a fully fledged branch of revenue management, albeit not particularly well known and poorly represented in the industry. As its name indicates, the goal of revenue integrity is to ensure the integrity of revenue, that is, the consistency of the entire commercial chain from price definition through price charging in booking systems, proper application of price conditions, and respect of yield-determined sales recommendations to final invoice clearance. In other words, revenue integrity ensures that the revenue received really does correspond to the revenue theoretically claimable and that the product sold at time t has been sold, invoiced, and cashed at the correct price and under the correct price conditions. The expected gains are high: from 1% to 3% of turnover.

The core of revenue integrity

This activity has been widely implemented in the air transport sector where price regulations are particularly complex and can easily be sidestepped. The cumulated losses were becoming critical for airlines. Fraud management through random checks at airports was proving ineffectual and manual checking of passenger lists had become prohibitive, thus preventing real-time fraud treatment and leaving the check-in agents powerless.

The air transport sector thus became the forerunner of the system. For instance, Air France has efficiently dealt with the well-known case of the 'cross-throwers'. The Pricing Department has segmented its price grids into 'Leisure Traffic' and 'Business Traffic' via a simple procedure based on the notion that a leisure traveller spends the night from Saturday to Sunday at his destination; this is the well-known Sunday Rule. If the night from Saturday to Sunday is included between both ends of the round trip, the company considers that the traveller falls into the leisure category and thus will offer an attractive price. Conversely, a business traveller is more likely to travel during the week and pay higher prices because the company is paying the travelling costs. The business airfare is thus often 6 or 7 times more expensive than the leisure airfare. Hence, business travellers might buy two low-cost leisure return tickets covering three weeks. Then, they throw away the first and the last coupon, which enables them to make the return trip within the week at lower cost than one business airfare (see Figure 1.1).

Cross-throwers can now be successfully identified and offenders stopped. Other types of airfare fraud have been identified. For instance, straightforward 'throwers' buy, from Paris, a Bordeaux-Paris-Boston ticket which is sometimes cheaper than a Paris-Boston one in order to boost local air traffic in Bordeaux; then, they simply throw away the Bordeaux-Paris coupon.

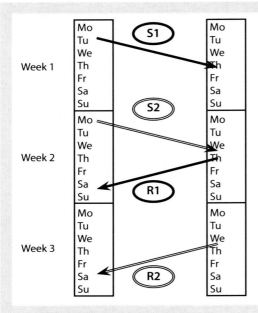

First leisure return fare: S1-R1

Second leisure return fare S2-R2

Abandoning coupons S1 and R2, the passengers can do the return trip in Week 2

Figure 1.1: Cross-Throwers

The Air France revenue integrity unit has set up a series of tools designed to track down these methods with controls placed at the Self Check-In kiosks to ensure that *'the coupons are used in the correct sequence'* as allowed by the sales conditions. Offenders are then sent back to the sales counter to buy a new ticket which, at the last minute, will often be full fare.

Other companies have followed suit, more or less timidly, and more or less successfully. Disneyland Resort Paris launched an Inventory Control and Regulation (ICAR) unit in 2006 to track down all anomalous sales. Pierre & Vacances set up its first Revenue Integrity System in 2008.

Problems in the hotel industry are not necessarily the same as in the air transport industry, but revenue integrity is far from powerless. For example, are the senior fares really used by seniors? Are cancellations or stay modifications being invoiced according to all applicable regulations? Are manual discounts applied to certain bookings controlled? Are the system fares accurately configured? The list of potential anomalies is a long one, and the sphere of revenue integrity operations covers a wide field of investigations.

The point is not to slip into an exclusively repressive mechanism through reinforcement of existing regulations and internal punitive measures against offenders. Rather, the point is to set up a series of indicators, to be shared with all stakeholders, and to find the most important improvement levers. Sale conditions should not be hardened but merely applied, even if that involves making them more flexible. For instance, if demanding a non-refundable deposit of 25% for a reservation made a year in advance does not appear to be a realistic condition, then it is best to relax the regulation rather than keep breaking it. Thus, Pierre & Vacances has relaxed the regulations concerning modifications and cancellations for leisure groups as these were inapplicable and off market. The new and more flexible regulations are widely understood and accepted, and it is thus much easier to insist on their proper application. Within one year, the modification and cancellation fees have increased by 60%.

The weaknesses in the sales and marketing operations must be identified, and then corrected. They fall into four categories:

- *Technical problems:* for instance, a package difficult to configure and which will not be sold at the correct price, fares that will not upload on the Internet.
- *Procedure problems:* sales instructions poorly applied by the providers, price conditions poorly transmitted by those who configure the systems.
- *Communication problems:* for example, 7 days for the price of 6. The provider could take advantage of the system by insisting that the most expensive night be the free one. If there is no clear specification in the communication concerning the deal, the provider is legally entitled to interpret the deal as he wishes:
- *Behaviour problems:* manually authorizing uncontrolled fare discounts, failure to comply with the sales instructions.

Here are a few concrete examples of situations which might lead to revenue integrity intervention: product code associated with the wrong fare; advocated yield poorly configured; retroactive application of special offers; 'no name change' rule being ignored; last minute offers code used for early bookings; firm order sales without regulations; abuse of the 'option' status; confusing conditions for remission of processing fees; tour operators' bookings for dates withdrawn from sales; no follow-up for length-of-stay; yield-decided recommendations; 'children' discounts with no child included in the booking; double bookings; non-invoiced no-shows; confusing regulations for concurrent special offers; management of free time constraints; erroneous bookings entry; and failure to collect penalties.

Here is one particular example of the retroactive application of special offers: while monitoring its Last-Minute Offers, the revenue integrity section of Pierre & Vacances discovered a flaw in the bookings system. Any reservation file, whatever its creation date, could be retroactively awarded the benefits of a currently valid special offer. When a reservation file was reactivated so as to add a related service, to prolong the length of stay, or simply to specify the children's age, the current special offer was automatically applied, even if the file was not eligible for it. The discovery prompted a thorough investigation. No less than €500k of discount had been awarded under the umbrella of 'special offers', long after the file creation date, and the clients had not asked for anything. A software modification enabled the blocking of special offers attribution by adding the file creation date and removing modification dates from the application criteria. Hence, revenue integrity saved €500k of turnover, and even gross margin in this specific case!

The virtues of revenue integrity

Revenue integrity implementation, beyond the net turnover savings, is virtuous, since it enables the levelling out of best practices from the top: one sales representative manages to obtain the full deposit from his or her clients; another is unsuccessful. A special report can be drawn up to provide the Sales Manager with specific figures so as to determine objectives based on high averages and capitalise on best practices. This process can then be extended to all types of objectives, particularly those that concern the collection of penalties or the various discounts which are more or less applied and integrated in the companies' fare systems.

In close collaboration with sales administration, revenue integrity may also help identify defaulters and integrate all these elements into subsequent sales negotiations. For instance, this is the case for tour operators' allocations or transport plans in the airline industry. End negotiations can then successfully take into account the difficulties experienced in obtaining deposits, managing cancellation fees, or invoicing no-shows. The process could also apply to other industries where revenue integrity has not yet been introduced, such as the media (e.g. permanent negotiations regarding campaign plans) or car rentals (e.g. annual company contracts). Revenue integrity would then enable defusing time bombs by cleaning up the processes upstream of the commercial chain so as to reduce the downstream potential dispute cases.

Revenue integrity activities then go well beyond the framework of revenue management. Whereas links to the chain of command are an essential part of revenue management, anybody can be involved in revenue integrity. For each new initiative, one can then ask oneself a number of questions: is my project operationally feasible? Who are the interlocutors who should be included in the project group? Which impact could the new initiative have on information systems? Which sales approach would sell this new product most successfully? If, through involvement in revenue integrity, staff members can contribute to facilitating, standardising, and documenting processes, and if they ensure that from beginning to end, that is, from clear concept definition through to concept implementation, configuration, and invoicing, the commercial chain is consistent and solid, then the whole company will benefit.

Under the impetus of revenue integrity, processes will be improved, tool development demands will be rationalized, and behaviours modified. For these reasons, revenue integrity is essentially a corporate approach. To function effectively, it needs to be understood and shared by all the services related to revenue management: commercial teams, distribution, operations, sales administration, and senior management.

Source: Pascal Niffoi, Revenue Management Expert, Founder & Manager, Apex Conseil.

Product revenue optimization, within the framework of a general approach (total revenue management), will always depend on the application of yield management techniques, but it should also enable the integration of all sources contributing to additional revenue generation. Various practices help meet this objective:

- Analysing overall consumer spending on a site so as to identify clients' real contribution and better select them. Genuine revenue optimization needs to take into account a client's value and the overall sales generated by this client. For instance, optimizing the green-fee selling price (the cost to play a round of golf) constitutes the first step in revenue optimization of a golf course. This approach, however, remains incomplete if the sales manager or yield manager does not take into account the client's other expenses, such as golf cart and equipment renting, practice tokens, bar and restaurant expenses, etc. The golfer who is willing to pay the highest green-fee is not necessarily the one who will generate the highest turnover for the company. The same link exists between a client's potential restaurant expenses and that client's hotel room purchase or leisure park entry ticket.

- Encouraging clients to take on new expenses:
  - ☐ For additional services to the main service.
  - ☐ For aspects of the main service which were previously included in the overall service (e.g. hotel parking, additional luggage in a plane). For instance, since November 2009, US Airways passengers may no longer check in the hold more than one piece of luggage for free on transatlantic flights. A fee of $55 per additional luggage piece is now charged (or $50 for online check-in). Thus, passengers who used to pay for extra weight only now have to pay for volume. The practice was then adopted by other air transport companies. The so-called traditional companies progressively tend towards hybrid revenue management solutions which bring them closer to low-cost companies for part of their client management.

"In order to respond to the threat constituted by low-cost companies, traditional air transport companies have had to set up hybrid revenue management solutions which enable them to avoid price erosion on the lower fares while preserving business and origin-and-destination (O&D) traffic. The current trend for airline companies is thus to develop a hybrid model where a strictly low-cost product, for which all services are optional, co-exists with a premium product, for which all services are included. This model has led to the success of JetBlue in the United States, which has been followed by numerous European airline companies such as EasyJet, Vueling, Aer Lingus or Norwegian." (Christophe Imbert, Solutions Partner)

Box 1.4: Revenue management – from technician to strategist

In the hotel industry, behind the obvious sophistication, the revenue manager pursues a goal that is actually quite simple: orient sales to maximise the property's revenues during a given period through the use of the most profitable clientele segments, their purchasing habits, and the calendar and distribution channels. This attempt at defining areas already shows the broad array of fields to be explored by revenue managers, who must absorb a large variety of information, attempt to fit it to their software without cutting themselves off from the commercial realities of the field and to do so while finding their position within the hotel's or hotel chain's organisation chart.

At first, revenue management was often associated with yield management, which identifies market segments, evaluates potential and sets room rates. The current trend aims at a better understanding of the inter-relations between market segments and their effects on the company's profits. This more global approach no longer concerns only room revenues, but places the emphasis on the total value of a potential reservation. Revenue managers concern themselves with the effective contribution of potential clients to the profit made by each of the services. "Today, we go beyond accommodations and also take hotel revenues from all its divisions into consideration,'" explains Katrin Doliwa, Revenue Manager IHG for Continental Europe. "Our expertise has been proven with regard to room revenues and now we are being asked to apply it to the Banquets-Conferences and F&B divisions as well", adds Etienne Faisandier, Revenue Manager Hilton for France and Eastern Europe.

Thus, whereas the yield manager was more of a technician with expertise in historical policies and rates, the revenue manager is increasingly becoming a strategist who recommends commercial options for optimizing all the property's revenues. He must obtain the best balance possible between occupancy rate and revenue generated by each of the clients at hand. The seminars market offers a new field of action for revenue management. An analysis report makes it possible to accept a group or not, by taking into consideration revenues and spending in all the services used in the hotel, and thus the total value of the reservation in terms of how much individual customers can generate.

Bruno Courtin, HTR, N° 157/158, May/June 2008, pp. 102-103.

In the hotel industry, the 'traditional' revenue management approach has focused on maximization of the revenue generated by the sale of rooms. Hotel groups have understood the need to develop this approach and to identify and analyse all the client-related revenue sources, which will enable them to achieve client segmentation more finely according to the clients' value. Additional revenue sources, hotels believe, originate from catering facilities, the bar and room mini-bars, the spa, shops, parking space, events and entertainment, the casino and golf courses.

One of the major difficulties lies in tracking successfully the commercial data essential to the application of revenue management methods to all of the hotel's profit sources. The loyalty programs set up by hotels/casinos have been used very successfully because clients have to use their card and identify themselves in order to benefit from the numerous advantages linked to the products they consume. Clients' buying behaviour and the generated revenue are then successfully identified. However, in the great majority of hotels, data aggregation for all the client-related data is simply not done, either because the commercial procedures and computerised systems have not been configured for that purpose (e.g. the golf course commercial file and its accounting system remain independent of the hotel's, although the hotel is located in the same area), or simply because clients do not identify themselves (e.g. clients who dine at the hotel restaurant but who decide to pay their meal directly without putting the cost on the overall bill for their stay). When information does not appear on the commercial file, the clients' value is under-estimated. Conversely, when the data capture is possible and well done, the data transmitted into the relational databases feed into the marketing analysis of the company which can then acquire a complete and up-to-date view of its clients' profiles. This knowledge will aid the commercial decision-making processes (segmentation, fare adaptation, evaluation of booking requests, etc.).

The total revenue management approach has been thoroughly examined by many hotel groups. Not only does the real contribution of each client occupy a central place in the search for a hotel's overall revenue optimization (indeed, there appears to be a movement from the traditional RevPar to new formulae such as GoPar or TotalPar), but the sources of additional revenue are often seen to bring revenue maximization opportunities which are greater than those offered by rooms. One of the consequences of this shift is the reassessment or improvement of the management of the traditional optimization levers such as the management of groups (rather than individual clients) and the clients' length of stay.

The total revenue management approach has to integrate the problems linked to the space management of the various sales sites. These include not only the rooms but also for example the spaces dedicated to catering (spaces occupied by clients and time spent in those venues), to a spa (staff time and space occupied for one treatment), to the seminar and event spaces (duration and type of services in terms of specific time indicators such as hour or day, or area indicators such as the notion of RevPas or revenue per available square foot), to golf (average time spent on the greens and management of departure intervals).

The TotalRevPar indicator (or any other acronym) rests on the analysis of all the sources of revenue generated by clients in the context of the overall potential of the whole hotel site. Upstream, the complete and detailed tracking of clients' commercial profile and of their real contribution level lead to client segmentation optimization and to fine-tuning the acceptance decisions regarding the 'client - fare level' pair. Thus, on a high occupancy evening, a client who is willing to pay the high fare of €180 for one night would be considered high-priority within the traditional revenue management approach. However, a client who regularly uses various services (restaurant, spa, etc.) may well prove to be more profitable, even when given a preferential fare of €150. The Total Revenue Management approach enables a more precise assessment of the €150 client, which will contribute towards a greater turnover optimization of the hotel site. An identical analysis can be applied to all the service sale situations which correspond to different profit sources for a company (leisure parks, cruise ships and ferries, theatres or show venues, etc.).

Cost analysis constitutes another performance optimization lever. The objective of revenue maximization, which is the stated objective of revenue management, focuses on the receipts segment and uses the notion of capacity occupancy rates at the best price. The notion of cost is partly ignored by the traditional revenue management approach because the fixed cost portion is considerable in the service industry companies whereas variable costs are considered of lesser importance. The Total Revenue Management approach, which we define as "the search for revenue maximization through combining the cross-selling of various services within the same profit centre" integrates the notion of cost analysis and particularly the impact of costs on the real contribution of all the purchases of the consumers. For instance, variable costs are likely to be negligible in the analysis of the maximization of a client's contribution for the purchase of a room, but they may have a more significant impact on the catering products or spa treatments. The cost analysis integration thus becomes considerably more relevant within a general approach of revenue maximization and contribution to the company's results.

■ # Summary

■ Yield/revenue management appeared in the air transport industry in the United States during the 1980s. Thereafter, the approach was extended to other sectors such as accommodation, car rentals or advertising space management.

■ This innovative management approach has become a fully fledged function within service companies. It involves joint management of pricing levels and of a company's fixed capacity towards turnover maximization.

■ The goal of revenue management is commercial decision-making optimization (e.g. offer the right fare to the right client, never selling at a price that is too low) taking into account service intangibility and fixed capacity constraints.

■ Revenue management has already been adopted in various sectors and various structure types and continues to develop through adapting to new sectors and tending towards a more comprehensive approach called Total Revenue Management.

References

Littlewood, K. (1972). Forecasting and control of passenger bookings, 12nd Annual AGIFORS Symposium, October, 95-117.

Smith, B., Leimkuhler, J., Darrow, R. & Samules, J. (1992). Yield management at American Airlines. *Interfaces*, **1**: 8-31.

2 The Components of Revenue Management

Patrick Legohérel, Elisabeth Poutier and Alan Fyall

Learning outcomes

After reading this chapter, you should be able to:

- Understand that revenue management techniques are based on key elements of the marketing approach: customer analysis, segmentation, pricing policy.
- Recall the key concepts of revenue management and highlight an evolution in the services sector, namely dynamic pricing and its consequences for the consumer.
- Identify the analysis elements and components linked to revenue management: performance indicators, optimization levers, quota restrictions and overbooking.

◼ A preliminary step: market analysis and pricing policy

☐ Understanding demand and market segmentation

Pricing: a strategic variable

Pricing is a variable the strategic importance of which has increased significantly in recent years. There is a direct relationship between pricing and the positioning of a company and its products, turnover, and market share (smaller or larger depending on the prevailing prices).

A demonstrated strategically important variable, pricing also has a crucial operational role. It is worth recalling that the mix design needs to be perfectly coherent. Pricing is thus not a free element; rather, it is a variable that needs to correspond to marketing choices such as positioning, or adaptation to client segments, regardless of the variations prices undergo during the different marketing stages of the services offered.

Pricing has been playing a different role since the development of high price variation practices: its job is to best adapt the services offered to the market conditions and fluctuating demand. There should be a direct effect of pricing and pricing variations on the consumers' purchase decisions. A thorough understanding of demand is thus essential to determine optimal price and relevant pricing variations, which are also effective in terms of their impact on demand.

Value analysis

Economic theories contribute to a fuller understanding of consumers' reactions when faced with price variation: they show weaker or stronger sensitivity to pricing - an economic principle - or to quality - a psychological principle. Pricing analysis needs to be placed in a much larger context which incorporates pricing as not just an economic sacrifice made by the consumers, but also one of the factors included in the analysis of value.

The way clients determine value may be personal and subjective (Zeithmal, 1988). Value may be determined in the following way: value corresponds to what one receives for what one gives. Lovelock and Wirtz (2004) used the expression 'net value': the sum of all perceived benefits minus the sum of all the product costs. The greater the positive difference between the two, the greater the net value. Advantages correspond, inter alia, to service quality, accessibility, image, secondary/supplementary services, and the environment/atmosphere of the place of service. The perceived costs are embodied in the price paid, but also in the risk, expectations, difficulties in obtaining the service, etc. The greater the positive difference, and the more willing the consumer, the higher the final price. When determining the selling price, one thus needs to consider the whole situation and incorporate the selling price in an overall cost-benefit analysis concerning the perceived value of the service offered, taking into account the importance of the principal service but also that of all its secondary dimensions. Additionally, the consumers' pricing perception represents not only their value analysis but also other exogenous variables such as the intensity of the competition, the communication activities, or the distribution practices.

Market segmentation

Market segmentation is based on the entire set of elements that indicate the consumers' expectations regarding the products and on variables indicating their consumption patterns. To take one example, a new class appeared in the aviation sector at the end of 2009, illustrating the need to adapt products to the market. A class corresponds to a first level segmentation, and each class is targeted at different sub-segments. The traditional configuration is as follows: First Class - Business Class - Economy Class. At the end of 2009, a new intermediate class, called Premium Economy (or Economy Plus), was offered to travellers. This was a rather exceptional event made necessary by the clients' changing expectations. A sustained trend of the high-end clients who no longer insisted on travelling First Class was combined with a contextual phenomenon linked to the economic crisis that resulted in restricted travel expenses for the Business Class clients. The new Premium Economy class thus responds to the needs of (mainly business) clients forced to downgrade and of (mainly leisure) Economy Class clients desiring to enjoy a little more comfort without paying the high First Class fares.

The new Premium Economy class meets the dual expectation of product and price from a portion of the clientele; at the same time, it contributes to maintaining acceptable price levels for some First Class clients who might otherwise have downgraded to the Economy Class and to upgrading Economy Class clients to Premium Economy. This example illustrates the need to adapt segmentation and product and tariff offers to the clients' changing expectations.

How can one determine optimal pricing?

Market orientation or cost analysis: two complementary approaches.

The analyses of demand, competition and costs represent the key elements of any pricing policy. The analysis of costs was and has remained a crucial element in determining the optimal selling price. Market-linked elements, however, now play a predominant role, particularly those relating to the appreciation of demand. It has become essential to know the clients' expectations and reactions regarding selling price to enable the price variable to play its part successfully as an information signal (in terms of quality, promotions, etc.) concerning consumers and to guide demand. The studies of acceptable price, value, and price sensitivity feed into the rationale for determining the optimal price, the pricing grid (the various prices for the same product or service), or the numerous selling prices.

Appraising and monitoring the competition

It is essential to monitor competitors' prices, for two main reasons:

- Optimizing one's own prices when there is an upward market pricing trend.
- Modifying, if need be, one's pricing policy if results are down (one should always avoid, as far as possible, any price drops and one should instead favour the reopening of quotas in the low-rate bands or launch special offers).

There are various tools and methods for tracking prices. Certain traditional methods are still in use, such as the direct contact with a mystery client or the straightforward exchange of information with competitors; there is, however, the risk of being accused of price collusion if the 'contacts' lead to price uniformity. It is thus preferable to ask a third party to collect the necessary marketing information as part of one's competitive intelligence strategy regarding one's market.

The information that companies themselves offer to the public is another source of relevant information. It provides a view of the competitors' pricing position and promotional offers. However, it does not permit understanding of the pricing variation mechanisms, nor of revenue practices.

Finally, increasingly successful price-tracking tools can be found on the Internet (mainly representing the new application of the real/false client old practice). For instance, QL2 is a price-tracking tool used by numerous companies (Europcar, Pierre & Vacances - Center Parcs, Air France - KLM, iDTGV, Eurostar, SNCF, Irish Ferries, etc.). This is how it works: using the weekly (or daily, if necessary) queries, the QL2 tool tracks Internet prices. Product types and business competitors to be investigated need to be carefully chosen so as to obtain a pertinent comparative analysis. QL2 is a type of investigation tool that can be configured internally by the client company.

For instance, the French iDTGV rail transport company tracks air transport companies for those train trips over 4 hours (e.g. between Paris and the Côte d'Azur/French Riviera) and rail transport for all markets. The top priority information is that which concerns the lowest fare available for the targeted time slots. Transport companies' websites and distribution sites are tracked. Well over 10,000 queries are launched every night, and over 150,000 returns are received. Every morning, once analyzed, the information is incorporated into decision support tools.

☐ Differential pricing

Demand is not homogeneous, and there are groups of clients with different price sensitivities and expectations regarding the services on offer. Hence, clients must be grouped into homogeneous segments regarding price sensitivity and expectations. Differential pricing requires following a number of rules:

- *Price sensitivity:* client segments need to reflect the various levels of price sensitivity.

- *Hermetically-sealed segments*: each client is related to one segment, one price type, and a specific service. Sometimes, when clients find a way of obtaining a more attractive price, they try to escape from their segment. Let us take one example: a businessman tries to obtain a reduced-price ticket reserved for the leisure clientele. The transport company will thus impose spending the Saturday night locally and booking several weeks ahead. Those constraints should thus be enough to dissuade the businessman from requesting the attractive price as generally, he prefers going back home on the Friday and has to book his seat late given the demands of his occupation. Barriers and constraints help keep the segments as they were defined when setting up the pricing grid.

- *Flexibility*: for greater reactivity, pricing flexibility (i.e. downward or upward variations) has to be maintained as well as the reservation conditions linked to those prices. The company then maintains its reactivity capacity when confronted with unforeseen events, market changes, or competition attacks.

- *Degressive pricing*: each price on offer should not be too far from the price immediately below or immediately above. In this way, clients are able to move to a higher price at limited additional cost when the price category they could claim is closed. Everything must be done to observe the following principle: clients who are willing to pay a certain price or slightly more should never pay less.

☐   Why and how to differentiate prices: pricing dynamics

Service companies adjust their prices in real time. Information systems integrate all the new data and refine recommendations. Pricing decisions also integrate all the opportunities and market characteristics changes, such as event or demand changes and a competitor's action. Flexibility, on which dynamic pricing is based, thus becomes the rule when prices are determined or decisions are taken regarding price grid variations. The concept of pricing flexibility and price adaptation to market situations is well illustrated by the pricing policy system used by iDTGV, a rail transport company in France (see Box 2.1).

Box 2.1: What is the pricing system used by iDTGV?

Between two dates, an iDTGV Nice-Paris ticket price may vary from €19 to €199. How can one account for such price variation for the same trip? The system is simple: pricing is not determined by the cost of the service offered (the cost of using the TGV train in terms of the number of passengers); rather, it is fixed in terms of supply and demand considerations.

- **Demand**: it varies in terms of the season, week days, and the number of days before departure. Depending on those various factors, clients will be more or less price sensitive. For example, on Sunday, January 3, 2010, for returning from Christmas vacation, Nice-Paris iDTGV tickets easily sold at €199. The high number of passengers who had reached the end of their vacation and who had to go back to Paris contributed to such a price high. As all the TGV trains were full, iDTGV could thus ask for a price much higher than the full fare for 1st class TGV seats.

- **Competition** : a Nice-Paris ticket on Wednesday, 27 January, bought 35 days in advance, cost only €32.99 at EasyJet (airline), including taxes. Hence, iDTGV (rail company) had no other choice than positioning itself a few Euros below, for example at €28.90. Price positioning in relation to competition is all the more crucial as iDTGV is distributed only on the Internet. What is easier than comparing transport company prices on the Web? The launch of several price comparison websites for different means of transport (airline, train, car), such as voyages-sncf.com, Liligo, or Kelkoo illustrates the point. Competition plays an important role when demand is poor. Conversely, at peak times, demand exceeds supply (the TGV trains are often full), and iDTGV could then turn out to be more expensive than EasyJet, which will not affect sales.

The science of yield management is to select for each train a price that enables turnover maximization, that is, the average price multiplied by the number of seats sold. If the price is too low, the train will be full long before the departure time, and the company loses the opportunity of selling last minute tickets at the highest price; this is the phenomenon of revenue dilution. If the average price is too high, the train might leave half empty.

The analyst, or yield manager, will thus monitor both:

- The train occupancy rate and its evolution over the 6 months preceding the train departure.
- The competitors' prices on all train tickets for the coming 6 months.

To sum up, the price for an iDTGV ticket at a specific time is consequent on supply and demand at that time.

The entry-level price: an effective way of capturing attention

The SNCF announces very low prices for iDTGV, from €19 each way in second class, thus copying the entry-level price strategy that has been so successful for low-cost airlines. Then, prices go up as the train fills up. It should be noted that booking must be made long in advance in order to benefit from this very low price. Let us take the example of a person travelling from Paris to Marseille on IDTGV:

- If booking is made on Monday, 8 February, the first seat available at €19 (incl. taxes) will be for a departure on Tuesday, 3 March, namely 23 days after the search date for this entry-level price. The same price is in fact available only for three dates in March and two in April; the reduced availability in April, further away in time, can be explained by the school holidays, which have a positive impact on demand. The best price in February is €34.90. Prices offered at other times are higher, reaching a high of €89.90 in February, €84.90 in March, and €89.90 in April.
- In this upward pricing system, the later the traveller decides to travel, the higher the price offered.

We can thus note that the real availability of the entry-level price is about three months prior to departure, remembering that one can buy tickets six months in advance. At other times, not only is the entry-level price no longer available, but headline prices are considerably higher. The €19 entry-level price used in all marketing communications remains the attractive element aimed at guiding passengers to the product.

A simple yet strengthened price range:

In addition to an attractive €19 entry-level price, iDTGV offers a price structure based on a simple and understandable rule: a single price for all, which varies in terms of supply and demand. However, in order to capture the maximum potential demand and to be able to react to competitors' actions, this price structure has to enable a rich diversity of prices on offer.

Thus, each analyst can play with 22 price levels (10 in 1st class and 12 in 2nd class) that may be offered per train per day. This flexibility enables them to best establish the travellers' willingness to pay and their price sensitivity. The wide range of prices on offer is one of the strengths of iDTGV to adapt to an extremely competitive environment with different macroeconomic contexts. This expanded price range has enabled iDTGV to offer prices in line with travel budgets that have been reduced since 2008 and to thus maintain occupancy rates over 85% in 2009. iDTGV has obtained those results by applying a revenue management strategy adapted to the context: prices are open in off-peak times to maximise occupancy rates, and train-based revenue is optimised in peak times thanks to a 'tight' fare strategy.

Source: François Albenque, Pricing and Revenue Management Director, iDTGV (2010).

Dynamic pricing practices entail changes in the pricing information clients receive. How does the concept of 'headline prices' change? Companies no longer try to post the highest price (called 'rack rate' in the hotel industry) but rather the best price for clients. This headline price needs to meet the expectations of each clientele type (in terms of given market conditions) and the revenue optimization goals (that is, the highest price in terms of the client profile and market conditions), and all this without violating the principle of pricing parity.

The Best Available Rate is a headline price used by many operators, particularly in the hotel industry. Thus, on a hotel web site, clients are given the opportunity to search for the Best Available Rate (BAR) for the date of stay they have chosen. The BAR is determined by taking into account the elasticity as calculated according to pricing level and in terms of reservation dates. Kimes and Rohlfs (2008) have defined the BAR as an attempt to reduce confusion and to guarantee clients that they are offered the best price for each night of their stay. In a study designed to assess travellers' perception of the BAR, Kimes and Rohlfs (2008) showed that consumers prefer being given price information for each night, even if the price is different for each night, rather than being given an average price for the whole stay. The price per night or BAR is seen as more honest and acceptable than the average price. This trend is greater for the less travelled clients.

☐   # The consumers' reaction

2

Consumers are sometimes the first beneficiaries of the price variations when they understand the operational rules and take advantage of a lower price than the one they logically ought to be limited to. In many other cases, their response is not so clear-cut and sometimes downright negative, which can be explained by various circumstances. For instance, regular clients of a hotel chain may feel cheated when they find out that the hotel will not offer them preferential rates even though rooms are still available on the hotel website. Over the last few years, Last Available Room clauses have started appearing in contracts of negotiated prices; these clauses impose clients' permanent access to the inventory at the negotiated price until such time as there is not one available room remaining.

Another circumstance, which affects the leisure clientele the most, relates to the loss of points of reference and price opacity. The considerable upward or downward price variations no longer enable the consumer to make an accurate assessment of value for money. Which price might be a 'good price'? When I board a train or plane, how can I explain that some of my neighbours have paid more for their ticket, and others less? Am I the lucky winner of the most expensive ticket in the entire aircraft? How can I explain that I myself will pay different prices for the same trip at the same times but in different weeks? There is a very real sense of loss of points of reference among the leisure clientele, and sometimes, the business clientele. Consumers might have become fatalistic as they have partly integrated the concept of price variation, but this does not necessarily mean that they understand these variations, let alone accept them. The reality is that it is not prices that change, but the quotas of sale units for each pricing level. As far as the consumers are concerned, however, because they do not know the rules that govern the opening/closing of the 'boxes' or quotas, it is prices that are constantly changing. Hence, clients call into question the company's credibility and that of its products. To all this must be added the opacity that prevails concerning the price determination rules and the fact that companies refuse to explain those rules. One example might help: when looking for a room price, one might find that, on a particular occasion, the price for a 3-star hotel will be lower than that of the 2-star brand from the same group. Hotel groups, aware of the negative effects resulting from this type of dissonant information, try to remedy the problem by giving clearer positioning to the headline prices. In practice, however, difficulties remain, particularly those linked to the freedom of pricing adjustments that franchised establishments enjoy.

In an attempt to partly remedy the issue of price opacity and consumers' loss of points of reference, some players have chosen to provide stable yet limited information which may relate to a price range or an average price. Consumers are then free to compare the price they are offered at a given moment to the benchmark price the service provider offers. Regardless of the issues raised, the consumers' demand and the awareness of market actors and public authorities necessitate setting up solutions.

☐   Key elements of the analysis: performance indicators

Occupancy rates and average price

Service companies that manage fixed capacity traditionally use two indicators to assess their business efficiency. The occupancy rate was and has remained the information most companies favour. The policy of occupancy rate optimization implies the quasi-systematic use of low price practices in order to sell units that would remain unsold soon before the service delivery date. Other companies, usually offering high-end services, will rather consider the average price of units sold in order to maintain their image and market positioning. The practice of *discount* prices might give regular clients the impression that the service is deteriorating. Luxury hotels have long been following these business policies and consequently have sometimes accepted low occupancy rates.

Today, neither of these business practices is considered acceptable as they do not bring overall revenue growth. The strategy companies now seek is that of finding the balance between 'selling a maximum number of units' and 'keeping an acceptable pricing position'. New performance indicators are thus developed.

Revenue per available unit (RevPar) and other indicators

The revenue per available unit, called RevPAR (Revenue Per Available Room) in the hotel industry, is considered a good performance indicator for tourism and transport companies. It is found by dividing the turnover obtained over a specific period of time by the number of available sales units in the same period, or by multiplying the occupancy rate by the average price over a benchmark period to be determined.

A number of different activity sectors apply the principles of revenue management, or are considering integrating them in the near future. Each sector has its own specific characteristics, and performance indicators need to be adapted to the context (product, company, etc.). In the air transport sector, unit revenue per available seat kilometre (RASK) is a benchmark indicator as it enables comparison of the profitability of different destinations without considering the number of seats available for sale and the distance covered, which may vary from one destination to another. RPK (Revenue per Passenger Kilometre) is another key indicator calculated from the number of passengers flown rather than the number of seats on offer. Other indicators used to provide a comprehensive analysis of real performance include the rate of waste, the rate of disembarked passengers, or the diluted revenue indicator.

We present an example of the reasoning behind determining performance indicators: golf courses and RevPATT. This example shows that companies need to take product specificity into account in order to create an indicator able to measure business performance. The fundamental principles to build the argument, however, are the same regardless of the situation encountered: how to successfully analyze the relationship between available space/time (for selling) and the actual business performance (turnover). In the field of golf, the chosen solution to increase revenue involves reducing start intervals. The golf course manager seeks to optimise the duo, space (round of golf) and time (daylight permitting to play or any other item that would not permit to play). The performance indicator is Revenue per Available Tee Time (RevPATT). The problem in determining a performance indicator for a golf course is that capacity is affected by factors which are controlled (start intervals, average time needed to finish the round, maximum time accepted locally, etc.) and uncontrolled (weather, number of acceptable daylight hours, etc.). Kimes and Schruben (2002) showed that it is best to evaluate the players' maximum waiting time, which corresponds to the minimum service quality desired, and to deduce from it the minimum interval time. Revenue optimization then results from service quality, clients' satisfaction, and optimization of the course occupancy.

The above example shows that determining the performance indicators is not necessarily exclusively based on quantitative elements but also on more qualitative and subjective variables such as service quality and satisfaction. This conclusion sends us back upstream of the analysis process, namely to the previous, essential, step constituted by the analysis of the client value.

■ Optimization levers

☐ Quota restrictions

The company determines quotas which correspond to a certain number of sales units. Each quota is allotted to one of the price levels previously determined. It is worth remembering that selling prices are considered to constitute fixed input data in revenue optimization models. They are determined based on a marketing analysis of consumer expectations. Hence, they are not constantly changing, contrary to what consumers believe. What are constantly changing are the quotas of units for sale for each price level, which lead to the opening or closing of that price level.

Quota restrictions contribute to the effort against revenue dilution. They represent arbitration between unsold units or units sold at too low a price. The principle consists in always protecting the highest prices, hence gradually raising the low price limit (called *bid price*) beyond which the company no longer sells its rooms or aircraft seats. Through controlling forecasts and booking pickup increases, the revenue manager decides to continue raising the bid price until such time as only a few high prices are left or lower prices are reopened to stimulate demand if real activity does not correspond to the forecasts.

The bid price is the revenue expected from the last available unit used as the minimum price of access to a price class. A reservation will be accepted or not by comparing the revenue generated (the price paid by the client) to the bid price; the latter has to remain lower.

Determining the number of sales units allotted to each price level is mainly based on the analysis of the sales history. Considering the calendar of events and the specific market characteristics at a given time contributes to fine-tuning the quotas. More sophisticated methods of sales unit allocation are based on allocation and algorithm models (Belobaba, 1987, 1989; Belobaba & Weatherford, 1996). They involve different approaches to allocation methods (static analysis, independent or embedded price classes, dynamic analysis, etc.).

☐   Overbooking

Hotels, airline companies, or car rental companies regularly accept more clients than they have products to sell! This sales practice, called overbooking, consists in anticipating late cancellations (sometimes a few hours only before the service is due) or the absence of people who had reserved (no-shows).

How can companies fight against these unfair practices on the part of consumers? The solution is to anticipate the number of cancellations and no-shows and to overbook the same number of sales. The successful calculation of the overbooking rate needs to compensate the number of late cancellations and no-shows. This is where we can see a difference in the risk-taking strategies of yield managers. If five rooms may be unsold at a specific date in a specific hotel, overbooking two or three clients is considered normal practice and without risk. Conversely, overbooking four, five, or even six clients becomes more risky since the likelihood that one of the clients will show increases for each new client in overbooking.

If we overbook the likely five cancellations and no-shows, and in the end only four clients do not turn up, we are now confronted with a client who has duly booked his/her room and cannot be accepted. This situation, called refusal, implies the *book-out* (the term used in the hotel industry) of the client, which we are responsible for; the guest will be 'relocated' in another hotel, as close as possible, and imperatively under the same price and comfort conditions. This refusal is not without costs. There are direct costs, linked to the relocation costs if the hotel room is more expensive - as the difference is, of course, not paid by the guest - or if there are taxi or restaurant charges. There are also indirect costs linked to the dissatisfaction of the guest unable to obtain a service he/she had reserved in advance for. The correlation between yield practice and consumers' satisfaction/ dissatisfaction has been examined (Kimes, 1999, 2002). Wirtz, Kimes, Theng and Patterson (2003) have shown that refusing a client brings a gap between the quality expected and the quality the company aims to achieve. Clients' frustration must be taken into account. This explains why some companies, in addition to paying for the direct costs, will offer monetary compensations designed to reduce the clients' dissatisfaction. It should also be noted that, as far as possible, operators take great care not to have to deal with refusals with their best high-end clients and/or regular clients.

Determining the acceptable rate of overbooking is based on both a sales volume analysis (the overbooking must compensate for the cancellations and no shows) and the analysis of the marginal benefit brought about by the overbooking. In truth, overbooking, as arbitration between unsold units and refusal, is of value only if it contributes to revenue maximization; hence, a sales unit will be overbooked only if the additional benefit brought about by the sale exceeds the cost generated by a likely refusal situation.

In addition to overbooking practices, other approaches are used to fight 'empty' units when the service is realised. One seemingly simple method consists in imposing constraints/penalties on the clients. A number of service providers are reluctant to impose this constraint on their clientele, particularly their business clientele who require maximum flexibility in service access. Over the last few years, however, increased competition, economic difficulties, and clientele excesses regarding cancellations and no-shows have led some companies to review their position. Penalties for failure to show up or cancel a reservation are currently increasing, such as monetary sanctions or refusing to postpone the service (for example, refusing to postpone transport if the passenger arrives when boarding is closed or the train has just left).

Another method is to identify double bookings (within the limits of the multiple bookings made by a consumer within the same group) or unreliable bookings. For instance, within the Air France-KLM Group, unreliable bookings are systematically cancelled. Computer programs cancel the agencies' reservations that are not converted into the issue of tickets before the deadline or that have been made in a class different from that of the ticket purchased. The same process applies to multiple bookings made by the same person under different numbers.

☐ Itinerary or length of stay management

Air transport incorporates the principle of itinerary management, whether simple or multiple ('single leg – multiple leg'), which is also presented as the management of the origin-destination (OD) parameter. The 'simple' product, for instance, corresponds to a London-Paris flight. If the same flight, however, after stopping in Paris, continues to Hong Kong, it will then be called a multiple product, incorporating the origin-destination parameter: a passenger may board the plane at the beginning of the trip (London) and get off in Paris or else go the entire route to the final destination. A passenger may have a different origin if he/she does not board at the start of the trip but only during the stop. The company is then managing three products in one: London - Paris, Paris - Hong Kong, London - Hong Kong. For each of these trips, the passenger will be charged a contribution per kilometre that is different - there is a decreasing rate of charge according to the lengthening of the trip. Clientele combinations, with their expectations and booking behaviours, will be different according to each product/trip. Hence, it is the totality of these parameters that the company will seek to optimise, particularly regarding the contribution levels of each clientele, booking behaviours, and actual bookings pickup. Factors such as specific competition on part of the trip may have to be included in the analysis.

In the case of a hotel, selling too many rooms in the middle of the week to guests who stay one night only freezes up the bookings for guests who wish to stay for two or three nights. If the hotel receives a business clientele from Monday to Friday, optimization needs to cover four nights rather than just the one. The guest who stays one night only will pay more for one night than the one who stays several days, but his/her weekly contribution will be lower, and he/she will have generated revenue losses in terms of unsatisfied demand. Freezing up all the hotel rooms one night in the middle of the week (even at a high selling price) can lead to numerous refusals for longer stays, hence to revenue optimization failure over the week.

☐ Distribution

In a context of greater price variation and companies' search for increased price attractiveness to consumers, distribution plays an important role. Many role players in the tourism industry see it as an economic performance driver closely linked to price policy and revenue growth. Selling every day, and at optimal price, all the fixed capacity and related services is the key to the profitability of tourist structures. The company's objective are thus twofold when it considers the distribution options for its services: 1) sales optimization and revenue growth through choosing networks which are adapted to the clientele and commercially efficient, and 2) distribution cost control (i.e. reduction).

How can one choose one's distribution networks to enhance business development efforts optimization? Several criteria are used for network selection. The same provider may choose to distribute the same tourism services through different networks simultaneously, which is called multichannel distribution.

Cost

Several years ago, the battle began to reduce distribution costs. Several role players, including airline companies, fought to stop paying commissions to the 'traditional' providers in the world of tourism, namely travel agencies and Global Distribution Systems (GDS). Direct sales through call centres or the Internet enable airlines to avoid paying commissions to intermediaries. Direct sales, however, also generate costs (e.g. human, financial, technical resources). Nevertheless, the fixed costs related to their own agencies' networks or call centres involve considerable sales volumes and thus lead to a real advantage in terms of costs as compared to the commissions paid to travel agencies.

The cost reduction battle is fought on all levels. *E-ticketing* is yet another solution employed by airline companies, and today by other role players in the maritime and rail transport sectors or the accommodation and show venues industry, to reduce distribution costs. First, a ticket is booked via the Internet or a reservation centre. The reservation number enables travellers to go directly to boarding with no intervention whatsoever from sales personnel or sending a ticket as 'tangible proof' of the purchase. These new procedures contribute to the reduction of the cost of delivering the service, particularly in the distribution/sales phase. The same can be said of those automatic dispensers that enable hotel guests to gain access to their room while reducing the presence, and hence costs, of the reception/sales staff.

Development of distribution network

Network selection and control becomes a major concern for service providers. This problem is emphasized by network diversity and complexity, particularly since the advent of the Internet (OTA & OTLA – Online Travel Agent & Online Local Travel Agent). In addition, when the producer collaborates with a powerful provider, sacrifices may be necessary, particularly concerning the selling price/commission rate, in exchange for the capacity to reach a certain clientele and sales volumes. The provider then acquires a greater power and control of the sales phase (commission rate, access to the inventory…).

OTA & OTLA market share is increasing (OTA = 37% / others suppliers = 63%, 2010). Today, they are key players in distribution networks all over the world. One of the current concerns for service providers is the relation between them and the different OTAs & OTLAs. The choice of the OTA you decide to work with (mapping), and the cost and the control of those partners is important. The commission rate paid by hotels and other service providers often ranges (on average) from 15 to 20%.

Moreover, service providers must respect carefully the parity rule (i.e. rate information forwarded on the Internet should be the same for all OTA), in order to avoid conflict with their online distribution partners. Disparity rate is a dangerous game to play; but inventory disparity is accepted, for example, if a hotel wants to keep full control of the sales of a limited number of rooms or prestigious suites, it might prefer to sell those products itself (direct sales) instead of giving a full access to the inventory to all OTAs.

Examples of OTA:

- Main four OTAs in the USA:
  - ☐ Expedia (expedia.com, hotwire.com, hotels.com + tripadvisor)
  - ☐ Sabre Holding (travelocity.com, lastminute.com)
  - ☐ Orbitz Worldwide (orbitz.com, cheaptickets.com)
  - ☐ Priceline
- Some European OTAs:
  - ☐ Voyages-sncf, expedia
  - ☐ Opodo
  - ☐ Booking
  - ☐ Expedia (+ hotels.com)
  - ☐ Sabre Holding
  - ☐ Orbitz Worldwide (+ ebookers)

The 'international' OTAs (example: Expedia) operate worldwide. In the meantime, local OTAs have significant power on all markets. It is important for a hotel manager to find the best balance between the choice of local and more 'global' OTA for the sales of rooms.

Another important issue for hotel managers is the increasing number of OTAs they have to connect with to sell their rooms. Again, the problem of the control of the network is arising, that is they have to forward the right information to all their distribution partners, and this task often takes a lot of time for the staff. More and more hotels (not only the hotel chains, but also independent and/or small-and-medium sized ones) implement tools (Updater/Channel Manager) in order to forward automatically the right information to all OTAs without wasting time.

The issues of revenue management and distribution are closely linked. Differential pricing coupled with inventory management according to the determined price and associated with effective monitoring of distribution and its costs, contributes to greater economic effectiveness of service companies.

Box 2.2: Changing distribution patterns at Best Western

The Internet now accounts for 49.7% of sales, up by 10% from 2009, while the market has reduced by about as much. Well over 174,000 nights in Best Western establishments in France were sold through this channel, 16,800 of which were booked from the site Bestwestern.fr. The goal for 2010 was to double the number of visitors – 1.2 millions in 2009 – and the Internet turnover, so that it brings 60% of revenue in 2 to 3 years. This channel represents a considerable challenge because Best Western still have to convince 50% of clients to book online. In large cities, the channel already accounts for 80% of the establishments' turnover. In contrast, the call centre is losing 2.3% with only a 17% turnover share in 2009 while the GDS experience a 12.6% decline with a 32.47% share. The share of the Best Western national sites in the online turnover is 80%; the remaining 20% come from partner sites such as Hotel.de, Orbitz, Travelocity or Viamichelin in France. We enter into about two new partnerships a year, but the real growth comes from the Best Western sites.

The ambition is to build a distribution system that enables hotels to manage the availability of rooms and price on all channels – call centre, GDS, and the Internet – and all this via a single interface. The new system will offer greater coherence according to the various channels. And because the hoteliers will be able to choose the most effective providers and channels, the new system will enable them to maintain their margins in those areas where intermediaries are most greedy. The latter take a 15 to 20% commission, which weighs heavily on the profitability of the hotels. The idea is thus to increase the share of hoteliers' direct sales.

At the same time, one should not try to avoid intermediaries at all costs: it's a good thing to have such partners, particularly for cross-selling that our brand does not really lend itself to. But a happy medium must be found. Hoteliers should be able to say "no" to intermediaries or to use their services when needed, without being totally dependent on them. This tendency to disintermediation is found in the United Kingdom, where there is a very mature market as far as online tourism is concerned, as over 50% of the sales are made on the Internet; the trend should become more pronounced in France in 4 to 5 years.

Today, the Internet accounts for a greater share of the turnover than that of the GDS at Best Western. Companies, which are the main GDS clients, increasingly bypass travel agencies and use the Internet the way individuals do. But the GDS are not going to disappear; they are going to change and offer more Internet services. This is not the case though with call centres. Best Western used five of them throughout the world, and three have already closed. Today, their share of turnover is relatively stable in France, but when it goes to less than 10%, maybe they won't be necessary any more.

Stéphane Gauthier, CEO France, Best Western, 'Hoteliers should be less dependent on intermediaries'.   http://www.journaldunet.com/ebusiness/tourisme/stephane-gauthier-interview 11/04/2010

■   Summary

- ■ Revenue management is made up, on the one hand, of elements related to the marketing domain (clientele and value analysis, segmentation, pricing) but also, on the other hand, of specific components (performance indicators, optimization levers, quota restrictions, overbooking).

- ■ Revenue management implementation is based on combining these various components which are adapted to each domain of activity and to each company.

References

Belobaba, P. (1987). Airline yield management: an overview of seat inventory control. *Transportation Science*, **21**(2): 63-73.

Belobaba, P. (1989). Application of a probabilistic decision model to airline seat inventory control. *Operations Research*, **37**(2): 183-197.

Belobaba, P. & Weatherford, L. (1996). Comparing decision rules that incorporate customer diversion in perishable asset revenue management situations. *Decision Sciences*, **27**(2): 343-364.

Kimes, S. (1999). The relationship between product quality and revenue per available room at Holiday Inn. *Journal of Service Research*, **2**(2): 138-144.

Kimes, S.E. (2002). Perceived fairness of yield management, *Cornell Hotel and Restaurant Administration Quarterly*, **43**(1): 21-30.

Kimes, S.E. & Rohlfs, K.V. (2008). Best-available rate pricing at hotels: a study of customer perceptions and reactions, CRD Report.

Kimes, S.E. & Schruben, L.W. (2002). Golf course revenue management: a study of tee time intervals. *Journal of Revenue and Pricing Management*, **1**(2): 111-120.

Lovelock, C. & Wirtz, J. (2004). *Services Marketing: People, Technology, Strategy* (5th Edition). New Jersey: Prentice Hall.

Wirtz, J., Kimes, S., Theng, J.H.P. & Patterson, P. (2003). Revenue management: resolving potential customer conflicts. *Journal of Revenue and Pricing Management*, **2**(3): 216-226.

Zeithmal, V.A. (1988). Consumer perception of price, quality and value: a mean-end model and synthesis of evidence. *Journal of Marketing*, **52**: 2-21.

3 The Role of the Revenue Manager

Patrick Legohérel, Elisabeth Poutier and Alan Fyall

Learning outcomes

After reading this chapter, you should be able to:

- Understand that the integration by service companies of the techniques of revenue management has led to the development of a new function, usually referred to as the revenue manager.
- Appreciate the different components which will enable fuller understanding of the meaning and contents of the revenue manager function.
- Define the revenue manager's place in the general organisation of the company, its interactions with other functions, and its missions and skills in the various sectors which have adopted and developed revenue management.

■ Place of the revenue management function

In those companies entirely focused on reception and services, the revenue manager function is preeminent. It has progressively been established and developed through the influence of players in various economic and managerial contexts. The revenue manager function is a new one, compared to the traditional functions such as marketing, finance, or human resources management. At the beginning, during the 1990s, its positioning was rather nebulous, and the yield missions (the term revenue management was not used then) were often given to services already in place such as marketing or operations. Nowadays, the revenue manager function is clearly identified but remains variously positioned in the companies' organisation charts.

In some companies, the revenue management unit reports directly to senior management. The revenue manager function is central in the organisation chart and viewed as an essential and strategic function. It is attached directly to the decision-making organs and to senior management, and it is placed on the same level as the other big functions, namely the marketing, sales, financial, and human resources functions.

Its expertise in the company's revenue optimization, the discriminating analyses it contributes to, and the strategic and operational recommendations it elaborates, influence and determine the company's strategic orientations in such sectors as the hotel industry, theme parks, airlines, and advertising agencies.

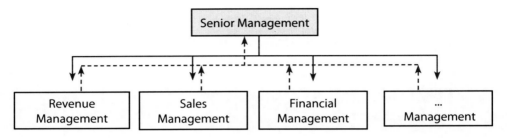

Figure 3.1: Organisation Chart

Downward (top-down) and upward (bottom-up) communication flows will follow the chain of command, and the final decision-making processes are eventually corporate, made by a management or executive committee that meets more or less often depending on the company.

In other companies, the revenue/yield management unit reports to a sub-directorate or assistant management position. The levels of responsibility are shared between the general management function and the various assistant management functions. Even though the revenue manager function does not occupy a pre-eminent position in the company, it does exert *de facto* influence through its distinct expertise.

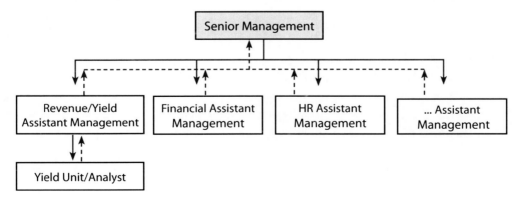

Figure 3.2: Organisation Chart with Revenue Management Function

There is a difference between the revenue manager function and the yield/revenue analyst function. The yield/revenue analyst function retains an operational role:

the objective of the yield/revenue management unit, placed at an operational level, is site optimization. It is responsible for market awareness, forecasting, budget fine-tuning of a site (e.g. hotel), pricing arbitration and sale quotas related to price levels, decisions to open or close fares, and distribution network management.

Hence, whereas yield managers used to be technicians, history and pricing experts, revenue managers increasingly take on the role of strategists who recommend commercial options to optimise the entire company revenue. Their job is to reach the best possible balance between occupancy rates and client-generated revenue.

Let us consider the specific example of the hotel industry. In the large hotel groups, each region comprises a certain number of hotels that do not all necessarily have a revenue manager. In each regional head office, several revenue managers handle each hotel in the place/region and formulate recommendations regarding the fare policy and capacity allocation to the hotel managers who ultimately make the decisions. Head office deals with the group's brand management and quality control, and each hotel manager is fully independent regarding sales, makes decisions without necessarily automatically referring back to head office, and consequently is fully in charge of business profitability. Numerous examples in the field of transport and the purchase of advertising space can help illustrate the place of the revenue manager function and its strategic positioning in a company's general organisation chart.

In the transport industry, we can look at the case of a new player in the railway transport sector, iDTGV. Created in 2004, iDTGV is a subsidiary of the SNCF Group, part of the SNCF Travel branch, one of the five Group branches. The subsidiary was created for two main reasons: competing with the low-cost airlines and anticipating the legal opening of the passenger traffic to competition from January 2010. The reality is that, for a number of years, low-cost airlines such as EasyJet or Ryanair have been gaining market share at the expense of the rail transport sector, particularly for the long trips the SNCF operates in the domestic market. These companies offer increasingly low fares with few services which enables them to reduce their production costs. iDTGV is a young company which has integrated yield management from its beginnings. The yield management unit reports to senior management. The head of the yield management and pricing unit leads a team composed of a pricing manager, an iDTGV transport plan manager collaborating with the SNCF, and analysts. The yield management strategy, fully adapted to the market context, is two-fold:

- Off-peak price relaxation in order to maximise the trains' occupancy rates.
- High season train set revenue maximization, driven by a tight fare strategy.

Another interesting example, this time in the air transport industry, is that of Corsairfly, the second French airline after Air France. Corsairfly's marketing positioning strategy is to target a family clientele under the slogan "The sky's the limit for families." Corsairfly's organisation chart is as follows:

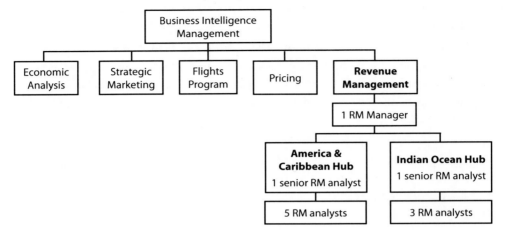

Figure 3.3: Corsairfly Organisation Chart.
Source: Julie Adam, Revenue Analyst America & Caribbean, Corsairfly

The revenue management unit is attached to Business Intelligence Management. It has 11 staff members, including one manager and senior analysts. The team collaborates with other units on an ongoing basis regarding the following:

- Pricing.
- Flights program.
- Economic analysis.
- Strategic marketing.

Corsairfly operates 20-odd destinations (among others, to Guadeloupe, Martinique, Montreal, Dakar, Réunion Island, Tel-Aviv, etc.) and flies nearly 2 million passengers annually.

■ Interactions with other functions in the company

The revenue manager function is trans-disciplinary, and links in a privileged way to the other functions in the company. Hence, it aims to create a climate of trust with its privileged interlocutors in the company: this is an essential factor in order to reach its objectives. One of the revenue managers' key skills is being able to get the other functions to share their convictions. Revenue control, which is part and parcel of their mission, requires that, at the organisational level, the revenue managers should also handle it, which involves decision-making autonomy. The art of being a good revenue manager is to bring teams to understand the principles of revenue management. This represents personal investment on the ground so as to establish one's credibility in terms of one's talk and expertise, but also in terms of the tools one will put in place that will be used by other functions in the company.

iDTGV can be used to illustrate the organisational interactions. The yield management and pricing unit, a strategic unit within iDTGV, interacts with the marketing unit. It determines the areas to be focused upon during the communication campaigns. It is regularly asked to prepare data, particularly regarding occupancy rates, which the marketing unit will then forward to potential partners as selling points. The yield management and pricing unit provides weekly occupancy rates data to the production unit which should then be in a position to anticipate the personnel required in each train and transmit all necessary information to the train crew. The production team keeps permanent contact with the transport plan manager within the yield management and pricing team, with whom the team conducts daily updates of the 'rotations', that is, the route each train travels in the course of a whole day. The revenue management and pricing unit also keeps regular contact with the data-processing systems unit responsible for developing the software and interfaces and for managing the iDTGV website maintenance.

The revenue manager's goal is to maximise revenue through fixed capacity optimization and average price increase. The implementation of revenue management could bring about the destabilisation of systems that have been in place for years. A hotel's principal aim is to sell a maximum number of rooms so as to fill its total capacity as much as possible. The sales team is always working towards accomplishing this task by finding new clients and signing new contracts. However, the revenue manager's aims are different from those of the sales teams. The practice of flexible pricing often conflicts with traditional pricing policy accurately summed up in the well-known saying, 'first come, first served'. Indeed, sales people focus exclusively on occupancy rates. Senior management needs to avoid opposing the two functions and, instead, must get them to work together; decision-making processes are eventually corporate, and require regular, scheduled meetings.

Belobaba (2002) stresses that, generally speaking, revenue management requires constant investment in the system users' education and training. From an organisational perspective, it is crucial that sales and marketing units and staff who are in direct contact with clients should not sabotage the goals of revenue management through making decisions which go against the revenue managers' recommendations. To this end, the ACCOR Group has developed an important training program targeting not only revenue managers but also reception clerks, hotel managers, in fact anybody connected to turnover. The training aims to help staff master the essentials of revenue management and to harmonize the know-how and expertise across the Group's brands. The idea is to bring everybody to understand the importance of revenue management and to ensure that decisions are made at the right level of responsibility. The aim is to train and motivate teams towards greater revenue optimization of the subsidiary or managed hotels.

Finally, the weekly meetings (called yield meetings) organised by the revenue management units contribute to more effective communication between units. This practice, which is common in the hotel sector, enables the revenue manager to bring to the department heads and to senior management the results of regular monitoring of the hotel, to share information, and to take a number of corporate decisions. The information presented and discussed may include result forecasting of upcoming periods, performance graphs compared to the previous years, pricing fine-tuning taking the competition's prices into account, events, monitoring of groups, promotion activities, and the fine-tuning of objectives for forthcoming periods.

■ Missions of the revenue manager function

Revenue managers are strategic players, and their mission is to anticipate activity and manage the capacity, whether it is hotel nights, plane seats, advertising space purchases, or theatre seats. Unsold supermarket products may be put back on the shelves the next day, but a room left vacant for one night is lost. The revenue manager's task is thus to ensure that the service is sold every day while maintaining a certain level of profitability. Apart from all this, they are also managers who are in charge of a team bringing together individuals whose number varies according to the sectors. Just like each service company making use of revenue management, the function has its own style. It is highly dependent on sector characteristics; we are thus going to consider the missions of this function.

Whereas revenue optimization in a hotel is a question of maximising the average room revenue, or RevPar, through strict inventory control or price incentives, it is a different issue altogether for advertising agencies. Revenue optimization in the case of advertising space presents characteristics which enable the application of revenue management principles. The advertising space market is a mature and highly segmented market in terms of both supply and demand, the space offer is regulated both legally and by the market, and the offer constitutes a perishable service since unsold space is lost. The very nature of the service which advertising agencies sell will thus lead the revenue managers to work differently to achieve optimization. The inventory takes the form of advertising slots available for selling. Hence, the revenue managers' goal is to maximise the filling-in rates of slots to be sold (instead of maximizing the occupancy rates in a hotel) and to optimise the average price of a sold second pricing (corresponding to the average price of a hotel room).

In a hotel context, the revenue managers' mission is to analyze the hotel prospects and sometimes those of the geographic region he is responsible for. They need to use the levers at their disposal to grow the turnover and optimise the gross margin of the hotel or area.

What are the main thrusts of the revenue managers' mission? We can sum them up into three stages:

- Establishing a diagnostic.
- Analyzing.
- Searching for optimum results.

☐ Establishing a general diagnostic of the hotel/geographical area

The revenue manager will establish a general diagnostic per hotel and area; this diagnostic is essential when budgets are defined, contracts renewed, and pricing fixed for the following year. This tool will provide the managers with a general survey of the dynamics of the area by contrasting and comparing the good references (hotel/brand/category) which can be highly concentrated in one geographical area. The diagnostic can be seen in Figure 3.4.

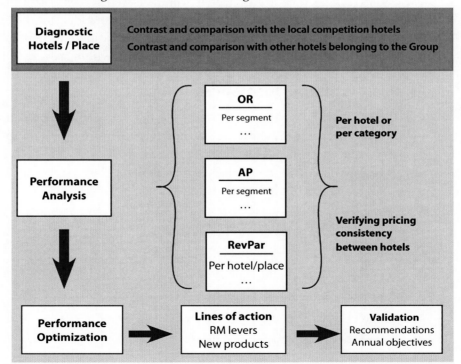

Figure 3.4: Revenue Management Diagnostic

■   The **occupancy rates (OR)** corresponds to the number of rooms sold divided by the total number of available rooms.

■   The **average price (AP)** is calculated by dividing the total room revenue by the number of rooms sold.

■   Finally, the **RevPar**, or Revenue per Available Room, is a highly relevant indicator since it combines the hotel occupancy rates and the average price. It can be worked out in two ways: either through multiplying the occupancy by the average price, or by dividing the total revenue by the number of available rooms.

This analysis tool enables revenue managers, particularly during times of pricing promotions, to ensure there is no cannibalism between the hotels in a particular area in a highly competitive context. For instance, a 3* hotel offering a 50% weekend discount could see its price positioning correspond to that of a 2* hotel. They should also ensure that these discount prices are offered to clients already identified, in order to build customer loyalty, or to newly targeted prospective clients, in order to attract them.

The revenue managers for a specific region thus need to take into account the specific characteristics of each hotel, namely, for instance, a hotel's share of so-called "corporate" contracts, that is, contracts signed with local or national companies, or contracts with airline crews, in order to put forward the best possible hotel revenue optimization. Each hotel caters for a different client mix, which implies different booking behaviours, even for hotels within the same brand.

☐   Analysing the performance

The revenue managers' analysis is based on the performance indicators of the specific hotel and area. The analysis is conducted along the following lines: the hotel performance in terms of its category, the comparison with local competition, and the comparison with the Group's other hotels in the area, if any. Each hotel analysis is based on the following parameters:

■   Occupancy rates/average price (OR/AP) per representative time period including special event, ordinary, or holiday weeks.

■   Changes in the key indicators: OR, AP, and RevPar.

■   Client mix in terms of the representative week.

■   Importance of constrained days in terms of the representative week.

■   Changes in occupancy rates and average price over the year.

■   Assessment of the annual objectives.

The geographic region analysis is based on the following parameters:

- The RevPar per geographic area.
- Pricing consistency.
- Performance in terms of inter-hotel referrals depending on constrained days.
- The importance of constrained days compared to no-vacancy days (when the hotel is full).

This analysis enables revenue managers to identify weak points or those marked for improvement regarding mix optimization on constrained days, filling rooms on certain days through the search for supplemental clients, optimizing certain market segments, such as the leisure group, etc. Concrete action opportunities need to be identified and decided upon for each hotel. The aim is to:

- Optimise the constrained days mix (the notion of an ideal mix) for hotels.
- Optimise occupancy rates on event days (length of stay) for those hotels involved and located in the tourist centre and the city and its periphery.
- Find additional clients for ordinary days (business groups, negotiated pricing, opportunistic pricing).
- Focus efforts on the leisure groups.

☐   Optimizing results

Finally, revenue managers need to define optimization annual objectives by means of the various revenue management levers and to quantify the financial gain these may bring if they are well executed. The activated levers can increase the gross profit margin. Some will bring quickly visible results, such as overbooking, while others bring long-term improvement, such as the management of annually negotiated contracts. Depending on places, geographic areas, brands, and chosen strategies, the revenue management levers will not be equally effective. For instance, length of stay management will have a greater impact on a tourist hotel than on an airport area hotel where the average length of stay is one night.

In order to better understand the revenue managers' missions and their sector-based variants, we will now present:

- Two players representative of the transport sector: iDTGV, subsidiary of the SNCF and the airline Corsairfly.
- Two players' representatives of the hotel sector: the ACCOR Group and The Carlton Hotel in Cannes.

In the transport sector, the revenue/yield managers' strategy choices and sphere of operations will differ.

Box 3.1: The case of iDTGV: The yield manager function and pricing

From the beginning, the yield management and pricing unit at iDTGV has been offering an extremely simple and clear pricing policy to enable clients to understand the system easily. We will expose its three major thrusts.

1   A simple and attractive pricing offer

Price grids are the same for all client types. It is a convenient, easy-to-use, Internet-only offer, proposed at the aggressive entry-level price of €19, which is the same for all destinations. Thus, the yield manager at iDTGV does not apply any client segmentation, or any service level-based distinctions. However, the targeted clientele for iDTGV trains is a highly circumscribed leisure group; the core target is composed of 26-59-year-olds. In other words, these are travellers who do not have any SNCF discount card, who constitute a highly volatile and opportunistic clientele constantly searching for the lowest possible fares, and who are thus willing to change their mode of transport frequently, from aircraft to train to car. The objective of iDTGV is to put forward a competitive rail offer to attract this client segment and then to secure customer loyalty with a winning price-service combination.

2   iDNight specificity: group pricing

The reduced rate system granted to groups is available only in the iDNight trains. This is how it works: clients who wish to book train tickets for a group of between 4 and 6 people are granted a 15% discount on the whole booking, and those who wish to book for a group of between 7 and 12 people are granted a 25% discount. One cannot book for a larger group. These prices are extremely attractive for consumers, and enable the company to secure minimum occupancy rates.

3   Origin-destination (OD) specific pricing

iDTGV rewards passengers who travel the longest routes in order to compete with airlines. Hence, one can find Paris-Biarritz tickets that are cheaper than those for a Paris-Bordeaux trip. The company seeks to maximise the profitability of its trains.

Source: François ALBENQUE, Yield and Pricing Manager

Another player is the airline CORSAIRFLY, for which the revenue manager function needs to integrate the hotel capacity handled by the tour operator Nouvelles Frontières within its sphere of operations.

Box 3.2: The case of Corsairfly: The revenue manager function

Within the company Corsairfly, the mission of the revenue management unit is to optimise the daily revenue through price and capacity adjustments. The unit is a major player in all the processes related to reporting, sales trends analysis, definition and launch of promotional campaigns, and the listings of groups. It needs to interact daily with the sales management unit so as to ensure maximum efficiency of all optimization measures.

Moreover, Corsairfly revenue management specificity involves not limiting revenue optimization to the sphere of airline capacity but also integrating the hotel capacity handled by the tour operator Nouvelles Frontières, which sells both airline and hotel capacity in the form of packages. All capacity allocation decisions are thus guided by the principle of contribution maximization from the perspective of an integrated Corsairfly and Nouvelles Frontières group.

This implies that the major decision-making tools connected to the airline revenue management are used equally for the package section of sales (promotion, demand forecasting, benchmarking, etc.).

Source: Julie Adam, Revenue Analyst America & Caribbean, Corsairfly.

In the hotel sector, the ACCOR Group, European leader in the hotel and tourist industry and one of the world'd leading groups, operates in nearly 100 countries with over 150,000 employees. The ACCOR Group brings several brands to the hotel market, from luxury to economy (Sofitel, Pullman, MGallery, Novotel, Mercure, Suite Hôtel, Ibis, All Seasons, Etap Hotel, Hotel F1, Formule1, Motel 6), and can thus offer hotel stays tailored to the needs of its clients. Like its competitors, over a number of years, the ACCOR Group has developed revenue management within its subsidiary and managed hotels. In certain areas, the Group can make use of a network of numerous hotels with differing capacity and distinctive pricing policies; and thus promote synergies aiming to give clients a diversified and worthwhile offer, particularly through its online booking site www.accorhotels.com.

Box 3.3: The case of ACCOR: Place or subsidiary and managed hotel revenue managers

Revenue management is a fully fledged function within the Group, and a considerable number of subsidiary and managed hotels are provided with a full-time revenue manager. Two types of positions can be distinguished:

■ - The *subsidiary or managed hotel revenue managers* are individuals who work in and for a hotel. They play an active role in the definition and monitoring of a hotel strategy and report directly to the hotel manager.

■   - The *place revenue managers* are individuals who work for a set of subsidiary or managed hotels which are geographically grouped under the appellation of 'place'. Their task is to perform demand forecasting for the whole of the place, and they will determine the sales instructions aimed at maximising the place subsidiary and managed hotels' accommodation performance, while complying with brand strategies and observing country customs, place and hotel regulations, and client needs. The revenue managers are responsible for coordination, activities and support given to subsidiary and managed hotels within a market place or an area.

A hotel revenue manager's general mission is to increase the RevPar (Revenue per Available Room), from the detailed analysis of performance history right through to the strategic sales and planning adjustments decisions. Revenue management development, whether within a hotel or for a group of hotels, requires more or less sophisticated tools which enable a specialised analysis of past data, so as to anticipate demand and thus offer day-by-day sales instructions while complying with brand and place strategies. The core of the revenue manager's role is forecasting. The Group ensures that all hotels, at their specific levels, are provided with appropriate teams and tools. This can go from a simple Excel file with a macro right through to highly sophisticated Revenue Management Systems (RMS) which enable the revenue managers in place in strategic hotels to make the best decisions on a daily basis.

The revenue manager function is trans-disciplinary and enjoys privileged links with the other hotel functions. Creating a climate of trust with the other teams is an essential factor towards reaching objectives.

Source: Frédéric Toitot, ACCOR Training Manager

Another example in the hotel sector is that of the Carlton Hotel in Cannes. The Carlton is a well-known *Belle Epoque* hotel, and has remained a legendary palace reigning over the Croisette and providing a magnificent view of the bay of Cannes. Behind the symbolic hotel façade are 343 rooms including 43 suites and apartments occupied throughout the year by diverse clients who all share the same demand for high-end service. The prestigious image the Carlton enjoys, whether in France or internationally, is strongly linked to its privileged situation at the heart of the Côte d'Azur social life. In this context, it is essential to remember that Cannes hosts a number of international events every year; the most well-known is the International Film Festival.

Box 3.4: The case of the Carlton Hotel: The revenue manager function

3

A revenue management unit has been operating at the Carlton for a number of years. Its mission is the maximization of the total revenue generated by accommodation and catering. The Carlton's revenue manager takes responsibility for a large range of missions. He holds a key position within the hotel management structure and collaborates closely with the Paris-based place revenue manager. Thus, he reports directly to the hotel general manager. His role is to handle forecasting, pricing, and capacity allocation. In addition, he supervises the four-person reservations team and one other person whose main task is to assist in the revenue management tasks.

The revenue manager collaborates with all the revenue-generating departments, giving instructions and advice designed to select the optimal revenue opportunities for the hotel. He sets results and performance against objectives and modifies the current strategy if need be. He monitors the Carlton Hotel's competitive set, and sets up tactics designed for market share maximization. He shares in the hotel's strategic decision-making in terms of budgeting.

Thus, the revenue manager works in close collaboration with the general director, the operations director, the financial director, and the marketing and sales director. In particular, he is involved in budgeting; this difficult exercise presupposes forecasting activity in terms of nights and average price, per segment and per day (micro-economic projection) for a period of one year, and all this in the medium-long term with visibility for several months. This means long-term forecasting, taking an important variety of parameters into account. What are required are thus both finely-tuned orientation towards detail and an overall vision of the future. At the Carlton, budgeting starts as early as June or July and continues until September or even later. Once set up by the revenue manager, the budget must be validated by head office which usually will request modifications and justifications. Hence, as for short-term forecasting, the manager will use past history, exogenous events such as events in the Palais des Festivals, confirmed and still negotiating groups, etc.

An overall vision is particularly important, as each change of forecasted number of rooms for a specific date will bring about revenue modifications.

Source: Jad Aboukhater, Revenue Manager

■   The profile and skills set of the revenue manager function

In general terms, competence involves the mobilisation of an individual's resources within a specific situation which requires from that individual a specific activity designed for specific ends. Competence is thus a skills set; it means everything that is involved in organised action and that which accounts for the organisation of action.

We shall use a simplified yet more operational definition of the notion of competence, one which involves the professional skills, the management skills, and the interpersonal skills necessary to carry out an activity.

■ *Professional skills* relate to the general or specialist knowledge set needed in order to carry out an activity.

■ *Management skills* relate to the mastery of tools and methods needed to carry out an activity. The revenue manager needs to know how to use the IT tools, the software chosen by the company, and the various optimization methods specific to revenue management.

■ *Interpersonal skills* relate to abilities and behaviour at work, the desirable ways to act and interact. The revenue manager is in permanent contact with the other functions in the company.

We propose setting up a competence frame of reference for the revenue manager function; it is restricted to the most important activities and/or tasks and summarised on one 'competence card'. The function of this competence frame of reference is to articulate standards and to underpin the development of a shared representation of required knowledge and behaviours. It is recommended that companies integrate this competence frame of reference in order to identify the competence mastery level required for this particular function.

When considering the revenue management function profile, the ideal candidates need to demonstrate qualities such as a keen eye for detail and precision (that is, they need to enjoy working with statistics and numbers). They need to know how to:

■ Analyse and synthesise.

■ Provide concrete propositions to senior management and the other company functions.

■ Communicate and persuade the other company players.

■ Manage a team.

Their missions centre on expertise, support, and analysis.

Box 3.5: Proposition : A competence frame of reference for revenue managers

Professional skills:

Knowing one's field:

- Theories of revenue/yield management (background, pole of activity, results)
- Revenue/yield management optimization levers
- Marketing techniques
- Sales techniques
- Distribution: the major players of electronic distribution (and links between them), the functioning of Global Distribution Systems (GDSs).

Management skills:

Knowing one's job:

- Projected budget management
- Sales: contract negotiation, marketing and sales action plan
- Pricing: segment-based grid development, product knowledge
- Systems – example in the hotel industry: mastery of the hotel industry Performance Management System (PMS), the hotel's Central Reservation System (CRS), the various connectivity platforms, and the Internet site (hotel and Group).

Interpersonal skills:

Knowing one's role:

- Ability to communicate and negotiate
- Thoroughness
- Ability to carry out accurate and detailed analysis
- Clear reporting and presentations
- Ability to project oneself into the future.

Source: E.Poutier, Essca Management School, and E.Scuto, WeYield Consulting

■ **Summary**

- ■ The revenue manager, attached to senior management, is a pre-eminent role in companies that have adopted revenue management.

- ■ The role is a trans-disciplinary function which establishes privileged links with the other functions in the company. Creating a climate of trust with the other teams is an essential factor towards reaching objectives.

- ■ The revenue manager's missions centre on expertise, support, and analysis. The revenue manager function is a fully fledged stakeholder in the company strategy. Its sphere of operations, strongly linked to sector specificity, extends to the whole set of company functions dedicated to turnover development.

- ■ The role involves a skills set and requires particular qualities that give it specificity.

References

Belobaba, P. (2002). Future of revenue management: back to the future? Directions for revenue management. *Journal of Revenue and Pricing Management*, **11**(1): 87-89.

4 The Revenue Manager's Approach

Patrick Legohérel, Elisabeth Poutier and Alan Fyall

Learning outcomes

After reading this chapter, you should be able to:

■ Understand that to maximise turnover, a company will often confront two price orientation options: reaching a volume target and offering numerous low-price seats in order to increase its sector market share; reaching a turnover target and maintaining its high-price product or service, even if this means not selling its entire production, in order to ensure the highest possible average selling price (ASP) per client.

■ Appreciate that the objective of revenue management is to enable permanent arbitration between the two above solutions. It falls to the revenue manager to set up a specific pricing policy and to be continuously monitoring the bookings activity in order to be able to take corrective actions regarding stock management if necessary.

■ Understand the various steps of this approach: history analysis, demand forecasting, revenue optimization, and performance monitoring.

■ Integrated revenue management systems

The revenue manager follows a four-step approach: database analysis, demand forecasting, revenue optimization, and performance monitoring. Figure 4.1 shows the specific ordering of those steps.

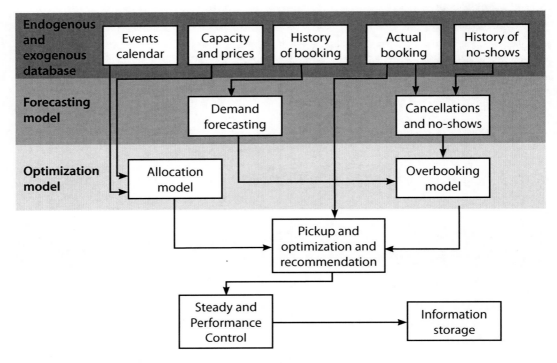

Figure 4.1: Integrated Revenue Management Systems

Here are the details of this approach

☐   Endogenous and exogenous database analysis

The first step in this approach is the analysis of the history and portfolio bookings databases. This constitutes an essential step for the revenue managers as it gives them access to the full reporting of past activities. Function expertise is crucial so that the data are contextualized (in terms of the market, past events, etc.), and certain differences are accounted for. The information, extracted from the various computer systems dealt with in the next chapter, has to be reliable. Both past data and portfolio data are needed for the analysis.

The study of past data

Past data analysis reflects the demand over a past period. The analysis concerns rooms, sold seats, or the turnover figures. The data can be broken down by product type, preferably by clientele segment, or according to day/month/season, market/product type such as the history of:

- Cancellations.
- No-shows (failure to show up or cancel a reservation).
- Go-shows (passengers who booked less than 3 hours before departure).

- Selling refusals.
- Occupancy rates.
- Bookings from the opening day to service realisation (that is, the pickup).
- Results.
- Events linked to the activity, special events (public holidays, strikes, etc.).

After the history analysis, the company activity is segmented into 'representative days'. Each representative day is a date with specific characteristics (occupancy rates, average price, clientele mix, events that have had a special impact, etc.). For instance, there are representative days labelled 'events', 'holidays', 'ordinary day –low', 'ordinary day – high', etc. Each future date is related to a representative day. In concrete terms, there are four or five representative days, defined by each establishment in terms of its activity. The year is divided into several seasons, determined according to the activity levels expected over the months. Determining these seasons is crucial, because this division will enable senior management and the revenue manager to work out the pricing strategy to adopt.

Generally, four types of days are selected:

- *Trade show days* which are highly constrained. Prices are high because space is rare. Trade show days may be occasioned by professional or leisure shows but also concerts or sports events.
- *Ordinary days*, which are days when demand is low, and clients need to be attracted by promotional offers.
- *Holiday days*, which are periods of high activity for hotels situated in cities visited during this period.
- Certain years, types of *supplementary days* may be found, such as the Olympic Games in London in 2012

Once the representative days have been decided upon, the calendar will be used by the revenue manager throughout the year for pricing decisions, acceptance or refusal of groups, etc. Then, the revenue manager determines an 'ideal mix' for each representative day: the clientele mix is defined as number of nights, segment per segment, for each representative day. For instance, for an 'ordinary' type day, 20 full price guests and 45 guests in the leisure group are expected. The aim is to find the best quantity/price combination for a specific date in a realistic fashion, taking into account the market characteristics, the history, and in a more proactive fashion, the ideal mix that reflects the hotel strategy for the future.

Finally, the chosen software solution will match the ideal against the actual reservation situation. The rule to conform to is the following: as soon as a segment has reached the number of nights that were assigned to it, it is closed to further sales. For instance, if for a given date, X hotel had calculated 120 rooms allotted to groups, as soon as this number is reached, the group prices will be closed. Segments are prioritized in terms of their revenue generation for the hotel. Thus, the 'full price for individual guests' segment generates more revenue than the 'negotiated price for business guests' segment. The last segment to be closed will be the one that generates the highest revenue for the hotel.

The study of portfolio data

Whereas the history is based entirely on past data, the portfolio indicates, at a specific time, the level of reservations for the future. The study of pick-up, or increase chart, is carried out daily to enable thorough analyses, particularly by comparing current data with those from the previous year. A graphic analysis or statistics table will show pickup at a specific D date.

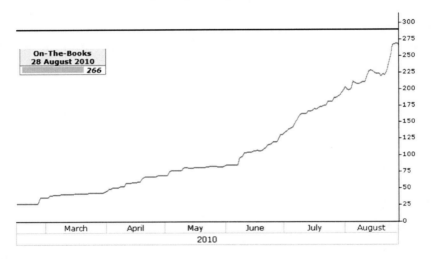

Figure 4.2: An Example of Pickup for a 5-star Hotel
Source: EzRMSTM – Hôtel Normandy Barrière - Deauville

It shows that pickup is gradual until the beginning of June. From that point on, reservations accelerate until the beginning of August.

At M-1, pickup is at its strongest with 50-odd rooms booked within a few days. The last minute booking is significant at D-10. Explanations may include the fact that the hotel is near the Paris region from which most of the French hotel guests come and who travel for the weekend.

This type of pickup only serves as an example, as many external elements may modify the pickup shape: resort, Paris-region school holidays, weather, events, type of rooms available, etc.

The graph in Figure 4.3 shows that pickup is gradual until the month of July. From August, bookings increase and progress rapidly until D-0. For this date, most guests have booked at the last minute.

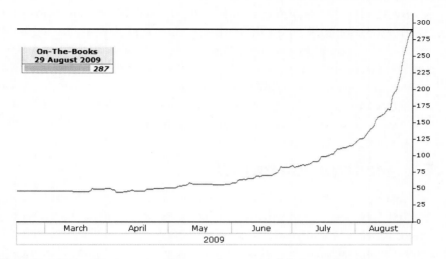

Figure 4.3: The Pickup for the same date at N-1 (same hotel, same period)
Source: EzRMSTM – Hôtel Normandy Barrière - Deauville

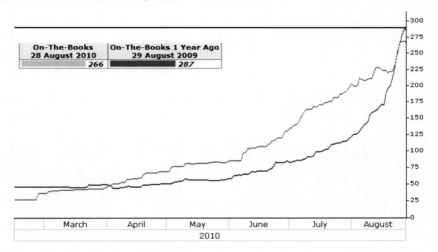

Figure 4.4: Comparison of 2009 and 2010 Pickup Curves
Source: EzRMSTM – Hôtel Normandy Barrière - Deauville

Both graphs, then, show differences from one year to the next. The Saturday pickup in 2009 comes later than the 2010 one (in 2009, at M-1, 100 rooms only were On Book as opposed to 200 rooms in 2010). It should also be noted that, despite the late reservation pickup for 2009, the realised return for that year is greater than that for 2010 (287 rooms were occupied in 2009, against 266 in 2010). This demonstrates that in terms of the level of demand and the selling instructions given, among other things, pickup may develop differently. Moreover, the booking window is greater in 2010 than in 2009, which means that upstream booking is higher in 2010 (for example: at the beginning of July 2009, 75 rooms were booked against 125 for the beginning of July 2010). Hence, last minute booking is lower for 2010 than for 2009. Thus, the current pickup for bookings is compared to past trends for the same type of day. This type of analysis enables the revenue manager to understand better the behaviour of the clientele resulting from the nature of decisions taken; for instance, are prices too high? Have certain price classes been closed too soon? The point of the analysis is to avoid repeated past errors, if any, and catch up on any possible lag by setting up a well adjusted pricing policy.

■ Forecasting demand

Forecasting is at the core of the revenue manager's approach and underlies any effective revenue management system. Forecasting enables decision making based on what is known rather than what is supposed. The essential thing is to choose an approach that is adapted to the size of the company. The most relevant data concerning consumer and market behaviour are collected, sorted, sifted, and analyzed; then, precise, advanced forecasting techniques are applied via a software package in order to anticipate the company's future activity more successfully. Forecasting aims to anticipate demand, cancellations and no shows.

☐ Demand

Based on calculation methods, the forecasting of demand per hotel/area/segment enables revenue managers to develop a clearer vision concerning future sales.

Box 4.1: The case of the Carlton Hotel: The function of the revenue manager and forecasting

Revenue managers carry out several forecasts at different intervals and with different objectives:

1   The first forecast is that of budgets, done annually;

2   Then, once a month, there is the 'Last Forecast', which is the official forecast of the month for the rest of the year, validated by InterContinental;

3   The third forecast, called 'weekly forecast', is carried out weekly for the current month. It is an adaptation of the last forecast in terms of the hotel's real activity, and it is used to justify results to the shareholders. It is validated during a revenue meeting by the General Manager and the Financial Manager. The Catering Manager will carry out the same activity for his operations. The forecast is sent to head office, where it is validated; justifications are demanded for any differences with the Last Forecast;

4   Finally, the non-official, daily Current Forecast is used to anticipate as closely as possible the situation for the next few days in terms of the number of bookings, bookings pickup, expected cancellations, etc. All the forecasts must be entered per day and per segment in the overall database, or Integrated Business Plan (IBP).

Source : Jad Aboukhater, Revenue Manager, Carlton, Cannes (France)

Budgeting is an essential step to start a new fiscal year. The process is based on the analysis of the past year data, which constitute the benchmark. Certain dates/periods, however, need to be taken out of the benchmark values so as not to distort the forecasting. These are, for example, special events days, such as the launch of a new attraction or the 20-year anniversary of Disneyland Resort Paris, bad weather affecting the occupancy rates of the amusement park and hotel revenue, etc. Revenue managers need to compare upcoming dates with past data to deduce calendar impacts. For instance, the gap between the holiday dates of a particular zone/country may have a positive or negative impact on the volumes of the week under scrutiny.

Should they succeed in forecasting demand for each market segment, the revenue managers will be able to deduce whether a low price class needs to be closed to sales because demand will exceed the hotel/park capacity, or it should be kept open because, instead, it will attract clients should demand be low. For those companies that have adopted revenue management, daily forecasting is essential, as a monthly-netting effort is not sufficient. Analysing time sequences is particularly interesting as these make possible the description of a data sequence to throw light on underlying mechanisms and to forecast the future of the sequence. The expression 'time sequences' refers to both real chronological time sequences and a theoretical succession of time-indexed random variables. Revenue managers will daily take into account the updated bookings or cancellations, per segment.

As far as forecasting methods are concerned, two major method groups are contrasted: those based on the past, called endogenous, using mainly internal company variables and those called exogenous, which combine internal and external variables. The latter may correspond to a multitude of variables such as service price, communication budget, consumer trends development, and events.

Two endogenous quantitative methods coexist: the one is called simple exponential smoothing, and the other, called Holt-Winters, is more complex exponential smoothing. Both methods are designed to find in the data history some pattern including a trend, seasonal fluctuation, and a hazard.

Simple exponential smoothing

This short-term forecasting method is based on three principles: the increasing devaluing of information over time, synthesizing information, and the permanent realization of parameters.

Its mathematical expression is as follows:

$$\hat{x} = \hat{x}_{t-1} + \alpha(x_t - x_{t-1})$$

where $\hat{x}$ = forecast, α = the smoothing constant between 0 and 1, and $(x_t - x_{t-1})$ = the gap between the forecast and the actual value. This approach can be used only for stationary chronological sequences, with neither trends nor seasonal fluctuation.

Holt-Winters exponential smoothing

This corresponds to an extension of the previous model and carries out a single forecast involving three types of smoothing: smoothing of the mean, trend, and seasonality. This is done with three constants α, β, γ that successively smooth these three elements so as to minimize the sum of the squares of errors in terms of the real data. This method is simple, easily adaptable and fast, while incorporating all the key parameters of data development.

The choice of a forecast method is related to the issue of whether the revenue management system (RMS) is developed internally or not. Should the company choose to develop forecasting tools with Excel, it could then select an endogenous quantitative method, which is easy to set up.

Cancellations and no-shows

Information regarding coming cancellations and no-shows over several dates is essential to supplement the information resulting from the demand forecast. Thus, knowing that, at a certain date, demand will be high and no-shows low will not carry the same strategy consequences as knowing that both demand and no-shows will be high. In the latter case, the revenue manager will be able to accept a greater number of overbookings since the no-show margin is higher.

■   The search for optimization

Optimization involves monitoring and controlling reservations and prices for different types of clients. Monitoring, in turn, involves accepting or refusing booking demands to maximise the company profits. The issue is capacity allocation and optimization *via* the various levers of revenue management.

□   Capacity allocation

Capacity allocation involves attributing for each period type a certain number of rooms, aircraft seats, or places for each clientele segment. This method requires thorough understanding of the behaviour of clients in the different classes and of their reactions to price modifications. The baseline hypothesis is that the low-end clients will book earlier than the others. Hence, they are attributed a limited number of rooms/seats/places, considering that they enjoy reduced prices.

Conversely, business class clients are not price sensitive, but they are subject to time schedule changes. They plan or cancel reservations at the last minute.

Some heuristics can help determine the optimal capacity allocation in terms of the various price classes. The first ones are based on the estimate of the probable demand distribution; they are the Expected Marginal Seat Revenue (EMSR) heuristics developed by Burth from 1982 and improved by Simpson (1985) and Belobaba (1989). It is a system that determines quotas per price class. At first, EMSR heuristics did not take into account the relationships between classes, which brought the risk of waste since one could then have to refuse demands. Indeed, if there is no demand for the higher class right up to departure, one could then refuse demand for lower classes, the protection level for which has been reached. The heuristics were then modified so as to take into account the relationships between classes, as each class contains the classes that are lower than itself. In 1992, Belobaba improved EMSR heuristics through working with virtual classes according to their contribution; these heuristics are called EMSRb, in contrast to previous heuristics, renamed EMSRa.

Other heuristics do not use the quantity variable as in the EMSR; rather, they use the price variable. These heuristics bring greater flexibility through a comparison between the selling price offered and a floor price: the Bid Price. Some Bid Price heuristics are based on EMSR calculations (Bid Price heuristic) while others are based on linear programming calculations (deterministic heuristic), and yet others combine both methods such as the pseudo-price heuristic. These Bid Price heuristics are widely used in the hotel industry. In order to carry out quota restrictions in the transport industry, the aircraft/train is split into several price classes. Initially, the allocation is determined in terms of the historical data; then it changes according to the bookings flow. Two types of price classes are considered when a flight is open to bookings: independent classes and nested classes.

For independent classes, the quota restrictions are predetermined. A particular quota is attributed to each class, and one sale in a class reduces the availability in that class without affecting the number of seats allocated in the other classes. For nested classes, a particular quota is attributed to each class, and one sale in a class reduces the availability in that class and the classes that contain it. Thus, when a reservation is made in one of the nested classes, the other classes are immediately affected. There are different types of nesting: standard, protective, and virtual.

The aviation sector, which has the greatest expertise level in this domain, has to face the complexity of products and operational situations, data volume, information systems, and also that of the decision-making process regarding optimization. What follows in Box 4.2 provides a synthesis of the decision-making processes in terms of inventory optimization and price levels in the air transport sector.

Box 4.2: Decision making processes in the air transport sector

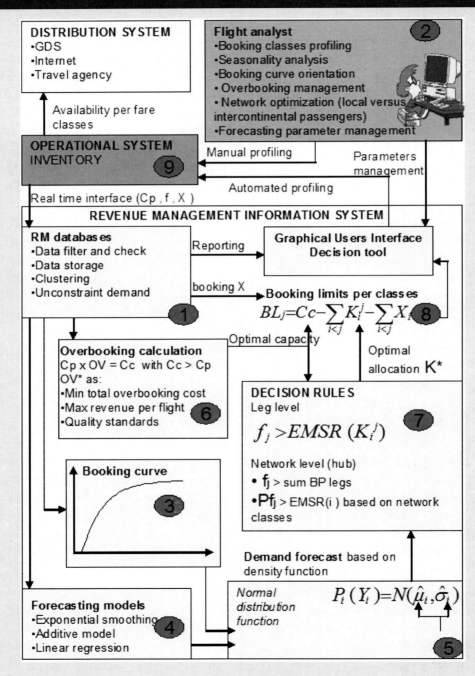

DISTRIBUTION SYSTEM
- GDS
- Internet
- Travel agency

Flight analyst ②
- Booking classes profiling
- Seasonality analysis
- Booking curve orientation
- Overbooking management
- Network optimization (local versus intercontinental passengers)
- Forecasting parameter management

Availability per fare classes

OPERATIONAL SYSTEM INVENTORY ⑨

Manual profiling

Parameters management

Automated profiling

Real time interface (Cp , f , X)

REVENUE MANAGEMENT INFORMATION SYSTEM

RM databases
- Data filter and check
- Data storage
- Clustering
- Unconstraint demand

Reporting

Graphical Users Interface Decision tool

booking X

Booking limits per classes

$$BL_j = Cc - \sum_{i<j} K_i^j - \sum_{i<j} X_i$$ ⑧

①

Optimal capacity

Optimal allocation K*

Overbooking calculation
Cp x OV = Cc with Cc > Cp
OV* as:
- Min total overbooking cost
- Max revenue per flight ⑥
- Quality standards

DECISION RULES
Leg level

$$f_j > EMSR\,(K_i^j)$$ ⑦

Network level (hub)
- f_j > sum BP legs
- Pf_j > EMSR(i) based on network classes

Booking curve ③

Demand forecast based on density function

Forecasting models
- Exponential smoothing ④
- Additive model
- Linear regression

Normal distribution function

$$P_i\,(Y_i) = N(\hat{\mu}_i, \hat{\sigma}_i)$$ ⑤

Key

Cp : Aircraft capacity

f: fare

X: Booking

BL: Booking limits per booking class

BP: Bid price per leg

I, j : booking class index with fj > fi

Cc : Saleable capacity

Pf: pseudo fare

K: allocation per booking class

Y: demand

OV: Overbooking factor

4

In this section we offer a step by step synthesis of all the tools involved in a Revenue Management information system.

Step 1 – Yield management databases

The databases of a Yield Management system deal with real time information coming from operational systems and with historical data which are aggregated in order to reduce their volume. The storage of information is organised by filtering and automated correction (e.g. of discrepancies, or odd values). The demand is not constrained by induced effects of supply variations (opening / closing of booking classes). Data are classified by standard profiles that describe the number of reservations usually observed depending on the date of flight departure and some seasonal criteria (time slot, day of week, peak, holidays etc.). This step is crucial according to the principle of garbage in / garbage out.

Step 2 – Daily work of a flight analyst

The flight analyst is generally someone with a strong commercial background. He performs some multi-purpose analysis and deals with opening/closing of booking classes, customer rates and dates of flight in order to maximise the revenue of a set of flights. At ease with Intelligence Technology, he initiates and tunes the flight profiling (capacity allocation per booking classes). For each flight he monitors the information system outputs and chooses the seasonal parameters, booking curve profiles, level of overbooking and number of seats to be allocated to connected passengers. Flight analyst excellence is fundamental and remains the key to success.

Step 3 – Demand forecast based on booking curve

A booking curve is the relationship between the number of reservations and the number of days prior to departure. Its origin comes from the inventory control considering RCN (t), the cumulative number of bookings net of cancellations in t as an initial stock, cancellations as outputs, new reservations as inputs and RCN $(t +1)$ the net cumulative number of bookings in $t +1$ as the final inventory. Thus we get:

RCN $(t +1) = RCN$ $(t) + bookings$ in $t - cancellations$ in $t.$

Booking curves are often at booking class level i and can be displayed as a percentage of the final point, namely the day of departure of flight $(t = 0)$ as $PROI$ $(t) = RCN$ $(t) / RCN$ $(0).$

Moreover, they help in assessing the number of reservations on the day of departure by projecting from the number of reservation observed in t.

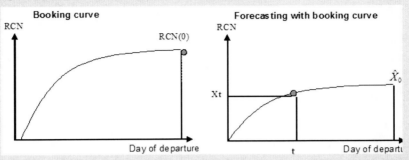

Booking curves are widely used and provide information related to customer behaviour (are bookings coming linearly over time or otherwise massively in the last days before departure?).

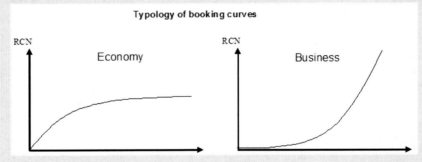

Step 4 – Forecasting models

Many models are available to estimate $\hat{X}_0$ the number of booking on the day of departure: exponential smoothing, moving averages, linear regression, the additive model, the predictive neighbourhood, etc. The information system includes several models to be chosen by the flight analyst.

Step 5 – Parameter estimates of the demand density function

Demand forecasting models described in Step 3 and Step 4 are used to estimate the parameters of the demand density function (binomial, gauss, fisher, gamma, etc.). In a Yield Management system the parameter estimate is often made up of combined forecasts with the current bookings which is calculated by:

$$\hat{X}_0\left(1 - \frac{RCN(t)}{RCN(0)}\right) + X_t$$

with $\hat{X}_0$ the number of reservations on the day of departure estimated by one of the models from Step 4 and X_t the current number of reservations (the observed value in real time) in t. Thus the observed value is more weighted when close to flight departure and vice versa.

Step 6 – Determining the overbooking level

It is assessed that a 1% increase in load factor corresponds to several million euros in turnover on a yearly basis. In this case an overbooking policy is almost mandatory for an airline. The overbooking level is measured by the number of additional seats to be sold to overcome the effects of potential cancellations and no-shows (passengers who book and who do not show up on the day of departure and who do not cancel their reservation in advance). Aircraft capacity Cp is the physical number of seats per cabin (first, business, economy). Saleable capacity Cc, which is the number of seats to be sold per cabin, includes overbooking. Overbooking is defined by OV an overbooking factor which is calculated according to different possible criteria:

- minimize the total cost of overbooking (cost of denied passengers + loss of revenue coming from the empty seats);
- maximise revenue per cabin;
- or adjust the level of overbooking as we respect the airline quality standards of service (no more than x reserved passengers can be denied for boarding).

The problem of overbooking is mathematically modelled by dynamic programming and conditional probabilities. In practice there are strict procedures both for the flight analyst in order to reduce the risk of denied passengers and for the check-in agent for managing the denied passengers in compliancy with the regulations. In the information system the optimal capacity to be sold per cabin (CC) that includes overbooking, will be used as input for capacity allocation per booking classes.

Step 7 – Determining the allocations by booking class

The optimal allocation between several booking classes is calculated with decision rules. Should we continue to sell a seat to a passenger with low contribution (leisure passenger) or should we stop the sale and protect the seat for a later but higher contribution (business passenger)? Littlewood (1972) proposes the following decision rule that the reservation requests from discounted f2 passengers must be satisfied till:

$$f_2 = f_1 \, P[Y_1 \geq C_C - K_2]$$

the discount fare f_2 is higher than the full fare f_1 multiplied by the probability of rejection of the sale of a full fare paying passenger lacking for an available seat. Belobaba (1989) generalized this decision rule with j booking classes:

$$f_j > EMSR\left(K_i^j\right)$$

with

$$EMSRi(K_i^j) = f_i \int_{C_C - K_i^j}^{\infty} P_i(Y_i)\partial_i$$

and

$$f_i > f_j$$

This means that the reservation requests for class j must be satisfied as long as the fare j is greater than the expected marginal seat revenue in class i given that fare j is less than fare i.

According to Belobaba (1992) the tradeoffs between booking classes must be based on a set of booking classes, namely protected capacity for class i should not be the result of a direct arbitration between class i and class $i+1$ but should be result of tradeoffs between the first set of I higher contribution classes and class i +1 with:

$$f_i > f_{i+1}$$

That is why Belobaba introduced the concept of EMSR type b, built on joint density functions that significantly increase the revenue per flight by shifting EMSR curve to the right. These decision rules are helpful in determining the optimal allocation between several booking classes for a single leg of a flight without any network approach.

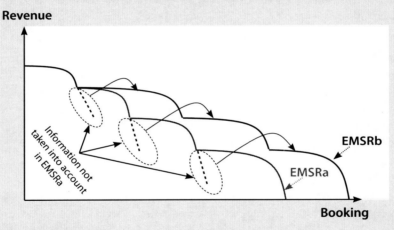

Revenue versus bookings

In case of an airline network built with one or several hubs, the trade-offs are to deal with local passengers versus connecting passengers. These trade-offs are based on bid prices calculation per leg. To calculate bid price: the first step is that a linear program has to be solved for determining the optimal allocations as a solution of the maximization of the network revenue under capacity constraints and demand constraints which can be written as:

$$\underset{K_{(i,j)}}{Max}\, N.R = \sum_{(i,j)\in H} f_{(i,j)} K_{(i,j)}$$

$$\sum_{(i,j)\in S} K_{(i,j)} \le C_S\ \forall s \in S$$ Capability Constraints: With S the set of flight leg of the airline network

$$K_{(i,j)} \le Y_{(i,j)}\ \forall (i,j)\in H$$ Demand constraints: with H the set of classes/origin & destination itinerary of the airline network.

$$K_{(i,j)} \ge 0\, \forall (i,j)\in H$$ non- negativity constraints:

In a second step, the Bid Prices are determined using a post-optimal calculation. The Bid Prices are the Shadow Prices (Lagrange multipliers) for each capacity constraint. At the optimum, for each segment s, the Shadow Price *SPs* is calculated as:

$$SP_S = \frac{\partial NR^*}{\partial C_S}$$

The Bid price (or shadow prices) of a leg *S* is the revenue variation generated by the increase of an additional unit for sale (1 seat) on the leg *S*.

To manage a network organized around a hub, there are two types of decision rules:

- The rules using bid price values directly, which are based on an overall network optimization by accepting or refusing the booking requests of local passengers and passengers in connection. The fare of the entire itinerary of a connected passenger must be higher than the sum of the bid prices for the legs which make up the itinerary. Theoretically bid prices should be re-calculated after each event (reservations, cancellations) but in practice, for reasons of performance, the bid prices are pre-calculated in advance and updated as far as technically possible.

- The rules using expected values calculation that remain at the leg level (local optimization) but that integrate network information to arbitrate between local passengers and connected passengers on the leg. The pseudo fare (fare of the entire itinerary minus the bid prices in other legs of the itinerary) must exceed the expected marginal revenue of local passengers. In some cases, this decision rule is limited to verifying that the added revenue of a connected passenger on the leg is sufficient (especially compared to the average fare of a local passenger).

Decision rules (at leg level or for complex network) are the core of a Yield Management system.

Step 8 – Determining booking limits

Booking limits' calculation takes into account the current reservations (real time). The set of booking limits corresponds to a flight profiling.

Step 9 – Interfacing the operational systems

While the tools defined in steps 1-8 are part of the information system of revenue management and/or modules for decision support, inventory is included in operational systems. Flight profiling in the inventory can be performed manually by the flight analyst or be proposed by decision tools as a recommendation. The flight analyst also deals with upgrading possibilities and overbooking policy. When a booking class contains available seats in the inventory, its associated fares are open in the distribution systems (GDS, internet, travel agencies) for sale. When there is no seat left in a booking class on the inventory, its associated fares are closed for sale.

Even if the flight analyst's work is widely supported by a dedicated information system, the optimization is guaranteed by human decisions, especially regarding the integration of seasonality, overbooking and network optimization. The information system is monitored daily by technical support. Human intervention can also monitor the results with reporting, and build the yield management policy in an overall strategy integrating the other optimization levers such as aircraft schedules, pricing, marketing, in-flight service policies, partnership policies, etc.

As regards the Information System, there is plenty of room for improvement: extending network optimization by combining deterministic models (linear programming) with stochastic models (based on expected values), dealing with the multi-hub companies involved in alliances, better integrating supply shifts by modelling of dependency links of booking classes in rules decisions, incorporating more current real-time information to improve optimization calculation especially for forecast auto-updating and finally, dealing with customer profiles for forecasting and overbooking.

The new challenges of yield management are:

- Adapting to a context of airline merging by aligning the business processes with the other partners. The information system is often the crucial point in this business alignment, each partner pushing to generalise its own IT system. A neutral choice could be the purchase an external system with some specific development or in-house development.

- Coping with the crisis by focusing on the airline fundamentals: strengthening the most remunerative segments, the implementation of new product lines and fares and the rationalization of schedule and capacities.

Source: Frederic Specklin, Air France (2001).

☐   Optimization

To increase revenue, the revenue manager can use a certain number of profit-generating levers. Levers are elements integral to the strategy determined by the revenue manager to increase the gross margin for the hotel/aircraft/train. What are those levers, that are part and parcel of the approach? The main levers adopted by the revenue manager are the following:

- Overbooking management.
- Pricing management.
- Length-of-stay management.
- Group management.
- Contract management.

Overbooking management

Overbooking involves offering for sale a capacity that is higher than the capacity actually available to anticipate the effects of cancellations and no-shows (a client's failure to show up or cancel a reservation). The fact is that booking a room or a flight seat means planning a trip, which could be cancelled or modified for any number of reasons. In the best scenario, the booking will be cancelled, which will bring a modification to pick-up forecasts. However, there are other situations which have a more negative impact on the forecast. Passengers may simply not show up at boarding and do not cancel their booking (voluntarily or not): they are called 'no-shows'. The phenomenon corresponds to revenue loss for the company. The loss involves the opportunity cost of the no-show ticket and in addition reduces the quota of seats offered to reservation. Conversely, passengers may arrive for boarding without a booking: they are called go-shows.

The revenue manager needs to take this type of behaviour into account to manage the uncertainty and the stochastic nature of demand. Hence, overbooking limits the risk of facing empty rooms/seats and consequently is part of revenue maximization. It also enables a greater number of clients to book the service that constitutes their first choice. Figure 4.4 shows an application of overbooking. It is clear that the company, during pickup, permits far more bookings than the actual available capacity, but the cancellations and no-shows taking place a few days before the date bring the final number of bookings to optimal level.

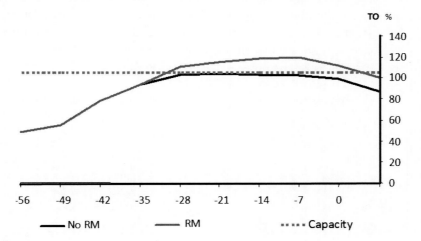

Figure 4.5: Overbooking

Overbooking remains one of the most delicate elements of the revenue manager's approach and involves ethical issues for numerous clients. Thus, in order to anticipate those phenomena that generate inevitable revenue loss, service industries use cancellations and no-shows forecasts to adjust the number of available units.

Those forecasts, though, are not always as reliable as in the example provided above, which generates an attendant cost. The company thus has to balance two risks before it can determine the optimal overbooking level: failing to sell all available units if too few bookings are accepted (the risk of revenue loss related to unsold rooms or seats) or having to refuse the offered service (the risk of refusal). In the case of refusal, the client's book-out may generate considerable costs. It is thus worthwhile comparing the costs of overbooking and the benefits generated, which would enable determining a theoretical optimum, hence the optimal overbooking rate.

Overbooking generates two types of costs:

■ The first corresponds to the loss generated by unsold units (hotel rooms, aircraft seats) remaining empty: this is the cost of waste.

■ The second is the refusal cost, characterised by two different types of cost. The first one corresponds to the financial cost of the compensation given to the client, including, for instance, the relocation, taxi ride, indemnity, etc. The second risk is related to the company's brand image; the amount of this hidden cost is very hard to assess.

In the hotel industry, the revenue manager has yet another lever at his disposal: inter-hotel referrals. The aim is to minimise those situations whereby one refuses a client while another hotel of the group in the same geographic area has free rooms. Transfer is the expression used to refer to a client's relocation at the time of booking and with the client's agreement. A second optimization step consists in sending the client to the hotel which can obtain the highest profit from the client. This step will not necessarily mean the hotel at the highest price but the one for which the costs of an empty room are the highest.

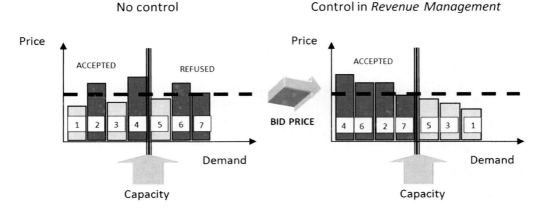

Figure 4.6: Ideal Control in Revenue Management

Pricing management

Pricing management involves authorising, or not, the sale of rooms at different prices. Successful pricing management entails offering several prices for the same room (in full compliance with brand policy) so that each client pays the price he/she is 'willing to pay'. The strategy pre-supposes that the optimum number of rooms per price class is allocated at revenue management level from the determined floor price (Bid Price) and the hierarchy of demand.

Length-of-stay management

Length of stay is to the hotel industry what the network effect is to the air transport industry. The principle is simple: working out whether the room should be sold immediately at €200 for one night only, or whether it is best to wait for a possible guest who would come for four nights, for instance. The decision is crucial, for the idea is to enable long stays, which are highly remunerative, and not to be constrained by poorly positioned short stays. Consequently, managing hotel capacity requires monitoring demand on three different axes: per day, per pricing class, and per length of stay. For instance, a hotel which experiences a peak in business activity on Wednesday should not accept all clients in booking order, for this would lead, in the end, to refusing clients wishing the stay the whole week. The issue is thus to keep some space for clients who will stay longer. To do so, two strategies are available:

- The 'closed-to-arrivals' strategy: give priority to clients who would fill the hotel on the low occupancy previous nights, as those nights will be below capacity.

- The 'length-of-stay' strategy: give priority to clients who would stay for extra nights and who otherwise would be refused because one of those nights is not available.

Group management

One of the many problems regarding service companies relates to group management. Group demands are often the fruit of negotiations around substantial volumes, but they disrupt the various optimization levers. Thus, in unconstrained periods, groups enable the filling up of available seats/rooms. They are then more than welcome. Conversely, in constrained periods, a group should be accepted only if its contribution is higher than that of the displaced individual demand.

Group management involves accepting or refusing groups in terms of the individual demand forecast and their financial contribution. Arbitration of a group demand is done by quotation and depends on a situation whereby the group should bring more revenue than potential individual clients. There exists the possibility of what is called 'client allocation', namely the contract-bound allocation of a certain number of rooms for potential reservation, as is usually the case with tour operators. The allocation should contain a release from booking commitment date, that is, the date on which the booking is automatically cancelled if confirmation has not been received.

The idea is to accept or refuse groups depending on the forecast of displaced individual demand. Before a group demand is accepted, a quotation needs to be carried out to determine whether that demand would bring in more revenue than that from the individual demand that will have to be displaced.

Contract management

Contract management involves accepting or refusing signing a contract in terms of the displaced individual demand forecast. The service company often works with partners with whom it is linked by contract. These contracts are important as they often ensure a minimum volume during the low activity periods in exchange for protections granted to the partner in constrained periods (permanent access to the stock/allocations/etc.) Signing the contract or its renewal or not, in terms of the displaced individual demand forecast, thus constitutes a real optimization lever. For optimizing turnover, the partner's contribution needs to be assessed after comparing the advantages obtained from the partnership to the disadvantages it brings. Are analysed contracts with tour operators or companies sometimes granted special conditions (guaranteed availability, release from booking commitment date, etc.)? The availability of each price is determined after the cross-analysis of the short- and long-term potential contribution, taking the price-related conditions into account.

For revenue optimizing, it is necessary to assess the potential brought by each client (contract) and to determine whether the production is worthwhile in terms of volume, but also of daily production. Contract management also involves introducing clauses that bring the highest leeway in terms of accommodation, possible prices given the period of activity and the maximum number of rooms which could be booked at the same date. These levers constitute an excellent means of increasing the revenue of a product while optimizing resources. To exploit them to the fullest, revenue managers use software tools that enable the treatment of the numerous parameters and thus constitute invaluable decision support tools.

■ Summary

■ Revenue managers use a structured approach based on the detailed analysis of databases that, in the end, enable them to optimise performance and make strategic recommendations to the company. To make a good assessment of the potential reservation demand, it is necessary to study the databases fully. The second step involves demand forecasting, drawing on the cross-analysis of the historical data (market change trend, analysis of time series, seasonal constant, etc.) and on the knowledge one may acquire of future events.

■ It is essential to state that one should take into account the so-called unconstrained demand without focusing on the final occupancy rate. Then, revenue optimization is a compulsory step in a revenue management system. Using specialised software or not, one must determine an estimated allocation per price class using unconstrained demand and in terms of capacity.

References

Belobaba, P. (1989). Application of a probabilistic decision model to airline seat inventory control. *Operations Research*, **37**(2): 183-197.

Belobaba, P. (1992). Optimal vs heuristic methods for nested seat allocation, AGIFORS, Yield Management Study Group, May.

Simpson, R.W. (1985). Setting optimal booking level for flight segments with multi-class, multi-market traffic, MIT Flight Transportation Laboratory Memorandum, Cambridge, MA.

Specklin, F. (2001). Le Revenue Management du transport aérien: Analyse et Synthèse scientifique des modèles du transport des passagers et du fret, Conception du Système d'Informations du Revenue Management à Air France Cargo, Thèse de doctorat en sciences de gestion (PhD), GRID Ecole Normale-Sup. Cachan.

5 Setting up a Revenue Management System

Patrick Legohérel, Elisabeth Poutier and Alan Fyall

Learning outcomes

After reading this chapter, you should be able to:

- Appreciate that in order for revenue managers to successfully complete their mission, they need high performance decision-support systems in place.
- Understand that companies using revenue management techniques need to monitor random demand which must be adapted to a fixed and perishable offer through a system of differential pricing. At stake is the ability to determine how many units (rooms, seats) should be sold at a full and at a reduced price.
- Acknowledge and understand the sophisticated techniques of demand forecasting that are available.
- Understand that a Revenue Management System needs to be usable, enable reliable forecasts and, if possible, offer its users automated or non-automated recommendations.

The purpose of a revenue management system (RMS)

The purpose of a RMS is to ensure turnover growth and company margin optimization.

- **Purposes of the tool for revenue managers:** In general, it enables them to analyze clientele behaviour and market changes. Revenue managers conduct analyses in terms of different detail levels, for a specific date and a fixed goal by:
  - ☐ Clientele segments.
  - ☐ Pricing levels.
  - ☐ Revenue management (RM) levels for the hotel industry.

Revenue managers need to access the information enabling them to monitor, in highly specific ways, the consistency with which the company's strategy is being applied daily. In the hotel industry, for instance, this implies the analysis of the daily revenue management production per class and its comparison with the ideal mix fixed for the day. Moreover, this task enables revenue managers to obtain specific information regarding the market and the clientele behaviour. For instance, the comparison of the bookings pickup for a specific day with the bookings pickup for the same type of day in the past (e.g. events day, ordinary day, and holiday day).

■ **Purposes of the tool for the end users:** The tool should enable hoteliers to manage their revenue management classes more effectively in their daily reservations system. The tool should provide four main benefits:

☐ Knowing every day the measures to be taken.

☐ Knowing the value of the client segments to be communicated.

☐ Adjusting the strategy / ideal mix.

☐ Possessing the main portfolio indicators (reservations and geographic area) for the hotel industry.

■ Architecture of the RMS

Constructing a RMS entails a certain number of operations (see Figure 5.1). The company wishing to integrate revenue management needs to consider the relevance of the constitutive elements of the RMS.

We will now consider the steps relating to the data and the system computerization, as the other steps have been dealt with in the previous chapter.

☐ The type and updating of data

The number of systems, software programs, and databases revenue managers use depends on the size of the company and the choices made by the executive: in-house development or purchase/leasing of software solutions. It is thus essential to ensure that the interface between all software elements is right, that all relevant information is updated, and that no gaps exist.

Using the historical data, the RMS will calculate and show graphically the pickup curves, which enable the revenue managers to monitor demand and bookings per contribution level and length of time at the time of the booking. It is worth noting that reservation periods vary in terms of the different sectors that come together to form the wider hospitality and tourism industries. By examining demand curves, revenue managers are able to determine their clients' reservation profiles and arbitrate the reservation demands accordingly.

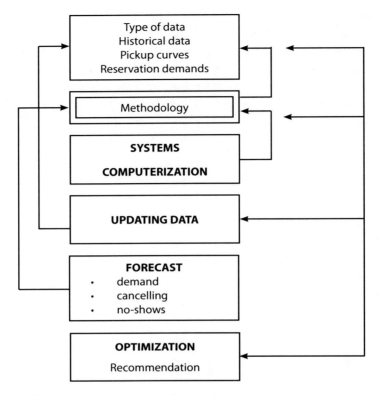

Figure 5.1: Architecture of the Revenue Management System

Collecting data, putting them into readable and usable formats, sharing information, and updating the data are time-consuming and tedious tasks which are best carried out monthly or once or twice a year by revenue managers or trainees. In numerous sectors across Europe and worldwide, workflows are linked directly to specific events. Examples include:

■ the hotel industry, in which activity is regulated by:

☐ The business sector events (in large cities or capitals): conventions, seminars, trade fairs, shows.

☐ The leisure business (tourist sites, seaside resorts, capitals): school holidays, public holidays.

■ The organisers of trade fairs and shows:

☐ Site owners.

☐ Organisers.

☐ Stand designers/suppliers for trade fairs.

■ Manufacturers desiring to show their products and services:

☐ Medical conventions (pharmaceutical laboratories, equipment companies).

☐ Industry shows (Motor Show, Paris le Bourget Air Show).

☐ Fairs (Paris Fair).

☐ Airline, railway, ferry, cruise companies whose activity peaks may be affected directly by school holidays.

■ Shops (sales or special events dates).

■ Advertisers who wish to communicate around a particular event.

The common threads of data updating for all these users are the following:

■ Tedious (the process can take days or weeks).

■ Repetitive (the update has to be carried out regularly).

■ Static (the information has to be collected from different sources).

■ Hard or impossible to share (at best, a database integrated into the information system, at worst, an Excel spreadsheet).

Box 5.1 demonstrates a web-based solution from Pricing iNSiDE/WeYield which enables revenue managers to access an online database that brings together all the elements necessary for the successful revenue optimization of airline companies, hotels, tour operators, cruise ships, trains, etc.

Box 5.1: PEC Professional Event Calendar: A Web-based application to focus on analysis and action?

After connecting to the platform www.thepec.net and identifying themselves, users may search for dates, countries, cities, and specific categories or else check the updates for recent events incorporated into the database.

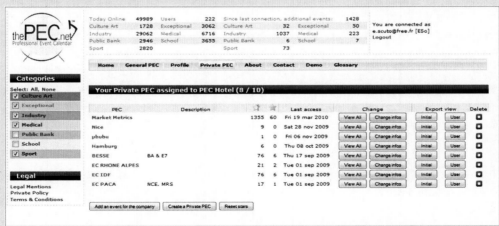

The list mode ensures that users will obtain permanently updated data when they launch a request.

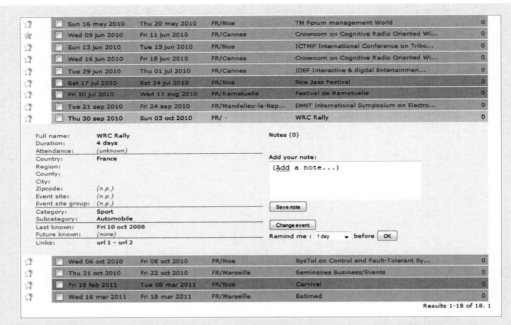

According to users, this web-based application offers numerous advantages:

"This application gives us considerable time savings and direct access to the principal European events. It enables our revenue management team to focus on the impact of the events highlighted by the PEC and to be kept informed proactively of the new events in a given market or region. The regular alerts make it easier for me to search for and identify events. I can instantly tick off those that will have an immediate impact on my hotels and those that will require a fine-turned marketing and commercial analysis towards a possible pricing measure."

Oriane Coquerel, Sales Manager - Hilton Hotels

"Adding the PEC to our yield tool box has helped us enormously. Sometimes, our hotels were full but we didn't know why. Moreover, thanks to the PEC, we can now anticipate demand several months or even years ahead, and the links to the URL of events' organizers give us the opportunity to be proactive in all our sales efforts. And then, the School section that gives details on school holidays throughout the world enables us to anticipate our clients' behaviour changes and to offer well targeted promotions. "

Florence Cohen, Yield Manager, Westminster Hotel.

The RMS can also play a role in the optimization process by giving revenue managers summary tables with the indicators they need for their analysis and the formatting that suits them so they can work as efficiently as possible.

Source : E.Scuto, Pricing iNSiDE/WeYield

■   Software solutions and information systems

We purposefully bring these two concepts together since they are often closely linked in their realisation. There is a wide selection of software packages (such as Excel) or integrated software solutions that can be bought or leased and that address revenue management optimization issues.

☐   In-house, Excel-based, company-specific software solution

The hotel, tourism, air transport and cultural sectors have access to Excel-based tools that are adapted to their specific needs and developed in-house. An Excel spreadsheet enables revenue managers to carry out a number of missions such as the projection valuation/estimation of the turnover, group and tour operators' quotations, among others. It works from two databases (for Year N and Year N-1) and enables the daily analysis of traditional indicators such as TO, ADR, and Revpar, according to room type and segment type. All the data are calculated for each client segment or for all segments and per room type. It is also possible to forecast the monthly demand without taking into account the pricing class, no-shows, and cancellations so as to obtain a more long-term, overall market forecast when the company's projected budgets are determined. Similarly, a number of role players in the air transport sector, such as the airline CORSAIRFLY, have chosen an Excel environment for their RMS.

Box 5.2: Corsairfly and revenue management Excel tools

Strictly speaking, the revenue management service at Corsairfly does not make use of a revenue management information system. Optimization is realised through the consolidation of a certain number of relevant settings within a central management process file designed in an Excel environment. The software advanced functionalities enable the use of the main optimization processes (formulae, filters, pivot tables, etc.). Consequently, the use and effectiveness of this revenue management system rest to a large extent on the presence and quality of information sources and on the capacity of the inventory section to realise the analysts' decisions.

The inventory system Corsairfly uses is the Amadeus software suite (Altea) which enables fine-tuning of the adjustments required by the revenue management service, particularly concerning the allocation of capacity shared between 'flights-only' clients and 'package' clients. A data warehouse consolidates the entire set of sales data found by client type and reservation class, and this for each individual flight.

Related systems feed into the central management process file to enable a comprehensive capture of the decision parameters. These systems include the following:

- information relating to the competitors' capacity and pricing (Innovata, QL2)
- information relating to the competitors' package prices
- information relating to sales performance in GDS (MIDT)
- forecasts relating to demand (Corsairfly in-house models)

Source : Julie Adam, Revenue Analyst, America & Caribbean

☐   Other software solution: an overall RMS

For example, in the airline sector, the market of revenue management solutions for airline companies comprises four major role players.

Figure 5.2: Airline Revenue Management Solutions

Solutions	Traditional Revenue Management	Low cost Revenue Management	Hybrid Revenue Management	Pricing
Sabre	✓	✓	✓	✓
PROS	✓	✓	✓	
Lufthansa Systems	✓	✓		✓
Navitaire		✓		

Source: C. Imbert, Solutions Partner

Sabre, the historical leader, and AirVision Revenue Manager (previously AirMax) constitute one of the more successful hybrid solutions on the market. Sabre was the first to develop a revenue management tool for American Airlines at the beginning of the 1980s, the first Origin & Destination (O&D) solution in 1985 and finally the first hybrid solution in 2004. Over 70 airline companies worldwide use Sabre solutions, including Air France, Alitalia, American Airlines, and Aeroflot. PROS is also an airline market leader, offering a O&D and hybrid solution used by many airline companies such as Iberia, Lufthansa, CSA, or Cathay Pacific. Lufthansa Systems offers a revenue management solution (Rembrandt/ProfitLine) to many regional European airline companies and to hybrid companies such as Spanair and Air Baltic. Finally, Navitaire offers a revenue management solution that is integrated to its inventory solution (SkyPrice) enabling low-cost companies to manage their low-cost revenue management. There are many other role players on the air transport market, such as SITA, Optix, and RMS.

In all sectors, the main question for a company committed to using revenue management techniques is as follows: should one buy or lease a RMS? The price of each revenue management solution depends on the complexity of the company network. Current trends tend towards leasing hosted software (Software As A Service, or SAAS) rather than buying locally installed licenses. As an implementation project generally takes from 6 months to 1 year, it is imperative to set up a project and consultant team to carry out the calibration, implementation, and validation of the tool. The critical steps usually concern the real time interface validation between the RMS and the inventory and the calibration of the revenue management system.

Box 5.3: Successful revenue management adoption at Aeroflot Russian Airlines

Aeroflot is one of the oldest airlines in the world. Founded in 1923, the old public company turned semi-privatised when the USSR collapsed in 1991. Over the past 10 years, Aeroflot has operated major transformations in order to remain a key player in the air transport. With a young fleet of 54 Airbus, Aeroflot decided to implement a Revenue Management System with a clear goal of improving its financial performance. In order to ensure an optimal revenue management culture, Aeroflot identified four areas to concentrate on:

- Work processes.
- Organisation.
- People.
- Reporting and measurement.

Aeroflot decided to implement AirVision Revenue Manager, one of the leading Revenue Management solutions developed by Sabre, and used by more than 70 airlines in the world (including Air France, Alitalia, Aer Lingus, and Norwegian). The system operates in a hybrid Revenue Management framework supporting traditional product based revenue management and price sensitive revenue management. The key factor for success of a Revenue Management system does not only rely on the forecasting and optimization's accuracy, but also on building a culture of performance that will make each analyst accountable and responsible for its routes and revenue target. It is essential to implement a system that will measure and assess each individual and global performance. The system offers the following functionality to Aeroflot:

- Forecasting and Optimization modules operating.
- Business rules engine to support commercial and marketing policy of Aeroflot.
- Exception based management interface.
- Real time connectivity with the inventory and sales channels.
- Capability to capture competitor's fares and data.
- Reporting.

The system was designed to assist the analyst in his decision process. While 80% of the decisions will be automatically undertaken by the system, based on rules defined by Aeroflot, 20% of the decisions will be flagged to the analyst based on 'criticality'. Each critical flight is flagged to the analyst. For example, a flight that is overbooked 10 days before departure will require the analyst's attention. The interface offers the analyst the possibility to review detailed information on the flight, but also historical, financial and competitive information. The analyst can access a complete set of data to support his decision:

- *Historical data.* How the flight behaved previously. In the case of a high overbooking forecast, it is essential to review whether the overbooking rate materialised or not in the past.
- *Competitor's fares.* It is essential to know how competition is behaving. Should a competitor increase its capacity, there is a risk that it would reduce its fares.
- *Financial data.* It is important for the analyst to make decisions that will support the revenue or profit target rather than pure load factor.
- *Group data.* The analyst can query the group data in order to adjust his decision based on group's materialisation rate.

Once the analyst has reviewed the options and made his decision, the inventory and sales channels will be updated in real-time. The analyst can then access a complete set of reports to support its daily tactical decision but also to define a strategy for future flights:

- Capacity offered.
- Seats booked.
- Booking activity (booking curves).
- Competitor's fare activity.
- Flights with a high load factor x days before departure.
- Flights with a low load factor x days before departure.
- Group booking activity.
- Revenue target.
- Deviation between forecast and actual to monitor forecast accuracy.

Additionally, the airline can build specific inventory rules to increase the benefits of its revenue management policy. For example, incremental revenue can be leveraged through a better Point of Sales Control (POS) management, allowing Aeroflot to display specific booking classes for specific markets or channels. In 2008, Aeroflot claimed a 10% incremental net revenue increase (US$145 million) thanks to their revenue management practices. This case demonstrates that implementing a revenue management system along with appropriate organisational changes and people management skills can lead to higher and more sustainable revenues.

Source: Christophe Imbert, Partner at Sabre Airline Solutions

■ A mixed solution: overall RMS and Excel

In the hotel industry, revenue managers are required to develop Excel-based tools to complement the overall RMS (see Box 5.4).

Box 5.4: The Carlton Hotel and the choice of a RMS combining an overall system and Excel

Excel is always used because it can complement the overall system or compensate for certain weaknesses. We thus see a variety of tools such as a database for rooms, a forecast support tool called Forecast, and a decision support tool for groups the sales section uses. In an Excel spreadsheet called 'Forecast', the revenue manager is provided with the 'On The Book' data (bookings entered) according to each segment for each month. He compares them to the 'On The Book' data of the previous year at the same date, which enables him to make quickly a comparison of pickup per segment. By subtracting the targeted Last Forecast data, he knows immediately how many rooms are still to be sold. At the same time, he also compares the Current Forecast figures to the last Forecast figures, so that he can see quickly the differences between the last official forecast and his own personal daily forecast. Thus, he can make a more detailed analysis of the explanations behind the differences.

The group management data are managed by in-house sales staff who use an Excel spreadsheet set up by the revenue manager. For each day, the tool shows the number of available rooms for groups and the average floor price required. The number of rooms allocated to groups is usually calculated in terms of the individual demand forecast. As the latter carries a higher average price than the price for groups, it is given priority regarding capacity. When the number of rooms required by a group exceeds or gets too close to the predetermined quota, the sales staff ask the revenue manager to authorize, or not, confirmation of the demand.

The latter needs to assess the consequent shift in individual demand to work out whether it is worth accepting it or not while taking into account the incidental expenses such as venue and restaurant renting, etc. If the group could be worth it, then the sales staff will negotiate the price, the sale of conference venues and banquet, and the number of rooms while remaining above the floor price.

The number of systems, software and databases used is very important. It is thus essential to ensure that they are correctly interfaced, that the information is updated, and that there are no differences. For instance, if Holidex indicates that there are 30 available rooms whereas, as is shown in Opera, there are only 15 rooms left, there is a 15-room overbooking risk! The reverse is also possible, with the risk of revenue loss.

5

All those tools produce the final outputs, namely the price adjustments, room allocations, or group acceptance or refusal, for instance. For this last step to be pertinent, it is essential that the data entered is accurate. Thus, all the individuals who enter the bookings data need to be made aware of the importance of their role, particularly by explaining the function of bookings, what segments refer to, etc. Then, monitoring needs to take place so as to identify any anomalies. To this end, every morning, the revenue manager consults a record of the bookings entered the previous day and, if need be, of the cancellations.

Similarly, the bookings data going from Opera to Holidex need to be checked. This effort is all the more important as the various sections use the systems for their activity and to take decisions: the managing director who receives reports and the sales staff who need to know room availability per date.

Opera is the hotel's Property Management System (PMS). It is central, as it enables the various sections to monitor activity. The two biggest contributors and clients of the PMS, apart from the revenue manager, are Bookings and Reception. All the hotel bookings are entered into the system, which shows room status, namely clients. Most of the data used for statistics and analyses come from the PMS. In the 'Room Plan' screen, Opera provides a visual presentation of room bookings in terms of dates; through inventory management, the screen enables revenue maximization.

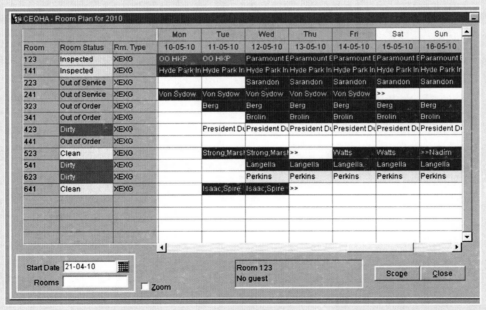

The Integrated Business Plan (IBP) is the hotel's general database. It brings together all the daily data relating to room and restaurant sales: budgets, forecasts, the Sales and Marketing Plan, and statistics per country and distribution channel. It is also an important source of reports. The advantage of IBP is that it enables the grouping of all strategic data into one system. It was developed by the InterContinental chain, which required standardised budget presentations. Finally, there is Holidex, the Central Reservation System (CRS) which centralises all the hotel bookings. It provides the unique confirmation number for each booking. Regardless of the distribution channel, all the bookings are entered into Holidex, either directly or through an interface. Pricing is entered directly and manually into the system.

Perform, the revenue management software, is principally designed to calculate the Bid Prices, called 'Hurdle points', in real time and according to pricing availability. As it is interfaced with Holidex and Opera, it will automatically close for them all prices lower than the Hurdle points.

To recap, here is a diagram showing how the various computer systems communicate with each other. The diagram illustrates well the complexity of the entire system.

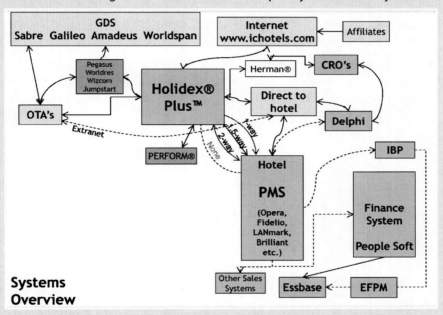

Source : Jad Aboukhater, Revenue Manager, Carlton Hotel, Cannes, France

■ Integration of systems and tools

A wide range of tools, including RMS, are used in hotel and other service companies. One of the main concerns for managers is the integration of all the systems. All tools and systems are (or should be) able to work together.

Here is a list of different tools a hotel manager may have to use:

- PMS (Property Management System) (Opera, Frontes, etc.)
- CRS (Central Reservation System)
- Data/rate tracking tool, rate shopper (QL2, EZ Complete, etc.)

- Channel manager/updater (Rate Tiger, Availpro, EZYield, etc.)
- Forecast and reporting tolls (IdeaS, Hotellingence, etc.)
- RMS (Revenue Management System) (Amadeus RMS, EzRMS, Fidelio-Opera RMS, Hubiz Revenue Management, etc.).

IT companies tend to provide on the market systems and software able to address all functions needed in hotels.

■ Summary

- RMS implementation involves linking a certain number of operations.
- The repetitive steps lead companies that have adopted revenue management to chose among the RMS solutions on the market and examine the relevance of the constituent elements in the RMS.
- To confront fluctuating demand and conduct arbitrations, the revenue manager function needs to make use of more or less sophisticated decision support tools that enable successful strategic management and turnover growth.

Part II

Revenue Management in Practice

6 Revenue Management for Fixing Quotas and Prices of Perishable Commodities under Uncertainty

SS Padhi

Learning outcomes

After reading this chapter, you should be able to:

■ Understand the dynamics of a decision making model and approach for the revenue management of perishable commodities under uncertainty of demand, through fixing quotas and prices of commodities.

■ Appreciate the superiority of the proposed approach by comparing the respective revenues generated through the new quotas and prices using the proposed yield maximisation model, with that of the old practised prices and quotas.

■ Understand the applicability of the model, which offers theoretical and real-time facilitation in hospitality management, through the case study of a hotel.

■ Introduction and literature

Revenue management (RM) refers to the strategy and tactics used by a number of industries to manage the allocation of their capacity over time to different willingness to pay end-users in order to maximise revenue (Burgess & Bryant, 2001; Phillips, 2005; Sanchez & Satir, 2005). According to Sanchez and Satir (2005), it is a holistic and systematic approach to maximise revenue through varying the rates offered to the end-users in light of forecasted demand and supply patterns. Shy (2008) defines RM as the utilisation of profit-maximising pricing techniques.

From several studies (e.g., Kimes, 2000; Phillips, 2005; Sanchez & Satir, 2005; Wang & Bowie, 2009), it emerges that RM is applicable when:

1 The provider is offering a fixed quantity of perishable capacity;

2 The receivers (or the end-users) book capacity prior to using the commodity;

3 The provider manages a set of price modules; and

4 The provider can change the choice of price modules over time.

The various approaches of RM are geared towards allocating the right percentage of capacity to the right end-user at the right time for the right price. Hence, market segmentation, timing (demand and supply management) and pricing are the three cornerstones of RM. Its successful implementation should benefit all the stakeholders. The provider of the service benefits in terms of increased yield and thus higher revenues, whereas the end-user has the option of taking advantage of reduced prices at non-peak times for the same service quality (Sanchez & Satir, 2005; Palmer & McMahon-Beattie, 2008).

Many industries have been reaping the benefits by employing the concepts of revenue management in their businesses (Wang & Bowie, 2009). In particular, the capacity- constrained service industry has been a popular area of research for many researchers for the last two decades. Predominantly researchers have applied revenue management in capacity-constrained service industries. For Example, Orkin (1988), Kimes (1989a), Brotherton and Mooney (1992), Weatherford and Kimes (2001), Burgess and Bryant (2001), Sezen (2004), Harewood (2006) have used the concepts of revenue management in the hospitality sector; Kimes (1989b) in healthcare; Goulding and Leask (1997) and Heo and Lee (2009) in theme parks; Hoseason and Johns (1998) in cruise lines; Hwang and Wen (2009), Noone and Mattila (2009), Guadix, Cortés, Onieva and Muñuzuri (2010), Padhi and Aggarwal (2011) in the hotel industry; Kasilingam (1997), Kuyumcu and Garcia-Diaz (2000), Gorin and Belobaba (2004), Luo and Peng (2007), Lindenmeier and Tscheulin (2008) in the airline industry; Bharill and Rangaraj (2008) in railways; and Tsai and Hung (2009) in Internet retailing. Although there is extensive literature available on applications of RM practices in various service industries, the literature is, however, scant in the field of RM under uncertainty for fixing of quota and price of hotel commodities (perishable commodities), where it is difficult to handle RM under stochastic market conditions, i.e., under uncertain customer demand, customer preferences, and commodity price. For example, the hotel industry faces problems while allocating different types of rooms – Standard, Deluxe, Junior Suite, Suite — to customers under various schemes, such as complimentary, honeymoon, season, summit, where hotel managements only have past information of the customers demand and market condition. Thus RM under uncertainty is an important field of investigation (Hwang & Wen, 2009; Morales & Wang, 2010; Padhi & Aggarwal, 2011), and many RM researchers have developed probability models or forecasting methods to reduce the level of uncertainty.

However, researchers have paid little attention towards competitive RM of the hotel industry under price uncertainty. Most researches in the past have assumed the hotel to be a price maker rather than a price taker under competition. Moreover, the hotel industry as an emerging business provides a typical pattern of competitive and dynamic pricing (Madanoglu & Brezina, 2008). The problem of RM in the hotel industry is complicated and challenging, not only because of a variety of commodity offerings, but also because of revenue uncertainty and complex cost structures (Padhi & Aggarwal, 2011).

For these reasons, this chapter aims to present a practical and flexible approach to optimise the competitive RM of the hotel industry under price uncertainty. The integrated real options approach developed by Tsai and Hung (2009) has been modified for the RM problem of Internet auctions to implement it in the RM of hotels. Since it is difficult to access the real option values of hotel rooms (commodities) and categorise them to poor, normal, and high prices commodities, the profit of each commodity was forecast, based on past trends using artificial neural network (ANN) methodology, and categorised accordingly. The analytic hierarchy process (AHP) methodology was adopted to assign quotas of each commodity (as a long-term goal), and the maximum expected profit (risk adjusted) of each commodity was used as a short-term goal to reap the multifaceted revenue performance under low risk and high expected profit setups (Reynolds & Braithwaite, 1997). Finally goal programming was used to fix the optimal quota and price of each commodity under each category for various schemes under uncertainty.

■ Dynamic revenue management framework with forecasted values

This chapter develops a forecasting approach to solve the dynamic pricing under uncertainty RM problem for a hotel. In each period, the hotel selects the optimal commodity mix with a fixed budget. For each commodity, the firm must fix prices (p) and number of bookings (x) having probability of cancellation of bookings (α) (Harewood, 2006; Morales & Wang, 2010). It can increase the quota of a commodity (such as high profit commodity, +1), keep it as it is (such as normal profit commodity, 0), or decrease the quota (such as for low profit commodity, -1). The hotels display the price of different rooms under different schemes. For setting up the price and number of rooms under different schemes, hotel management looks for the past trend of occupancy of rooms (demand), operating cost and service complexity associated with it and calculates the profit obtained under each category of commodities. The ANN based forecasting can help them to a better understanding and proper evaluation of the prices and quotas. In order to perform dynamic RM, the hotel scrutinizes the profit under each category in each period for allocating its fixed budget, optimally and in a timely manner.

For each commodity, the hotel has the right (under Indian Deregulation Act, 1956) to offer a fixed quota with favourable operating costs in each period. Each quota can only be replenished in the next period. If the hotel wants to increase the quota (or lower the quota) for a commodity, then the hotel has to incur additional operating costs to render service, and in case of decreasing the quota, it has to withdraw the operating cost for changing the capacities of the commodities.

From forecasting profit to fixing the optimal quota for each commodity, we have followed a three step approach as shown in Figure 6.1.

Forecast profit	Through forecasting the profit the lower and upper bounds of each commodity are determined. The average prices of the commodities in the last period are assessed by the forecast lower and upper bounds. If the price is larger than the upper bound (or lower than the lower bound), then the quota of that commodity should be increased or decreased respectively. If the price is within the bounds, the initial quota of the normal commodity should be maintained. This step is used to identify the commodity prices that are too low, and detect the commodities that have favourable performance.
AHP assessment	To determine the increments and decrements in the number of commodities under different categories, as a long-term analysis, the AHP methodology was used. Using a simple three levels AHP network the weights of the commodities are determined. Where the criteria — Duration of stay, Excess demand, Market share, Operations cost, and Revenue generated — to evaluate the commodities are assessed by the hotel managements. The five evaluation criteria are widely accepted as the long-term assessment criteria for hotel commodity management (Upchurch, Ellis & Seo, 2002; Harewood, 2006).
Fixing optimal quota	A portion of the budget is retained for diversification, customer services, and possible changes, so that the minimum quotas of the low and normal commodities will be reserved, and the minimum quota increments of the high profit commodities will also be reserved. The budget amount is first determined, and then allocated to the commodities by the AHP weights, as a long term indicator, to determine the minimum quota and minimum quota increment. The other portion of the budget is used for timely quota increment and decrement. For timely adjustment, the quota should be further adjusted based on the latest information. Therefore, a Goal programming approach was adopted where short-term lead indicators, such as risk adjusted expected profit (RAEP) and expected revenue, will be maximised after long-term performance has achieved a certain acceptable level. In this way, short-term indicators will be more reliable.

Figure 6.1: Decision steps for fixing of optimal quota

■ Case study and discussion

To handle the above-mentioned RM problem, the following three steps were taken to get acquainted with the past and current hotel commodity booking data:

1 Browsing the website of the hotel and studying the details regarding the types of rooms and facility provided by it.

2   Gathering information on the details of the pattern of commodity bookings, profit yielded by each commodity, types of expenses involved, such as operating cost, service complexity with each commodity, by interviewing the hotel's staff and management.

3   Collecting the past records and relevant data from the hotel log-books.

☐ Forecast profit using artificial neural network

An artificial neural network (ANN) is a computing system made up of an interconnected set of simple information processing elements (PE). The PE collect inputs from both single and multiple sources, and produces output in accordance with a certain transfer function. Some inputs to the neuron may have more relevance than others, and this is modelled by weighting. Generally, the main principle of neural computing is the decomposition of the input–output relationship into a series of linearly separable steps using hidden layers (Haykin, 1994; Padhi and Aggarwal, 2011). There are four distinct steps in developing an ANN-based solution. They are:

1   *Data transformation:* Large variations in the input data can slow down or even prevent the training and weight optimization of the network. To overcome these problems, the data are usually scaled or normalized (Haykin, 1994; Priddy & Keller, 2005: Padhi & Agarwal, 2011). For the case under consideration, the data sets were normalized between –1.0 to +1.0 to improve the weight optimization (Gunn, 1998). The data were normalized using the following equation:

$$\lambda_n = (\beta - \delta) \times \left[\frac{\lambda_0 - \lambda_{min}}{\lambda_{max} - \lambda_{min}} \right] + \delta$$

Where λ_n is a normalized variable; δ is the minimum range of the variable *i.e.,* (-1); β is the maximum range of the variable *i.e.,* (+1); λ_{max} is the maximum value in the time series and λ_{min} is the minimum value in the time series.

Table 6.1: Basic statistics of profit data sets for training and testing

Commodity	Training (2005-2008)	Testing (2009-2011)
Sample size	158 weeks	64 weeks
Minimum profit (million rupees)	81	67
Maximum profit (million rupees)	138	111
Profit range (million rupees)	61	46
Mean profit (million rupees)	114	78
Std. deviation (million rupees)	19	11

2   The number of hidden layers, the number of neurons in each layer, and the connectivity between the neurons are set. There are three basic layers or levels of data processing units, namely the input layer, the hidden layer and the

output layer. Each of these layers consists of processing elements (PE). The number of input PE, output PE and the PE in the hidden layer depends upon the problem being studied (Karunanithi, Grenney, Whitley & Bovee, 1994). Obtaining the optimum number of hidden neurons in the ANN architecture is a trial-and-error process, which depends on the quality of data and the type of problem.

Following the works of Haykin (1999), Sivanandam, Sumathi & Deepa (2006), Pramanik and Panda (2009) and Padhi and Aggarwal (2011) for this case, we have used multilayer perceptrons feed-forward neural network with three PE as inputs for predicting profit (output) of four types of commodities, shown in Figure 6.2. Where each connection between PEs is weighted by a scalar weight (*w*), which is adapted during model training, and a bias (*e*). The PE in the multilayer perceptrons generates the final output from the net inputs, using nonlinear activation functions. One hidden layer having five PE is used to develop the neural network architecture.

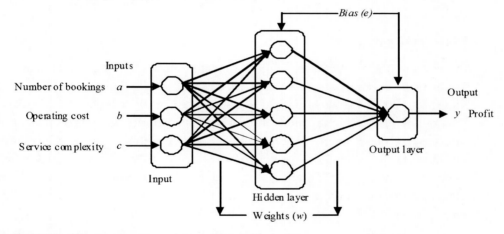

Figure 6.2: Multilayer perceptron with single hidden layer

3 To train the network to respond correctly to a given set of inputs, a learning algorithm is used. The training goal is to find parameters that result in the best performance of the network with unfamiliar data by updating connection weights through establishing a desired input–output relationship. For the case under consideration, we have used *Levenberg–Marquardt* algorithm (Charalambous, 1992; Wilamowski, Chen & Malinowski, 1999; Chen, Han, Au & Than, 2003) that works on back-propagation principles, for training a multilayer perceptrons feed-forward neural network as shown in Figure 6.2.

4 The performance of the trained ANN model is tested using some selected validation data sets. Validation can be employed to monitor the network error during training to determine the optimal number of training iterations. It can also be used to find out the optimal number of hidden neurons. For the case under consideration, training, testing, model validation, and overall performances of the trained networks were judged with respect to the modelling efficiency (*E*), correlation coefficient (*R*), and root mean square error (RMSE) using *MATLAB 7.1* software package. The difference between the observed and the ANN computed approximate profit was used to evaluate the prediction capability of the trained networks. The expressions of the model validation parameters – vindicate the model is reliable (Dawson & Wilby, 1999) – and forecasted average profit are presented in Table 6.2.

Table 6.2: Model validation and 10-week profit forecasting for various commodities

Commodity	Scale	ANN structure	R	E	RMSE (profit/ week)	Forecasted Avg. Profit (approx)/week
Standard	−1.0 to +1.0	3-5-1	0.876	0.810	83.03	0.83 ≈ +1
Deluxe	−1.0 to +1.0	3-5-1	0.846	0.827	82.31	0.85 ≈ +1
Junior suite	−1.0 to +1.0	3-5-1	0.817	0.803	78.13	-0.78 ≈ -1
Suite	−1.0 to +1.0	3-5-1	0.829	0.832	79.52	0.79 ≈ +1

☐   ## AHP assessment

To measure the importance weights of commodities for yield management, five evaluation criteria were extracted from past works (Upchurch *et al.*, 2002; Harewood, 2006; Tsai & Hung, 2009) shown in *Level 1* of Figure 6.3. By interviewing the management staff of three hotels, the priority weights of evaluation criteria were determined. To determine priority weights of evaluation criteria and importance weights of types of commodities (*Level 2* of Figure 6.3) Analytic Hierarchy Process (AHP) methodology (Saaty, 1980) was adopted. The logic of using AHP for measuring weights was due to the dependence between the evaluation criteria, shown by arrow heads in level 1 of Figure 6.3.

Table 6.3 provides the priority weights of criteria (*Level 1*) and its normalised priority weight in Column 1 and 2 of Table 6.3. Column 3 and Column 4 of Table 6.3 provides the type of commodity and its normalised importance weight. For calculating the Priority and importance weights of criteria and commodities we have used *Superdecision 2.0.8* software package employing nine point Saaty scale.

Table 6.3: Priority and importance weights of criteria and commodities

Criteria	Normalized priority weight	Commodity	Normalized importance weight
Duration of stay	0.104	Standard	0.285
Excess demand	0.210	Deluxe	0.304
Market share	0.107	Junior suite	0.158
Operations cost	0.131	Suite	0.253
Revenue generated	0.448		

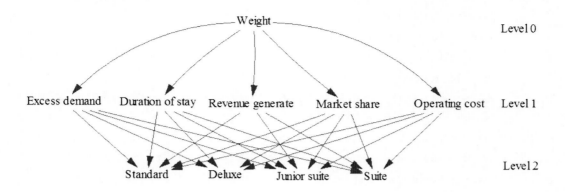

Figure 6.3: Network of criteria and commodities

☐   Fixing optimal quotas

Fixing optimal quotas for each commodity is a multi-attribute decision-making problem. Where individual commodities contribute to the total profit of the hotel differently on different parameters and increment or decrement, keeping fix of quota for each commodity makes the problem challenging. Additionally, when price elasticity is considered for a commodity to set favorable price of each commodity under increment or decrement of quota makes the problem more complex. To solve this problem, a goal programming approach was used.

Goal programming is a very widely used technique for multi-objective decision making. There have been a number of extensions of the basic goal programming approach. Here the decision makers set some acceptable aspiration levels to achieve a set of goals as closely as possible with preset goals. Of relevance to this paper is the goal programming (Özcan & Toklu, 2009; Padhi & Mohapatra, 2010). In these modeling approaches, decision variables are integers and reflect the number of commodities booking in a planned season.

Index

i	Index for the commodities, for all i = 1, 2, ..., I;
j	Index for the forecasted profit of each commodity, for all j = 1, 2, ...,
	where j = 1 below the normal profit, i.e. -1 extracted from ANN analysis.
	j = 2 normal profit, i.e. 0 extracted from ANN analysis.
	j = 3 above the normal profit, i.e. +1 extracted from ANN analysis.
t	Index for the time period (in week) for all t = 1, 2, ... , T
$P_{ij,\,t}$	Price of i-th type commodity under j-th category on week t;
$X_{ij,\,t}$	Number of bookings of i-th type commodity under j-th category on week t;

C_t Capacity of the hotel on t-th week

B_t Budget allotted for the t-th week

$\hat{R}_t$ Estimated revenue for the t-th week

G Objective function

$\theta_{ij,t}$ Importance weight of i-th type commodity (determined through AHP methodology) under j-th category on week t;

$AHPG_t$ AHP weight goal for commodities on week t;

$d_{g,t}^-$ Negative deviation representing under achievements of the targeted goals

$d_{g,t}^+$ Positive deviation representing over achievements of the targeted goals

$E(pft)_{ij}$ Expected rate of profit earned by i-th type commodity under j-th category in the last period

v_{ij} Actual past volatility of profit earned by i-th type commodity under j-th category in the last period

MEP_t Maximum expected profit (risk adjusted) on week t;

$SO_{ij,t}$ Number of i-th type commodity under j-th category on week t offered by the hotel under some schemes;

$\alpha_{ij,t}$ Probability of cancellation of bookings of i-th type commodity under j-th category on week t;

$PE_{ij,t}$ Price elasticity of i-th type commodity under j-th category;

$z_{ij,t}$ Increments (or decrements) in number of i-th type commodity under j-th category on week t;

$w_{ij,t}$ Operating cost of i-th type commodity under j-th category on week t;

$h_{i3,t}$ Increment in operating cost due to increase of i-th type commodity under j-th category (profit making $j=3$) on week t;

$l_{i1,t}$ Decrement in operating cost due to decrease of i-th type commodity under j-th category (profit making $j=1$) on week t;

Goals

The total revenue earned from booking of commodities should approximately equal the total estimated revenue for all the commodities in the planned season.

$$\sum_i \sum_j (1 - \alpha_{ij,t}) p_{ij,t} x_{ij,t} + d_{1,t}^- - d_{1,t}^+ = \hat{R}_t \tag{1}$$

where $d_{1,t}^-$ and $d_{1,t}^+$ are the under-achievement and over-achievement of the goal (the total estimated revenue).

The importance weight of each commodity, determined using AHP methodology, must not exceed the short term assigned cost indicator value.

$$\sum_i \sum_j \theta_{ij,t} x_{ij,t} + d_{2,t}^- - d_{2,t}^+ = ANPG_t \tag{2}$$

The ratio of expected profit yielded from the commodity to the volatility of that commodity, in the last period, is a major short term indicator of risk adjusted expected profit. So the hotel management wants to minimize the deviation from the maximum expected profit to the sum of risk adjusted expected profit of each commodity.

$$\sum_i \sum_j [E(pfi_j)/v_j]x_{j,t} + d_{3,t}^- - d_{3,t}^+ = MEP_t; \tag{3}$$

Constraints

Subjected to Constraint (Equation 4), which is the fixed budget sanctioned for the planned period, and the expenses against each commodity should not exceed the total sanctioned budget.

$$\sum_i \sum_j w_{j,t}(1-\alpha_{j,t})x_{j,t} + \sum_j h_{i3,t}(1-\alpha_{i3,t})z_{i3,t} - \sum_j l_{i1,t}(1-\alpha_{i1,t})z_{i1,t} \le B_t; \tag{4}$$

Subjected to Constraint (Equation 5), which is the total number of bookings over the planned period should not exceed the capacity of the hotel.

$$\sum_i \sum_j (1-\alpha_{ij,t})x_{ij,t} \le C_t; \tag{5}$$

Equations (6) through (9) are quota constraint, *i.e.* the number of rooms should be kept, for booking, under each category in the planned season, which should not be more than (eq. 6), equal to (eq. 7), and less than (eq. 8) the sanctioned quota based on the assessment of forecasted profit. Furthermore, number of rooms sanctioned under each category for a planned season should be higher than the quota increment of that commodity (eq. 9).

$$(1-\alpha_{ij,t})x_{ij,t} < so_{ij,t-1} \qquad for \qquad j=1, \forall\, i\,; \tag{6}$$

$$(1-\alpha_{ij,t})x_{ij,t} = so_{ij,t-1} \qquad for \qquad j=2, \forall\, i\,; \tag{7}$$

$$(1-\alpha_{ij,t})x_{ij,t} \ge so_{ij,t-1} + \Delta sq_{ij,t} \qquad for \qquad j=3, \forall\, i\,; \tag{8}$$

$$(1-\alpha_{ij,t})x_{ij,t} \ge \Delta so_{ij,t} \qquad for \qquad \forall\, i\,; \tag{9}$$

Equation (10) is for decrement in quota for the low profit commodity and Equation (11) for the maximum price decrement limit considering price elasticity of 1, *i.e.* neither elastic nor inelastic price under change in quota of the low profit making commodity.

$$so_{ij,t-1} - x_{ij,t} = z_{ij,t} \qquad for \qquad j=1, \forall\, i\,; \tag{10}$$

$$[(-z_{ij,t}/so_{ij,t-1})/(P_{ij,t} - P_{ij,t-1}/P_{ij,t-1})] = PE_{ij,t} \quad for \qquad j=1, \forall\, i\,; \tag{11}$$

Equation (12) is for increment in quota for the normal and high profit making commodities and Equation (13) is for the maximum price increment limit considering price elasticity of 1.

$$x_{ij,t} - so_{ij,t-1} = z_{ij,t} \qquad for \qquad j=2,3, \forall\, i\,; \tag{12}$$

$$\left[(z_{ij,\,t} / so_{ij,\,t\text{-}1}) \; / \; (P_{ij,\,t} - P_{ij,\,t\text{-}1} / P_{ij,\,t\text{-}1}) \right] = PE_{ij,\,t} \qquad for \qquad j = 2,3, \; \forall\, i \,; \qquad (13)$$

Non-negative restrictions equation 14

$$d_g^- \geq 0, \; d_g^+ \geq 0 \quad \forall g \tag{14}$$

Objective function

The objective function (Equation 15) is to minimize the deviation derived from the bookings over the planned season.

$$Minimize \; Z = (d_{1,t}^-) + (d_{2,t}^+) + (d_{3,t}^-) \tag{15}$$

■ Results and discussions

Using equations (1) through (15) and considering the parameter values observed for the planned season of the hotel and the requirement sate by the hotel management for each parameter (provided in Table 6.4 and Table 6.5 respectively) the optimisation problem was solved.

Table 6. 4 gives the observed parameter values for each commodity of the hotel. Column 1 of Table 6.4 gives the index of various types of parameters. Columns 2 through 5 of Table 6.2 give the details of the corresponding commodity values for different parameters.

Table 6.4: Observed parameter values

Parameters	Standard	Deluxe	Junior suite	Suite
$P_{ij,\,t}$	6.835*	9.750*	14.825*	18.275*
j	3	3	1	3
$\theta_{ij,t}$	0.283	0.306	0.156	0.255
$E(pft)_{ij}$	1267*	2354*	-3113*	5098*
v_{ij}	311*	544*	749*	919*
$w_{ij,t}$	4.113*	7.466*	12.684*	15.761*
$l_{i1,t}$	2.665*	3.926*	7.467*	9.795*
$h_{i3,t}$	3.251*	5.134*	9.235*	11.324*
$(1\text{-}\alpha_{ij,t})$	0.94	0.95	0.95	0.96
$so_{ij,t\text{-}1}$	85	75	35	25
$PE_{ij,\,t}$	1	1	1	1

* Thousand rupees (Indian currency)

Table 6.5: Value of parameter goals and constraints set by hotel management.

Estimated revenue	Diversion cost (ANPG)	Maximum expected profit	Maximum operating cost	Capacity of the hotel
2150*	65*	750*	1750*	220

* Thousand rupees (Indian currency)

This problem has been formulated as a goal programming model (mentioned in section 3.3). We have used the LINDO 8 software package (Schrage, 1999) to solve the problem. The objective function value $Z^* = 9.478$ and the optimal values of the decision variables are given in Table 6.6. The results imply that the quota of standard, deluxe, and suite commodities should be increased and of junior suite should be decreased, and the respective favourable price of each commodity considering price elasticity of 1. The over-achievement and under-achievement values of each goal are the following: $d_1^- = 0, d_2^- = 5.73, d_3^- = 3.75$, and $d_1^+ = d_2^+ = d_3^+ = 0$. The optimal solution meets the first goal, whereas the second and third goals are under achieved by a slight margin.

Table 6.6: Optimal quota and favourable price of commodity

Parameters	Standard	Deluxe	Junior suite	Suite
$\Delta so_{ij,\ t}$	7	4	-7	1
$so_{ij,\ t-1} + \Delta so_{ij,\ t}$	92	79	28	26
$Max\ P_{ij,\ t}$	7.398*	10.270*	11.860*	19.000*

* Thousand rupees (Indian currency)

Table 6.7 gives the following:

1 The total revenue that could be earned by the hotel, considered in this paper, by keeping the old price and old quota, i.e. 2287.98 thousand rupees (Indian currency)

2 The total revenue that could be earned through implementing new price of hotel commodities with old quota, i.e. 2289.18 thousand rupees, which is better than the previous case.

3 The revenue obtained for the case when the old price of hotel commodities is kept as it is and with new quota of commodities are allotted, i.e. 2289.32 thousand rupees, which is better than the previous both the cases.

4 Finally, the revenue yielded when the new price for each commodity with new quotas are allotted, i.e. 2318.03 thousand rupees, which is the maximum and also superior to all the three cases. Thus fixing the optimal quota and price, using the proposed model, for hotel commodities would yield superior outcomes.

Table 6.7: Comparison of optimal parameter values

Parameters	Total Revenue
Old price with old quota	2287.98*
New price with old quota	2289.18*
Old price with new quota	2289.32*
New price with new quota	2318.03*

* Thousand rupees (Indian currency)

■ Summary

- In order to earn higher yield, hotels are practicing RM through dynamic pricing to capture the diversified 'willingness to pay' customers. RM of hotel commodities under price uncertainty is an increasingly important issue in practice. Considering the importance of the research, this chapter tries to optimise the quota and price of hotel commodities for improved RM.

- RM is a multi-attribute decision-making problem and as such an artificial neural network, analytic hierarchy process, and goal programming approaches were used to solve the RM problem. For fixing of optimal quota and price both lead and lag indicators (AHP weights and risk adjusted expected profit) were used in the goal programming model.

- The model is credible because it yields superior outcomes in terms of revenue when the new quota and new price are considered. When solved with the consideration of old quota and price, the model yields inferior revenues compared to the new quota and price. Based on this observation, the chapter concludes that hotel management should adopt the modelled outputs to reap higher revenues.

- The model can be used to evaluate other service industries having uncertainties of allotments and complex cost structure. Using this model, an online decision support system could be developed to fix optimal quota and price of commodities. Data must be stored for monitoring bookings, rebooking, and cancellation by customers and preference shown by customers against each commodity. An online database can be developed to store the past records of the customers and can be used to analyze customer behaviour.

References

Bharill, R. & Rangaraj, N. (2008). Revenue management in railway operations: a study of the Rajdhani Express, Indian Railways. *Transportation Research Part A: Policy and Practice*, **42**(9): 1195-1207.

Brotherton, B. & Mooney, S. (1992). Yield management – progress and prospects. *International Journal of Hospitality Management*, **11**(1): 23–32.

Burgess, C. & Bryant, K. (2001). Revenue management – the contribution of the finance function to profitability. *International Journal of Contemporary Hospitality Management*, **13**(3): 144-150.

Charalambous, C. (1992). Conjugate gradient algorithm for efficient training of artificial neural networks. *IEE Proceedings*, B(3): 301-310.

Chen, T. C., Han, D. J., Au, F. T. K. & Than, L. G. (2003). Acceleration of Levenberg-Marquardt training of neural networks with variable decay rate. *IEEE Trans. on Neural Net.*, **3**(6): 1873 - 1878.

Dawson, C. W. & Wilby, R. B. (1999). A comparison of artificial networks flow forecasting. *Hydrol. Earth System Sci.*, **3**: 529–540.

Deregulation of price Indian Company Act. (1956), www.legalserviceindia.com (accessed 24 April 2010)

Gorin, T. & Belobaba, P. (2004). Impacts of entry in airline markets: effects of revenue management on traditional measures of airline performance. *Journal of Air Transport Management*, **10**(4): 257-268.

Goulding, P.J. & Leask, A. (1997). Scottish visitor attractions: revenue versus capacity. In I. Yeoman & Ingold, A. (Eds), *Yield Management: Strategies for the Service Industries*. London: Cassell, 160-82.

Guadix, J., Cortés, P., Onieva, L. & Muñuzuri, J. (2010). Technology revenue management system for customer groups in hotels. *Journal of Business Research*, **63**(5): 519-527.

Harewood, S. I. (2006). Managing a hotel's perishable inventory using bid prices. *International Journal of Operations & Production Management*, **26**(10): 1108-1122.

Haykin, S. (1994). *Neural Networks*. Englewood Cliffs, New Jersey: Macmillan.

Haykin, S. (1999). *Neural Networks: A Comprehensive Foundation* (2nd Edition): New Delhi: Prentice Hall.

Heo, C. Y. & Lee, S. (2009). Application of revenue management practices to the theme park industry. *International Journal of Hospitality Management*, **28**(3): 446-453.

Hoseason, J. & Johns, N. (1998). The numbers game: the role of yield management in the tour operations industry. *Progress in Tourism and Hospitality Research*, **4**: 97-106.

Hwang, J. & Wen, L. (2009). The effect of perceived fairness toward hotel overbooking and compensation practices on customer loyalty. *International Journal of Contemporary Hospitality Management*, **21**(6): 659-675.

Karunanithi, N., Grenney, W. J., Whitley, D. & Bovee, K. (1994). Neural networks for river flow prediction. *J. Comput. Civil Engng ASCE*, **8**(2): 201–220.

6

Kasilingam, R. G. (1997). Air cargo revenue management: characteristics and complexities. *European Journal of Operational Research*, **96**(1): 36-44.

Kimes, S.E. (1989a). The basics of yield management. *The Cornell Hotel and Restaurant Administration Quarterly*, **30**(3): 14-19.

Kimes, S.E. (1989b). Yield management: a tool for capacity-constrained service firms. *Journal of Operations Management*, **8**(4): 348-63.

Kimes, S. E. (2000). Revenue management on the links: applying yield management to the golf industry. *Cornell Hotel and Restaurant Administration Quarterly*, 41(1): 120-127.

Kuyumcu, A. & Garcia-Diaz, A. (2000). A polyhedral graph theory approach to revenue management in the airline industry. *Computers & Industrial Engineering*, **38**(3): 375-395.

Lindenmeier, J. & Tscheulin, D. K. (2008). The effects of inventory control and denied boarding on customer satisfaction: the case of capacity-based airline revenue management. *Tourism Management*, **29**(1): 32-43.

Luo, L. & Peng, J. (2007). Dynamic pricing model for airline revenue management under competition. *Systems Engineering - Theory & Practice*, **27**(11): 15-25.

Madanoglu, M. & Brezina, S. (2008). Resort spas: how are they massaging hotel revenues?, *International Journal of Contemporary Hospitality Management*, **20**(1): 60-66.

Morales, D. R. & Wang, J. (2010). Forecasting cancellation rates for services booking revenue management using data mining. *European Journal of Operational Research*, **202**(2): 554-562.

Noone, B. M. & Mattila, A. S. (2009). Hotel revenue management and the Internet: the effect of price presentation strategies on customers' willingness to book. *International Journal of Hospitality Management*, **28**(2): 272-279.

Orkin, E.B. (1988). Boosting your bottom line with yield management. *The Cornell Hotel and Restaurant Administration Quarterly*, **28**: 52-56

Özcan, U. & Toklu, B. (2009). Multiple-criteria decision-making in two-sided assembly line balancing: a goal programming and a fuzzy goal programming models. *Computers & Operations Research*, **36**: 1955–1965.

Padhi, S. S. & Mohapatra, P. K. J. (2010). Centralized bid evaluation for awarding of construction projects – a case of India Government. *International Journal of Project Management*, **28**: 275-284.

Padhi, S. S. & Aggarwal, V. (2011). Competitive revenue management for fixing quota and price of hotel commodities under uncertainty. *International Journal of Hospitality Management*, **30**(3): 725-734.

Palmer, A. & McMahon-Beattie, U. (2008). Variable pricing through revenue management: a critical evaluation of affective outcomes. *Management Research News*, **31**(3): 189-199.

Phillips, R. L. (2005). *Pricing and Revenue Optimization*. Stanford, CA: Stanford University Press.

Pramanik, N. & Panda, R. K. (2009). Application of neural network and adaptive neuro-fuzzy inference systems for river flow prediction. *Hydrological Sciences Journal*, **54**(2): 247-260.

Priddy, L. K. & Keller, E. P. (2005). Artificial Neural Networks: An Introduction. Bellingham, WA: SPIE Press.

Reynolds, P. C. & Braithwaite, R. W. (1997). Whose yield is it anyway? compromise options for sustainable boat tour ventures. *International Journal of Contemporary Hospitality Management*, **9**(2): 70–74.

Saaty, T. L. (1980). *The Analytic Hierarchy Process*. New York: McGraw Hill International.

Sanchez, J-F. & Satir, A. (2005). Hotel yield management using different reservation modes. *International Journal of Contemporary Hospitality Management*, **17**(2): 136-146.

Schrage, L. (1999). LINGO Release 6.0, LINDO System, Inc., USA.

Sezen, B. (2004). Expected profit approach used in discount pricing decisions for perishable products. *International Journal of Retail & Distribution Management*, **32**(4): 223-229.

Shy, O. (2008). *How to Price a Guide to Pricing Techniques and Yield Management*. New York: Cambridge University Press.

Sivanandam, S. N., Sumathi, S. & Deepa, S. N. (2006). *Introduction to Neural Networks using MATLAB 6.0*. New Delhi, India: Tata McGraw-Hill Publishing Company limited.

Tsai, W-H. & Hung, S-J. (2009). Dynamic pricing and revenue management process in internet retailing under uncertainty: an integrated real options approach. *Omega*, **37**: 471-481.

Upchurch, R. S., Ellis, T. & Seo, J. (2002). Revenue management underpinnings: an exploratory review. *International Journal of Hospitality Management*, **21**: 67-83.

Wang, X. L. & Bowie, D. (2009). Revenue management: the impact on business-to-business relationships. *Journal of Services Marketing*, **23**(1): 31 – 41.

Weatherford, L.R. & Kimes, S.E. (2001). Forecasting for hotel yield management: testing aggregation against disaggregation. *Cornell Hotel and Restaurant Administration Quarterly*, **42**: 63-4.

Wilamowski, B. M., Chen, Y. & Malinowski, A. (1999). Efficient algorithm for training neural networks with one hidden layer. *In Proc. IJCNN*, **3**: 1725-728.

6

7 Revenue Management in China's Lodging Sector: Practices and Challenges

Larry Yu and Huimin Gu

Learning outcomes

After reading this chapter, you should be able to:

- Understand hotel revenue performance in China by ownership, management, level of services determined by star-ranking system, and major hotel markets in China.

- Appreciate a macro review of hotel financial performance which demonstrates the diversity and complexity of hotel ownership structures, management organisations and regional variations in hotel revenue generation.

- Understand the challenges facing China's hotel industry for implementing effective revenue management systems, including insufficient forecasting based on past performance data, lack of a uniform system of accounts for the hotel industry, inadequate market segmentation for developing a differentiated pricing structure to capture consumers of different price points, inefficient management structure and knowledge of revenue management facing many state-owned enterprises (SOE) and domestic private firms.

Introduction

The lodging sector in the Chinese tourism industry became one of the earliest businesses to be exposed to international hotel management standards, when China first instituted joint-venture hotel development initiative in the early 1980s and later granted sole foreign investment of hotel development. Such knowledge transfer of hotel management from international management to hotel operations in China benefited, to some extent, from the effectiveness and efficiency of Chinese hotel operations, particularly in functional areas of financial management: budgeting, internal cost control, yield or revenue management. However, due to the extreme complexity of hotel ownership structure, brand affiliation, variations of demand and supply in regional markets and business practice influenced by social and cultural factors in China, a myriad of business practices in hotel revenue management in China has been shaped by the complex set of political, business and cultural factors. This chapter reviews the array of hotel ownership structures and compares their associated financial performances. It then examines hotel revenue management practices determined by different cultural and business factors. Finally, it identifies and analyses the challenges facing revenue management in hotel operations and presents recommendations for effective revenue management in China's lodging sector.

■ Financial performance

☐ Hotel ownership and financial performance

The current hotel ownership structure in China provides a living testimony to the phenomenal economic reform and transformation from the state owned enterprises (SOE) to a highly diversified ownership portfolio of public, private, joint venture and sole foreign investment, with different variations of ownerships under each structure. Table 7.1 exhibits the diverse and complicated ownership and business structures in the lodging sector in China. It is evident that hotels owned by the government have been reduced significantly compared to 35 years ago. Replacing the SOE hotels are the hotels developed by domestic private and collective businesses, organized in various legal forms. Only a very small proportion of the hotel stock in China is owned and financed by investors from Hong Kong, Macau, Taiwan and foreign countries. Absent from a national uniform system of accounts for hotel operations, one could just imagine that there must be many different standards and practices used for revenue management in China.

The financial performance of Chinese hotels at different star ranks demonstrates revealing aspects of revenue management at the national level (Table 7.2). Nationally, four of the five star-ranking categories were reported at quite similar performance levels of low 60% occupancy, except for the 2-star hotels reporting 57% occupancy in 2011. The average daily rate (ADR) and revenue per available room (RevPar) showed clearly differentiated lodging product supply by star ranking system. However, the rates and the revenues generated were considerably lower than countries in Europe, North America and some neighboring Asian countries such as Japan, South Korea, particularly in the 5-star and 4-star segments.

Table 7.1: Hotel ownership in China, 2011

	Ownership	5-Star	4-Star	3-Star	2-Star	1-Star	Total
Domestic Assets	SOE	152	658	1711	1079	47	3647
	Collective	6	50	225	185	9	475
	Stock cooperative	4	55	117	73	1	250
	Joint SOE	1	1	5	3	0	10
	Joint collective	0	2	10	8	0	20
	Joint SOE & collective	0	1	4	5	0	10
	Other joint ownership	0	3	1	1	1	6
	SOE – Sole ownership	33	109	161	68	2	373
	Other limited liability co.	19	65	141	60	4	289
	Equity trading company	29	137	298	129	9	602
	Private – sole ownership	31	137	709	694	51	1622
	Private – partnership	11	35	149	147	7	349
	Private limited liability co.	56	323	851	389	18	1637
	Private equity trading co.	11	45	90	56	1	203
	Other	9	35	142	89	4	279
Joint & sole assets from Hong Kong, Macau and Taiwan (HKMT)	Joint-venture from HKMT	41	43	41	8	0	133
	Cooperative with HKMT	8	10	11	3	0	32
	Sole ownership by HKMT	19	33	23	3	0	78
	HKMT equity trading co.	8	6	9	0	0	23
Foreign Assets	Joint-venture with foreign investor	32	42	30	4	0	108
	Cooperative with foreign Investor	9	9	11	0	0	29
	Foreign sole ownership	26	19	19	7	0	71
	Foreign equity trading co.	6	1	10	1	0	18
	Total	615	2148	5473	3276	164	11676

Source: China National Tourism Administration, *2011 Statistical Bulletin of Star-Ranked Hotels in China*. China Travel & Tourism Press, June 2012.

It is interesting to note that the Chinese hotels at all five star categories gen-erated significant revenues from food and beverage services, with over 40% of the total sales from food and beverage operations for the 4-star, 3-star and 2-star hotels. Such food and beverage revenue performance indicates that hotel food and beverage outlets are an essential part of the local society providing dining services and event functions for local residents, particularly so considering the low utilisation rates of the hotel rooms nationwide. When examining the efficiency of revenue generation measured by fixed asset turnover, the lower ranking hotels performed better than the 4-star and 5-star hotels: the 2-star hotels generated the highest revenue, ¥63 for ¥1 in fixed assets while the 5-star hotels had the lowest ratio of generating ¥45 revenue for every ¥1 in fixed assets. The different ratios of fixed asset turnover by different star-ranking categories reveal that the upscale and luxury hotels in China face the challenge of reducing capital intensity by efficiently utilizing the property's fixed asset to produce sales.

Table 7.2: Hotel capacity and financial performance by star-ranking categories, 2011

	Total	5-star	4-star	3-star	2-star	1-star	Average
Number of hotels	11676	615	2148	5473	3276	164	
Number of rooms	1474900	217600	424600	610600	214400	7700	
Total revenue (billion ¥*)		73.1	78.5	65.8	13.4	0.3	
% room revenue		44.46	41.37	40.81	45.50	52.82	42.44
% food & beverage revenue		34.89	42.82	43.34	43.03	37.69	39.17
ADR (¥)		689	350	208	140	118	313
Occupancy (%)		61	62	60	57	62	61
RevPar (¥)		430	220	130	80	60	190
Total revenue per room (¥)		336	186	108	63	39	157
Fixed asset turnovr (¥)		44.78	50.57	55.95	62.88	51.93	50.46
Total profits (billion ¥)		6.5	0.21	-0.61	0.054	0.011	
Taxes (billion ¥)		6.66	6.93	5.56	1.62	0.064	

Note: *The Chinese Renminbi *yuan* (¥) fluctuated from ¥ 6.6:$1 in early 2011 to ¥ 6.3:$1 in late 2011.

Source: China National Tourism Administration.*2011 Statistical Bulletin of Star-Ranked Hotels in China.*China Travel & Tourism Press, June 2012.

☐   Hotel geographic locations and financial performance

The national data provides a macro view of hotel financial performance in China. Table 7.3 shows the next level to examine the cities ranked by ADR, occupancy and RevPar.

Table 7.3: Chinese popular tourist cities by hotel performance, 2011

City	ADR (¥)	City	Occupancy (%)	City	RevPar (¥)
Sanya	724.95	Changsha	83.28	Sanya	520
Shanghai	633.63	Sanya	71.39	Shanghai	350
Beijing	494.85	Nanjing	70.12	Beijing	310
Guangzhou	472.82	Guiyang	69.55	Guangzhou	300
Shenzhen	443.35	Lanzhou	69.32	Shenzhen	290
Dongwan	430.54	Xiamen	68.99	Xiamen	290
Xiamen	421.26	Qingdao	68.95	Qingdao	290
Qingdao	417.31	Chengdu	68.78	Changsha	270
Changchun	395.47	Fuzhou	68.33	Nanjing	270
Wuhan	393.50	Nanning	68.15	Chengdu	260

Source: China National Tourism Administration. *2011 Statistical Bulletin of Star-Ranked Hotels in China.* China Travel & Tourism Press, June 2012

Cities with higher average daily rates include the major political and commercial centers (Beijing, Shanghai and Guangzhou) and coastal destinations (Sanya, Shenzhen, Dong Wan, Xiamen, Qingdao) except for Changchun in northeast China and Wuhan on the Yangtze River in interior China. Sanya, the capital city of Hainan province and also known as the Hawaii of China, is a popular year-round coastal resort destination in southern China and enjoyed the highest ADR and

RevPar in 2011. Cities with the highest occupancy rates reflect a mixed geographic distribution: coastal cities (Sanya, Nanjing, Xiamen, Qingdao and Fuzhou), interior cities (Changsha, Guiyang. Lanzhou. Chengdu and Nanning). The relatively high occupancy in some of the interior cities, particularly Guiyang in Guizhou province and Lanzhou in Gansu province, may indicate significant seasonality and supply and demand imbalance in these heartland destinations.

☐ Hotel management and financial performance

When examining revenue performance by management, data for the three main types of management in China: international management, domestic chain management and domestic independent management, were available for 2002 – 2009. Figures 7.1 and 7.2 show RevPar performances of the three types of management.

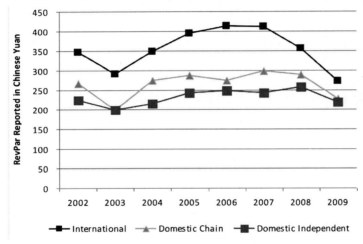

Figure 7.1: 4–star hotel RevPar performance, 2002–2009

Source: China Hotel Industry Study 2003-2010, China Tourist Hotels Association.

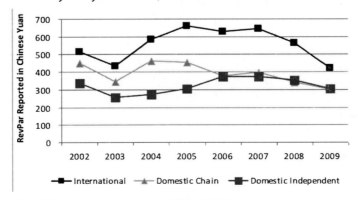

Figure 7.2: 5–star hotel RevPar performance, 2002–2009

Source: China Hotel Industry Study 2003-2010, China Tourist Hotels Association.

Clearly, Chinese hotels managed by international companies have consistently outperformed their Chinese counterparts of equal star-ranks managed by domestic management companies or domestic independent operators from 2002 to 2009.

Revenue management practices

Due to the complexity of ownership and management structures of hotels in China, as discussed in the previous section, this section attempts to provide an overview of revenue management practices in Chinese hotel operations. It focuses on pricing, room inventory management, food and beverage revenues, and accounts receivable management.

Pricing

Hotel room pricing is determined by a myriad of external and internal, cost-based or market-based factors (Steed & Gu, 2004). To determine the optimal pricing structure by utilizing the fixed room inventory and finding consumers who are willing to pay for different types of rooms and service, hotel management needs to understand consumers' value functions and behavior by clearly defining different market segments and targeting these market segments using a mix of price, amenities, purchase restrictions, and distribution channels (Chiang, Chen & Xu, 2007). Hotel pricing in China, in general, fluctuates with supply and demand as influenced by latent demand, e.g., mega events (2010 Shanghai World Expo), seasonality, or any negative events such as health concerns or government policy to restrict visitors to a particular destination. For instance, international and domestic visitors were discouraged from visiting Beijing during the 2008 Beijing Summer Olympic Games due to security concerns. As a result, hotels in Beijing had a mixed performance due to reduced visitors and increased supply leading up to the Olympics (Mayock, 2008). Intense market competition also affects hotel room pricing in China as discounting has been a common tactic in competitive markets. However, deep discounts have been discouraged and value adding approach has been recommended as effective revenue management, such as including amenities, food, or parking in the room price, or buy certain number of room nights get one night free, or using opaque price service (Wang, 2010; Liu, 2011). However, in some destinations, local government may interfere with market mechanisms by issuing decrees for setting up minimum regulated pricing management for different star-ranked hotels in its jurisdiction. The rationale for such government intervention in hotel operations was to protect consumers' interest and prevent hotel operators from reaping huge profits (Sun, 2009).

☐   ## Room inventory management

Overbooking as revenue management is also practiced in hotel operations in China. Overbooking by hotel management during the peak season is built on the forecast of mixed uncontrollable consumer decisions: the consumer does not show up on the registered date of arrival; the consumer cancels a reservation and registered guests decide to check out a day early (Wang, 2011; Song, 2009). Since credit cards are not used as widely in China as in many other countries, hotel reservation guarantees are still problematic since the hotel management cannot claim any damage from lost room sales if the consumer does not show up. Therefore, overbooking is practiced to protect potential revenue loss due to no-shows, cancellations and early check outs.

Revenue management by leveraging technology applications in improving distribution channels has been extensively pursued by hotel management. Online travel agencies (OTA) have grown rapidly since the late 1990s. At present, 71.6% of online travel business was generated from air ticket bookings, 20.2% from hotel reservations and 8.25% from other travel related products (iResearch, 2012). Of the OTAs for hotel bookings, Ctrip.com, founded in 1999 and listed in Nasdaq in December 2003, is now the market leader in China with 32.5% of online hotel booking businesses (iResearch, 2012). Ctrip.com now lists over 39,000 hotels in the world for its 50 million registered members and non-members to select and book hotel reservations (Ctrip, 2012). Selling rooms by OTA enables hotel management to reach consumers who search travel product information online and feel comfortable purchasing products and services online. In addition to Ctrip.com, eLong.com is ranked as the second largest online hotel booking OTA with 10.5% market share and many other direct selling of online platforms (iResearch, 2012).

As China's financial system continues to transform consumers are beginning to be more open to credit use, however, hotel transactions are still commonly handled by cash payment. In China, hotel revenues are generally collected from three main types of payments: cash payment, credit sales extended to important and close business partners, and credit card sales (Jiang, 2010). Guests paying by cash are recorded in hotel's guest ledger and each guest is required to make a cash deposit upon check in. The amount of the deposit varies by the level of star-ranks and it is intended for covering incidental costs or damage to any objects in the room. Some hotels require the deposit to be the equivalent amount of room sales. If the actual spending by the guest exceeds the deposit, the front office staff will ask the guest to add more cash to the deposit on a daily basis (Jiang, 2010).

Hotels in China often extend sales credits to close business partners based on previously negotiated sales contracts for business travel and tour groups. This account is recorded as city ledger. Hotels then will collect the accounts receivable from these business partners after the hotel stay. However, accounts receivable collection can be a daunting task in China, particularly facing SOE and domestic private firms, since many companies tend to delay the disbursement of payment as late as possible. It is not uncommon for hotels to write off delinquent accounts. It is often recognised in China that the chance to collect outstanding balances is only 50% if the account is over one year and the chance is nil when the outstanding account is more than three years (Jiang, 2010). The last payment method is by credit card both by individuals and organisations which involves a time lag between when the bank issuing the credit card sends the payment to the hotel and the actual journal entry of the completed sales. However, the high credit card fees charged by the banks cut into hotel revenues substantially when credit card payments make up considerable portion of the payments. New legislation has been recently passed by the central government to require commercial banks to lower credit card fees to stimulate consumption by credit card.

Chinese hotel revenue structure

As discussed earlier, food and beverage sales in hotel operations contribute significantly to the total hotel revenues in China. A few studies reported that some hotels generated almost 60% of sales in hotel total revenues from food and beverage service (Kong, 2009). Revenue management is therefore a critical management measure for effective and efficient food and beverage operations in Chinese hotels. Hotel menu pricing, in parallel to room pricing, depends on location, level of star-ranking, and seasonality. Based on the 2012 *China Hotel Industry Study*, the financial performance of hotel food and beverage operations in the top two star-ranked hotel categories and by management types were reported for 2011 (Table 7.4). Table 7.4 reveals that the 5-star domestic operations generated higher food revenues compared to 5-star hotels by international hotel management. This could be probably attributed to the lower menu pricing offered by the food and beverage operations in domestic 5-star hotels which generated more food sales. Food revenues at the 4-star level showed no significant difference by the types of management. It is interesting to note that the 4-star and 5-star hotels by international management had considerably lower total cost of goods sold, a possible sign of better internal cost control measures in inventory management, less waste and internal theft prevention. However, international management spent considerably more on payroll and related benefits for hotel staff. The bottom line of hotel food and beverage financial performance therefore did not exhibit significant differences by types of management.

It is worth mentioning a unique aspect of the Chinese business environment directly influenced by social relations that has direct impact on food and beverage revenue management in Chinese hotels. Food service outlets in hotels, especially in upscale and luxury hotels, have been the preferred venues for various types of business, social and cultural functions. However, many clients, typically government agencies and business enterprises, request the hotel management to extend sales credit of varying amounts to them. To maintain a good business relationship, hotel management normally grants the sales credit to these clients. When the meal is finished, one person in the party simply signed the bill and the hotel is responsible for collecting the bill later. Sometimes, there is even confusion as who will sign the bill, so the service staff have to make sure to get the appropriate signature (Tang, 2008; Chen, 2009; Zhang, 2011). This phenomenon, intersecting business, politics and society in China, is unavoidable, but presents a challenge to revenue management in hotel food and beverage operations.

Table 7.4: Hotel food and beverage financial performance by star-rank and management, 2011

P&L (%)	International Management 5-star	Domestic Management 5-star	Domestic Independent 5-star	International Management 4-star	Domestic Management 4-star	Domestic Independent 4-star
Food revenue	68.2%	76.0%	74.4%	73.6%	78.9%	77.5%
Bev revenue	11.5%	10.0%	9.5%	8.34%	10.1%	8.6%
Other revenue	20.3%	14.0%	16.1%	18.03%	10.90%	13.9%
Total revenue	100%	100%	100%	100%	100%	100%
Food cost	36.66%	43.4%	43.7%	39.8%	44.27%	47.3%
Bev cost	24.7%	36.5%	35.7%	28.0%	38.61%	53.6%
Total Cost of goods sold	34.9%	42.5%	42.0%	38.54%	43.48%	47.04%
Payroll & related expenses	21.4.9%	17.2%	15.5%	24.71%	18.4%	17.32%
Other expenses	10.0%	7.6%	9.71%	10.5%	8.9%	10.3%
Total payroll & related expenses	31.42%	24.8%	25.2%	35.2%	27.3%	27.6%
Total F&B expenses	59.3%	62.4%	62.0%	65.9%	67.3%	70.1%
F&B Profit (loss)	40.7%	37.6%	38.0%	34.1%	32.29%	29.9%

Source: China Tourist Hotels Association. *China Hotel Industry Study 2012*, Financial Year 2011. China Travel & Tourism Press, June 2012, p. 20.

■ Challenges and recommendations for hotel revenue management

The main challenges facing effective revenue management in hotel operations are identified in this section and the necessary strategies for developing effective hotel revenue management in China are recommended.

□   Challenges

Hotel management in China faces many challenges for running profitable operations. Of the many challenging factors, four are identified and discussed: increasing competition; rising labour and product costs; facility upkeep; new distribution channels.

- First, the competitive hotel market in China has put great pressure on the management to effectively utilise current capacity to optimise sales. Hotel occupancy data at national and local levels reveal disparities in capacity utilisation and certain destinations with low occupancy have to deal with overprovision caused by optimistic business outlook and aggressive development by both international and domestic companies. Hotel operators are therefore challenged for finding ways to increase revenues by booking more customers and cutting operating costs through internal control.

- Second, inflationary pressure in the Chinese economy in the last decade has resulted in significant increase in operating costs on labour, food products, and energy (Kong, 2009). The rapid rise in these operating costs have eroded profit margins and presents challenges to the management for finding solutions to the rising operating costs when intense competition prohibits rate increase.

- Third, the development of consumerism in China has made the consumers more sophisticated, demanding quality and value when making purchasing decision for lodging service. Furthermore, in the era of social media networking, instant comments and images of lodging facilities can travel fast and wide among consumers. Therefore, hotel owners and operators have to invest in the physical facilities through renovations and maintenance which requires capital reserves on the annual basis.

- Finally, the rapid change of technology applications in hotel management further challenges the hotel management to keep abreast with innovative adaption of distribution channels and revenue management system.

Recommendations

The following recommendations for improving revenue management in hotel operations in China are proposed.

- First, an effective forecasting system needs to be established. A sound hotel revenue management is based on an effective forecasting system utilizing past hotel performance data. Reliable forecasting of differentiated hotel market segments and associated revenues is essential to hotel revenue management (Li, 2011). However, the function of forecast is absent in most hotel operations due to the lack of historical hotel performance data and appropriate information management system, this is particularly true of the SOE and domestic private hotels. Most Chinese hotels do not perform revenue bench marking and business analytics of sales data (Li, 2008). Without past performance data on room utilization and sales revenues, it is very difficult to develop a revenue management system that can determine optimal room revenues based on room availability, length of stay, days of the week, and market mix. Therefore, it is crucial for hotel management in China to keep reliable record of hotel performance data and conduct bench marking analysis of competitors' performance. China has made marked stride in the last decade in hotel performance data collection and standardization. Examples include the annual *China Hotel Industry Study* conducted by China Tourist Hotels Association and Horwath HTL since 2002 which established standard definitions and template for reporting hotel financial performance.

■ Second, it is essential to establish a uniform system of accounts for hotel accounting and financial management. A uniform system of accounts is essential for hotel revenue management. The hotel industry has been following the general *Enterprise Accounting System* used for all business enterprises in China. Though there is an accounting system for travel and food services, no standard reporting procedures and forms are provided (Liu, 2010). Great variations are found in hotel financial reporting forms and accounts for hotel operations are highly generalised. Detailed operational performance data are hard to come by and bench marking of hotel performances is almost impossible (Liu, 2010). Clearly, a national uniform system of accounts for the hotel industry in China will enable the industry to effectively measure and manage business revenues.

■ Third, hotels need to develop effective marketing strategies for optimal match of supply and demand. Another important aspect of hotel revenue management is to find the optimal match of fixed capacity of room supply and consumer demand conditioned by numerous factors. These factors influence consumers' decisions for hotel selection, time to travel and length of stay which all have direct impact on hotel revenue generation. Hotel management needs to clearly understand the differentiated market mix they serve and its position in the competitive set. Market knowledge and understanding of clearly differentiated customer segments: commercial, meetings and groups, and leisure, will enable hotel management to reach the consumers by using effective distribution channels to increase revenues (Du, 2012; Wei & Han, 2008). A well-defined market mix and past performance of such market segmentation data are the basis for revenue managers to effectively forecast and allocate fixed room inventory for sales for different days in the week, for weekend, for different number of nights, for holidays or non-holidays, and for different seasons.

- Fourth, it is critical to improve managers' competency in revenue management knowledge and technology systems. Great disparities have been found in hotel management structure and efficiencies in China, particularly comparing financial performance among international management and domestic management (Okoroafo, Koh, Liu & Jin, 2010; Liu & Zhang, 2011) and even comparing domestic hotel companies listed in the equity market (Zhang, 2012). Poor management or insufficient management system has been criticized as the hindrance for effective hotel revenue management in China by several previous studies (Yin, 2006; Liang, 2008; Xie, 2009; Hua, 2009; Liu, 2010; Jin, 2010; Yang, 2011). This refers particularly to many SOE hotels and domestic private hotels in China. Inconsistent management, lack of internal control and audit system, and lack of knowledge of revenue management on the part of the managers and staff are the critical management issues for effective implementation of revenue management system in hotel operations in China.

- Fifth, new computer programs need to be implemented for more effective revenue management. Various property management systems have been widely used in hotel operations in China, including domestic proprietary programs and international systems. However, revenue management systems have not been extensively adopted in hotel management in China. A few domestic hotel firms, such as Jinling Hotel Management Company in Nanjing and Tianlun International Hotels in Beijing, have now implemented IDeaS Revenue Solutions to better forecast demand and optimise price (Hotel Modernization, 2011). Other domestic hotel firms should follow these innovators to strategically adopt new revenue management systems to drive better revenue.

- Finally, hotel revenue management should be introduced in the curriculum of hospitality management programs in China. Future hospitality management professionals should be exposed to the knowledge and practice of revenue management which intersects several functional areas in hotel operations: rooms, food and beverage and marketing.

References

China National Tourism Administration (2012). *2011 Statistical Bulletin of Star-Ranked Hotels in China.* Retrieved September 12, 2012, from China National Tourism Administration website: http://www.cnta.gov.cn/html/2012-6/2012-6-28-8-42-36760.html

China Tourist Hotels Association (2003-2010). *China Hotel Industry Study 2003-2010.* Beijing: China Travel & Tourism Press.

Chen, Q. (2009). Analysis of hotel accounts receivable management. *Heilongjiang Science and Technology Information,* **31**: 127.

Chiang, W. C., Chen, J. C. H. & Xu, X. J. (2007). An overview of research on revenue management: current issues and future research. *International Journal of Revenue Management,* **1**(1): 97–128.

Ctrip (2012). Ctrip company profile. Retrieved September 9, 2012, from Ctrip website:

http://pages.english.ctrip.com/webhome/purehtml/en/footer/CompanyProfile.html.

Du, X. Q. (2012). Research on enhancing guest room revenue control in hotel financial management. *Operations Manager,* **6**: 194.

Hua, Q. (2009). Reflecting on improving financial management in the hotel industry. *Manager Journal,* **20**: 74.

iReseach (2012). China online travel market reached 44 billion yuan in Q1 2012. Retrieved September 30, 2012, from iResearch News wwebsite: http://www.iresearchchina.com/views/4202.html.

Jin, H. (2010). On how to strengthen the control of room revenues in hotel financial management. *Modern Economic Information,* **8**: 22–23.

Jiang, Q. (2010). Accounts receivable management in higher star-ranking hotels. *Science and Technology Association Forum,* **10**(b): 152–154.

Kong, Q. (2009). On the cost control of hotel food and beverage operations. *Friends of Accounting,* **3**: 42–43.

Li, Q. Y. (2008). Applications of revenue management theory in the hotel industry. *Hotel Modernization,* **11**, 42–43.

Li, W. L. (2011). Revenue management in China's hotel industry: barriers and strategies.

2010 International Conference on E-business, Management and Economics, Hong Kong, *IPEDR,* **3**, 144–143.

Liang, M. Q. (2008). On how to improve business income in hotels. *Friend of Science Amateurs,* **4**: 153–154.

Liu, J. (2010). Discussion on controlling hotel revenues. *Manager Journal,* **XX**: 232.

Liu, X. J. & Zhang, Y. (2011). Comparative analysis of operation performance between Chinese and foreign hotel management groups. *China Urban Economy,* **9**: 99–101.

Liu, Y. C. (2011). Will competition affect your price? *Hotel Modernization,* **4**: 60–61.

Mayock, P. (2008). Beijing hotels turn in mixed performance. Retrieved September 8, 2012, from *HotelNewsNow.com*: http://www.hotelnewsnow.com/Articles.aspx/77/Beijing-hotels-turn-in-mixed-performances

Okoroafo, S. C., Koh, A., Liu, L. L. & Jin, X. M. (2010). Hotels in China: a comparison of indigenous and subsidiaries strategies. *Journal of Management Research*, 2(1): 1–10.

Song, Z. Q. (2009). Research analysis of pricing management in hotel revenue management. *China Collective Economy*, 7: 58–60.

Steed, E. & Gu, Z. (2004). An examination of hotel room pricing methods: practiced and proposed. *Journal of Revenue and Pricing Management*, 3(4): 369–379.

Sun, M. Y. (2009). Research on hotel room pricing strategy. *Market Modernization*, **1**: 31–32.

Tang, M. J. (2008). Accounting and sales revenue control in hotel financial management. *Commercial Times*, **20**: 88–89.

Wang, X. S. (2010). How to be a winner in a price war? *Hotel Modernization*, **5**: 6–7.

Wang, Z. H. (2011). Applied research of overbooking in hotel management. *Brand*, **Z2**: 25.

Wei, W. & Han, J. J. (2008). Research on hotel revenue management based on economics. *Tourism Science*, **22**(6): 26–31.

Xie, J. (2009). Strength financial management and enhance hotel management effectiveness. *China Chief Financial Officer*, **4**: 128–129.

Yang, X. Y. (2011). On present operation and improvement of hotel financial management. *Manager Journal*, **23**: 133.

Yin, K. Y. (2006). On controlling hotel operation revenues. *Science Information*, **4**: 165.

Zhang, P. (2012). A cluster analysis of business performance by publically traded hotel companies in China using contingency factors. *Economic Forum*, **5**: 73–75.

Zhang, P. Y. (2011). Exploratory study of accounts receivable in hotels with food and beverage operations. *Foreign Investment in China*, **10**: 73–74.

7

8 Restaurant Revenue Management

Cindy Heo

Learning outcomes

After reading this chapter, you should be able to:

- Understand the issues of significance when determining revenue management strategies in the restaurant sector.
- Critique the concepts of capacity management, time management, menu management and price management in the context of restaurants, and be familiar with the concept of customer perception management.
- Appreciate that slightly different revenue management approaches are required in the restaurant sector when compared to hotels and airlines.

Introduction

Restaurants can improve their revenue by increasing the number of customers they serve and/or the amount of money that is spent by each guest. Additional seats or drive-through windows, extended operating hours, and additional food service units are all examples of restaurant efforts to increase their capacity to serve more guests. Conversely, suggestive selling by service staff, creative menus, and special discounts for very large purchases are examples of efforts to increase the amount of money each customer spends. Revenue management is one of the ways to increase revenue in restaurants.

The basic rationale of revenue management is the efficient use of fixed, perishable capacities by charging customers different prices for identical services in an attempt to balance the demand and revenue per capacity unit (Kimes, 1989; McGill & van Ryzin, 1999). Revenue management works in industries that typically have perishable inventories, fixed capacities, a high fixed and low-variable cost structure, variable demands, and a segmentable market (Kimes, 1989; Berman, 2005).

In addition, reservation systems can help manage demand forecasting because such systems can calculate inventory units in advance of consumption. Airlines and hotels, which are normally considered as traditional revenue management industries, have successfully adopted revenue management techniques; more service industries, which have similar business characteristics, have begun to adopt revenue management practices (Chiang, Chen & Xu, 2007). Non-traditional revenue management industries include restaurants, heritage sites, tourist attractions, ski resorts, golf clubs, cruise industries, resorts, casinos, theme parks, and healthcare facilities. Research has indicated that these industries share most of the common business characteristics of traditional revenue management industries. Thus, these industries have the potential to incorporate revenue management.

However, non-traditional revenue management industries such as restaurants have unique business characteristics. One of these unique characteristics is the service capacity, which is an important consideration for the implementation of revenue management. Examples of traditional and non-traditional revenue management industries are presented in Figure 8.1. The figure shows the typology of revenue management industries based on the flexibility of the service capacity. This service capacity depends on two characteristics: the physical constraint of the business and the duration of service use by a customer.

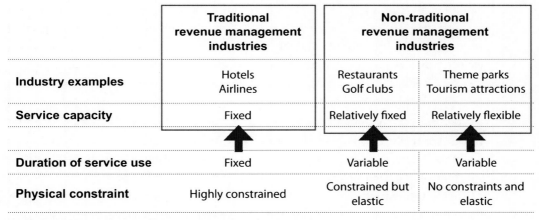

	Traditional revenue management industries	Non-traditional revenue management industries	
Industry examples	Hotels Airlines	Restaurants Golf clubs	Theme parks Tourism attractions
Service capacity	Fixed	Relatively fixed	Relatively flexible
Duration of service use	Fixed	Variable	Variable
Physical constraint	Highly constrained	Constrained but elastic	No constraints and elastic

Figure 8.1: Typology of revenue management industries

The physical constraints of non-traditional revenue management industries such as restaurants, golf clubs, and theme parks differ from those of traditional revenue management industries. Unlike hotels and airlines (e.g., the number of available hotel rooms or flight seats per day), the total service capacity of non-traditional revenue management industries (e.g., the total number of available table per day in restaurants) is not fixed because the duration of service use by customers is unpredictable. Likewise, the physical constraints in the non-traditional revenue management industry are elastic.

First, the duration of the service use by customers is unpredictable and variable in non-traditional revenue management industries. All passengers board and exit a flight together and the check-in and check-out time for a hotel has already been set. However, some people spend three hours in restaurants for their lunch, whereas others may need only one hour.

Some non-traditional revenue management industries, such as theme parks or tourism attractions, have relatively flexible service capacities because of the variable duration of service use and the relaxed physical constraint. Generally, no fixed number of attendees or visitors is imposed by theme parks or tourism attractions; the duration of their stay is not predictable. Those non-traditional industries tend to have an excess capacity during low-demand seasons and excess number of customers at high-demand seasons or on weekends. An excessive number of visitors, that is over the optimal capacity, during the high-demand periods often causes problems. Therefore, revenue management can be a useful strategic approach to alleviate demand fluctuation and to maximise revenue.

Other non-traditional revenue management industries such as restaurants or golf clubs have a limited space for their business activities and their temporal capacity is limited. However, they are likewise physically less restricted than traditional revenue management industries. For example, the addition of chairs or tables, as well as the changes to the table layout, is possible in restaurants, whereas the addition of one more seats in a flight (or one more room in a hotel) is not feasible. A restaurant may have an outdoor patio seating area during good weather to expand their capacity during peak periods. In a restaurant, therefore, the total available seating capacity per day is not fixed because of the variable duration of the meals of customers as well as their loose physical constraints.

Revenue management generally involves segmenting customers, setting prices, controlling capacities, and allocating inventories to maximise the revenue generated from a fixed capacity. Fixed service capacity is a key characteristic of successfully applied revenue management. Capacity limitation generally enables a firm to build variable pricing policies and proper rate fences. If the service capacity is not limited, businesses are less able to apply variable pricing, particularly imposing premium pricing during peak periods. For instance, customers believe the value of the flight ticket during peak period is higher and are willing to pay more because seats are limited during peak periods. Therefore, the core principles of revenue management pricing are based on the customer perceptions of value rather than of cost and their different valuations for service products of limited availability, according to the demand fluctuations. Thus, service capacity influences the customer perception of value for a service. These unique characteristics of restaurants pose special challenges to restaurant operators and consequently require more creative revenue management strategies.

Several restaurants adopt various revenue management approaches. Restaurants offer time related promotions such as 'happy hour' rates and 'early bird' specials. However, the revenue management strategies that are currently implemented by restaurants merely focus on discounting prices during low demand periods. Restaurants have most of the characteristics that allow successful revenue management implementation such as perishable service products, variable demands, relatively high fixed costs, and no inventory opportunities. Restaurants have relatively high fixed costs and fairly low variable costs that are similar to those of hotels. Even though restaurants have a higher percentage of variable cost than traditional revenue management industries, their potential revenue gains can be substantial (Kimes & Thompson, 2004). This chapter presents comprehensive strategic approaches to help restaurants become more effective and profitable from the revenue management perspective.

■ Capacity management

Capacity utilisation is a major concern for restaurants as they try to maximise revenue. However, the service capacity of restaurants is less constrained than that of hotels and airlines. The likely effects of capacity utilization in a restaurant are presented in Figure 8.2. The level of capacity utilization affects the quality of service and the restaurant's financial performance.

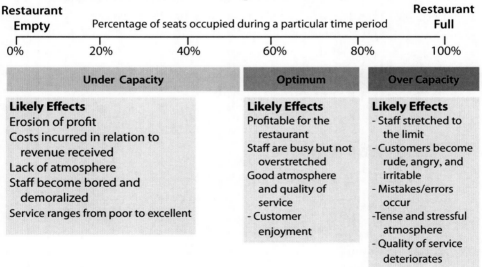

Figure 8.2: The Impact of capacity utilisation in a restaurant. (Adapted from Mudie & Pirrie, 2006)

Not all restaurants are concerned with limited space. For example, takeout restaurants that market the meal itself rather than space and time may have limited applications for revenue management to maximise revenue. Revenue management is more applicable to restaurants that have a higher demand than the capacity that they can accommodate during peak times (e.g., Friday dinner). The majority of the restaurants can increase revenue by the adopting revenue management approach.

Effective management of service capacity is the first strategy for restaurant revenue management. Restaurants should focus on extending their service capacity during high-demand periods to maximise revenue by serving more customers. The physical space of restaurants is usually limited. Thus, the flexibility of their table layout allows restaurants to increase their service capacity. Restaurants would rather offer a mix of table sizes and types. If a restaurant only has four-person tables but all of its customers come in pairs, restaurants must give four-seat tables to two people or wait for customers to finish dining. On the other hand, if restaurants can easily change a four-person table to two two-person tables during dinner hours, these restaurants can accommodate more customers quickly. Therefore, to maximise the service capacity during high demand periods, restaurants may determine the common sizes of customer groups at given parts of each day and accordingly set up their table layouts.

However, the dining space of customers is not only in terms of the physical constraints restaurants faced during high-demand periods. The capacity of a service firm is defined as "the highest quantity of output possible in a given time period with a predefined level of staffing, facilities, and equipment" (Lovelock, 1992, p.26). A variety of factors potentially limit service capacity in restaurants. These limiting factors include the kitchen facilities, staff, and parking space, as well as the number, size, and arrangement of tables. Therefore, restaurant operators should consider the dining space of customers and the various operational capacities to increase the service capacity during high demand periods. The optimal mix of tables for a given restaurant situation can increase the revenue.

■ Time management

The principles of revenue management can apply to restaurants given that the unit of sale in restaurants is the time required for service, rather than just the meal itself (Kimes, 1999). A special concern for restaurants is that they have to consider the length of time that is spent by groups of customers when they arrive at the restaurant. Restaurant operators seeking to maximise revenue should look carefully at how long their tables are occupied because restaurants can enhance service capacity by managing the meal duration. During peak hours, the meal duration facilitates serving more customers and accordingly enhances the revenue. Customers who unexpectedly linger even after their meal is finished may prevent the restaurant operator from seating the next party (Kimes, Chase, Choi, Lee & Ngonzi, 1998).

Kimes and Chase (1998), Kimes (1999) and Kimes et al. (1999) proposed the use of the revenue per available seat hour (RevPASH: revenue accrued in a given time interval divided by the number of seats available during that time) for restaurant revenue management. RevPASH indicates the rate at which capacity utilization generates revenue. RevPASH increases as the number of table turnovers increases and the duration of a meal decreases. Restaurants, however, typically face an unpredictable duration of the customer meals, which limits their ability to manage total service capacity and revenue. To improve the revenue management opportunities, restaurants should enhance their control over the time duration when customers occupy their tables. Research found certain approaches help shorten the meal durations of customers such as using background music, lighting, and interior color. For example, Miliman's study (1986) found that fast-tempo music reduces both the meal duration and spending. Kimes and her colleagues (1999) suggested giving visual signals to remind customers that the meal is over by bussing the table, delivering the check, or offering valet service.

Moreover, restaurants should make an effort to reduce the amount of time between customers to increase their service capacity and revenue. Researchers have proposed various approaches to increase the efficiency of restaurant operations. Sill and Decker (1999) proposed the use of capacity management science (CMS) as a systematic approach to evaluate a restaurant's capacity potential and process efficiency. CMS includes monitoring every element of the service and the production delivery process with quantifiable measurements. Quain, Sansbury, and Abernethy (1998) as well as Muller (1999) had previously identified the managerial factors that may improve the efficiency of restaurants; those factors include defining the profit centers, dispersing demand, reducing operating hours, and decreasing service time by making the restaurant operations as efficient as possible. Similarly, Kimes et al. (1999) suggested recommendations such as training employees, developing standard operating procedures, and improving table management to increase the efficiency of restaurant operation. A good communication system among staff can help to reducing the changeover time. The service blueprint, which is a detailed description of the people, processes, and systems involved in the delivery of a service, can be used to identify process bottlenecks and improvement opportunities. Service blueprinting is a process analysis methodology proposed by Shostack (1982), which allows for a quantitative description of critical service elements such as time or the logical sequences of actions and processes. This process also specifies both actions/events that happen in the time and place of the interaction (front office) and actions/events that are out of the line of visibility for the users.

■   Menu management

In hotels and airlines, the cost per unit sold (e.g., rooms or seats) is basically the same, because the production cost is evenly distributed across all sales unit. However, the production cost for each menu is different in restaurants because of the varied ingredients for each item. Therefore, restaurants need to consider the contribution margin of each menu item rather than total revenue. Traditionally, restaurant operators have been concerned about food cost. The food cost percentage (an item's ingredient cost divided by its menu price) is the most commonly used criterion for assessing effective cost control. For example, from a traditional perspective, a rib-eye steak with a 50% food cost may be regarded less profitable than the pizza with a 20% food cost. However, if the rib-eye steak sells for US$40 and has a cost of US$20 (50%), its margin is $20. On the other hand, if the pizza sells for $30 and has a cost of US$6 (20%), the margin is only $14.

Recently, menu engineering has been a popular tool in the restaurant industry, since it focuses strictly on dollars. Menu engineering, which was developed by Kasavana and Smith (1982), is based on the classification of the menu items, that is, to determine how to make the menu perform more profitably using the said items. The process of menu engineering begins with an evaluation of the popularity (sales volume) and contribution margin for each menu item. All items are then categorized into four basic categories: stars, workhorses, puzzlers or dogs. These categories are based on whether they are high- or low-volume and high- or low-gross profit. Consequently, a restaurant operator can increase the total gross profit and the bottom line profitability of the restaurant by changing the menu items or the menu itself.

- Stars – high popularity and high margins.
- Workhorses – high popularity and low margins.
- Puzzlers – low popularity and high margins.
- Dogs – low popularity and low margins.

Menu engineering is a useful tool but it does not take into account the restaurant's service capacity and the time issue. To maximise the profitability of a restaurant, menu engineering should be applied to the restaurant revenue management strategy. During peak hours, restaurants have more customers than service capacity, and thus they should focus on only a few superstar items. A superstar menu item refers those which are very popular and have high contribution margin. Concurrently, less time is available to prepare the said item and to be consumed by customers as well. Therefore, if a restaurant sells more superstar items during peak hours, the restaurant can serve more customers (enhancing service capacity) while it increases its profits by selling a high-margin menu item.

■ Superstars – high popularity and high contribution margins with less time required for them to be prepared and consumed by customers.

Superstar items should be featured and easily found by customers. Restaurants can highlight or put the superstar on the top of the menu so that customers are more likely to choose the said item. Restaurants may not provide all menu items during peak hours because offering all the menu items may impede efficient operation. A special set menu can be developed for peak hours, which can be seen as a value-added item from a customer's perspective. However, restaurants should not provide discounts during peak hours. By contrast, the aim of revenue management during off-peak hours is to promote demand because the service capacity is higher than the number of customers. Therefore, restaurants can provide discounts on star and puzzle menu items to attract price-sensitive customers. A special set menu which combines the workhorses and puzzlers can be priced lower to bring more customers or to increase the RevPASH by enhancing the revenue per customer.

■ Price management

Traditional revenue management industries apply demand-based variable pricing policies to increase revenues in two ways. First, the company can gain greater revenue by charging the less price-sensitive market segments premium prices during high-demand period. Simultaneously, charging discounted prices to price-sensitive market segments during low-demand periods can encourage increased sales, thereby offsetting the price reduction. Demand-based pricing has proven to be successful in traditional revenue management, where customers find it to be more acceptable or fair; by contrast, restaurants are more constrained in their use of demand-based pricing (Kimes & Chase, 1998). Restaurants cannot merely raise prices in response to high demand because of potential customer dissatisfaction. In practice, restaurants offer 'happy hours' or 'two-for-one' specials. However, discounting is only one part of the revenue management approach.

Demand-based variable pricing is based on the different customer valuations for the limited availability of service products. The service capacity of restaurants is not fixed as compared to airlines or hotels. Thus, a demand-based variable policy by restaurants is more likely to be perceived negatively by restaurant patrons. If restaurant patrons find different prices for the same menu based on the day of the week (i.e., Monday dinner vs. Friday dinner), they may think such a price policy is unfair because the practice does not seem to add any value to the service. In that case, customers may refuse to pay a higher price for the service, thereby deciding not to patronize the restaurant and to visit another restaurant instead.

Charging price premiums in restaurants solely based on a high demand is generally not acceptable, unless they perceive a fair reason for the price differential. One possible approach that restaurants can adopt to minimize the unfairness perception of a variable pricing policy by restaurant patrons is to develop different menus with different names that are based on the demand level. Menu items can differ in terms of the serving size or the side dish. Differentiating the menu is important; given a perceived price difference between two transactions, a high degree of transaction similarity leads to the high perception of price unfairness (Xia, Monroe & Cox, 2004). Price differences can be more easily be explained when the degree of similarity between the two transactions is relatively low.

Restaurants can utilize rate fences to differentiate menu items with different prices. Rate fences refer to the rules and policies that a company uses to decide who receives what price and to distinguish one transaction from another (Kimes & Wirtz, 2003). Kimes and Wirtz (2003) found that the perceptions of differential pricing in the form of coupons, time-of-day pricing, and lunch/dinner pricing were fair, whereas weekday/weekend pricing had a neutral to slightly unfair perception. Likewise, table-location pricing gained a somewhat unfair perception. Restaurants should develop additional rates to provide better value to the customers during high-demand periods and to prevent perceptions of unfairness by differentiating menu and service offerings from a customer's perspective.

Research found that the pricing policy in restaurants can be used to manage customer demand. Susskind, Reynolds and Tsuchiya (2004) found that customers would be willing to shift their dining time to off-peak hours in exchange for discounts on menu items. Incentive strategies can be used with a reservation system that can create demand shifting such that customer arrivals are managed to match the restaurant's capacity (Dickson, Ford, & Laval, 2005).

■ Customer perception management

Maintaining a good relationship with customers is a critical issue in a restaurant business. While only a few major competitors exist in the airline and rental car industries, many competitors populate the restaurant industry (Kimes, 1994). A customer who is not satisfied or who feels treated unfairly may simply go elsewhere or not return at all. Several researchers claimed the importance of profitable relationships with customers to maximise the lifetime value from current and potential customers (Mathies & Gudergan, 2007). Therefore, to survive in a competitive market, restaurant operators need to provide good value as well as quality food and services; a high level of customer satisfaction should be maintained to increase the customers' return visits and give them a greater market share (Kivela, et al., 1999). Therefore, if customers perceive revenue management practice as an unfair policy, such negative perceptions may engender dissatisfaction with the service or product; consequently, increased revenues accruing from revenue management practice may be short-term (Kimes, 2002; Hoang, 2007).

The fencing conditions (Wirtz & Kimes, 2007), framing of rate fences (Kimes & Wirtz, 2002), familiarity with revenue management practices (Wirtz & Kimes, 2007), and information disclosure of rate fences (Choi & Mattila, 2004; 2005) have revealed effects on the fairness perceptions of differential pricing. Framing effects refer to the phenomenon wherein people respond differently to different descriptions of the same condition (Frisch, 1993). Prospect theory posits that individuals value gains and losses differently even if their situations are economically equal (Kahneman & Tversky, 1979; Thaler, 1985). According to both framing effects and prospect theory, the customer is more favorably disposed and accordingly perceives a price to be fairer when prices are framed as a gain from a customer's perspective than when those prices are framed as a loss. Kimes and Wirtz (2002, 2003) examined the perceived fairness of five types of pricing in a restaurant. Their study found that framing demand-based pricing as discounts rather than as surcharges made consumers perceive the revenue management practices to be fairer. Moreover, customers' fairness perceptions increased when customers were aware of the various factors affecting different prices (Choi & Mattila, 2005). Customers who received no information generally thought the process was unfair. When informed customers knew how the various reservation factors affected a room rate, fairness perceptions ratings increased compared to the limited-information scenarios. Therefore, a restaurant adopting revenue management practice should develop reasonable rate fences with favorable framing from the perspective of customers to enhance fairness perceptions.

■ Summary

- Restaurants have the potential to incorporate revenue management practices in their operations, but cannot simply apply the same revenue management strategies as those used by airlines and hotels.

- The unique business characteristics of restaurants such as a relatively fixed service capacity due to variable meal durations and elastic physical constraints require restaurants to develop more sophisticated revenue management.

- Restaurants need to educate their customers about revenue practice by providing information or by adopting a step-by-step approach to create familiarity with the restaurant's revenue management practice among customers.

- Restaurant revenue management aims to determine the most effective ways of balancing restaurant demand and supply such that revenue is maximised without customer dissatisfaction. Revenue management for restaurants asserts selling the right seat to the right customer at the right price and for the right duration (Kimes, 1999).

8

- Restaurant operators should keep in mind that the determination of 'right' entails attaining the largest contribution possible for the restaurant while delivering the greatest value or utility to the customer (Kimes & Wirtz, 2003).

- Therefore, restaurants must balance their use of revenue management strategies with the creation of value for their customers.

References

Berman, B. (2005). Applying yield management pricing to your service business. *Business Horizon, 48*(2): 169-179.

Chiang, W. C., Chen, J. C. H. & Xu, X. (2007). An overview of research on revenue management: current issues and future research. *International Journal of Revenue Management, 1*(1): 97-128.

Choi, S. & Mattila, A. S. (2004). Hotel revenue management and its impact on customer fairness perceptions. *Journal of Revenue and Pricing Management, 2*(4): 303-314.

Choi, S. & Mattila, A. S. (2005). Impact of information on customer fairness perceptions of hotel revenue management. *Cornell Hotel and Restaurant Administration Quarterly, 46*(4): 27-35.

Dickson, D., Ford R. C. & Laval, B. (2005). Managing real and virtual waits in hospitality and service organisations. *Cornell Hotel and Restaurant Administration Quarterly, 46*(1): 52-68.

Frisch, D. (1993). Reasons for framing effects. *Organisational Behavior and Human Decision Processes, 54*: 399-429.

Hoang, P. (2007). The future of revenue management and pricing science. *Journal of Revenue and Pricing Management, 6*(2): 151-153.

Kahneman, D. & Tversky, A. (1979). Prospect theory: an analysis of decision under risk. *Econometrica, 47*: 263-291.

Kasavana, M. & Smith, D. (1982). *Menu Engineering - A Practical Guide to Menu Analysis. Okemos,* MI: Hospitality Publications, Inc.

Kimes, S. E. (1989). The basics of yield management. *Cornell Hotel and Restaurant Administration Quarterly, 30*(3): 14-19.

Kimes, S. E. & Chase, R. B. (1998). The strategic levers of yield management. *Journal of Service Research, 1*(2): 156-166.

Kimes, S. E., Chase, R. B., Choi, S., Lee, P. Y. & Ngonzi, E. N. (1999). Restaurant revenue management: applying yield management to the restaurant industry. *Cornell Hotel and Restaurant Administration Quarterly, 39*(3): 32-39.

Kimes, S. E. (1994). Perceived fairness of revenue management. *Cornell Hotel and Restaurant Administration Quarterly, 35*(1): 22-29.

Kimes, S. E. (1999). Implementing restaurant revenue management: a five step approach. *Cornell Hotel and Restaurant Administration Quarterly, 40*(3): 16-21.

Kimes S. E. (2002). Perceived fairness of yield management. *Cornell Hotel and Restaurant Administration Quarterly*, **43**(1): 21-30.

Kimes, S. E. & Thompson, G. M. (2004). Restaurant revenue management at Chevys: determining the best table mix. *Decision Sciences*, **35**: 371-392.

Kimcs, S. E. & Wirtz, J. (2002). Perceived fairness of demand-based pricing for restaurants. *Cornell Hotel and Restaurant Administration Quarterly*, **43**(1): 31-37.

Kimes, S. E. & Wirtz, J. (2003). Has revenue management become acceptable? findings from an international study on the perceived fairness of rate fences. *Journal of Service Research*, **6**(2): 125-135.

Kivela, J., Inbakaran, R. & Reece, J. (1999). Consumer research in the restaurant environment, Part 1: A conceptual model of dining satisfaction and return patronage. *International Journal of Contemporary Hospitality Management*, **11**(5): 205-222.

Lovelock, C. (1992). Seeking synergy in service operations: seven things marketers need to know about service operations. *European Management Journal*, **10**(1): 22-29.

McGill, J. & van Ryzin, G. (1999). Revenue management: research overview and prospects. *Transportation Science*, **33**(2): 233-256.

Mathies, C. & Gudergan, S. (2007). Revenue management and customer centric marketing: how do they influence traveler's choices? *Journal of Revenue and Pricing Management*, **6**: 331-346.

Miliman, R. E. (1986). The influence of background music on the behavior of restaurant patrons. *Journal of Consumer Research*, **13**(2): 286-289.

Mudie, P. & Pirrie, A. (2006). *Services Marketing Management.* Oxford: Elsevier.

Muller, C. C. (1999). A simple measure of restaurant efficiency. *Cornell Hotel and Restaurant Administration Quarterly*, **40**(3): 31-37.

Quain, B., Sansbury, M. & Abernethy, T. (1998). Revenue enhancement, part 2. *Cornell Hotel and Restaurant Administration Quarterly*, **39**(6): 71-79.

Sill, B. & Decker, R. (1999). Applying capacity-management science. *Cornell Hotel and Restaurant Administration Quarterly*, **40**(3): 22-30.

Shostack, L. G. (1982). How to design a service. *European Journal of Marketing*, **16**(1): 49-63.

Susskind, A. M., Reynolds, D. & Tsuchiya, E. (2004). An evaluation of guests' preferred incentives to shift time-variable demand in restaurants. *Cornell Hotel and Restaurant Administration Quarterly*, **45**(1): 68-84.

Thaler, R. (1985). Mental accounting and consumer choice. *Marketing Science*, **4**(3): 199- 214.

Xia, L., Monroe, K. B. & Cox, J. L. (2004). The price is unfair! a conceptual framework of price fairness perceptions. *Journal of Marketing*, **68**(4): 1-15.

Wirtz, J. & Kimes, S. E. (2007). The moderating role of familiarity in fairness perceptions of revenue management pricing. *Journal of Service Research*, **9**(3): 229-240.

8

9 RevenueManagement at Heritage Visitor Attractions

Anna Leask

Learning outcomes

After reading this chapter, you should be able to:

■ Define the term 'heritage visitor attraction' (HVA).

■ Appreciate the management challenges experienced by HVA managers.

■ Understand why revenue management might be suitable for use in HVAs.

■ Recognise the barriers to the adoption of revenue management (RM) within HVAs.

■ Understand how organisations such as the National Trust for Scotland make use of revenue management in practice.

■ Introduction

This chapter focuses on how revenue management might be suitable for use as a tool in developing the effective management of heritage visitor attractions (HVAs). It begins with an explanation of the terms to be used within the chapter and the challenges faced by managers at HVAs. It then provides a synthesis of existing research on the use of revenue management (RM) in visitor attractions in general and, more specifically, the challenges involved in its adoption in HVAs. A case study on the National Trust for Scotland's use of revenue management is provided as an example of a heritage organisation that makes increasing use of this management tool. The chapter concludes with a summary of the key issues in the adoption of revenue management in heritage visitor attraction management.

■   Managing heritage visitor attractions

☐   Definitions and categories

As stated by Loulanki and Loulanki (2011, p.839), "the relationship between heritage and tourism is well documented in the literature, most often described in terms of interdependency, complexity, inherent tensions, dynamics and conflicting values". This conflict emerges from the often multiple objectives of the stakeholders involved in the conservation and management of the heritage resource (Aas, Ladkin & Fletcher, 2005; Leask, 2010).

Visitor attractions are defined as "a permanent resource, either natural or human-made, which is developed and managed for the primary purpose of attracting visitors" (Hu & Wall, 2005, p.619). This definition can be further broken down to focus on heritage tourism, defined by Kaufman and Weaver (2006) as "the experience visitors seek to have at historic sites". The distinction between heritage and visitor attractions in general becomes significant when researching the differing issues and management practices entailed in their management objectives, management skills and ability to adopt new practices (Leask, Fyall, & Garrod, 2002; Leask, 2010), where key differences in their management priorities and practices can be observed. HVAs account for the majority of the whole visitor attraction supply (Boyd, 2000) and are defined for the purposes of this paper as those containing an aspect of historical interpretation. The majority of these heritage attractions are museums and galleries, mainly in the public sector and operated on a not-for-profit basis (Lennon & Graham, 2001). See Table 9.1 for a breakdown of HVA categories.

Table 9.1: Summary of HVA Categories (adapted from Leask, 2010)

Museums & Galleries Art, cultural, historical, collection-based, virtual, open air museums	Guggenheim, Bilbao, Spain Athens Acropolis Museum, Greece Tellus Science Museum, Georgia
Natural (with interpretation of resource) Gardens, national parks, forests	Karori Sanctuary Experience, N Zealand; Go Ape, UK Grand Canyon WHS, USA; Eden Project, Cornwall, UK
Animal (with historic/conservation interpretation) Safari, farms, zoos, aquariums	Longleat Safari Park, UK Edinburgh Zoo, UK Agricultural Tour, Argentina
Visitor Centres (with historic interpretation) Cultural, industrial, transport	Heineken Experience, The Netherlands Three Gorges Dam, China Ngong Ping Cultural Village, Hong Kong
Religious Sites	Rosslyn Chapel, Scotland; Notre Dame, France Angkor, Cambodia
Heritage Castles, forts, historic houses, monuments, industrial, dark, archaeological, military, music	Sovereign Hill, Australia; Hearst Castle, USA San Francisco Literary Tour, USA Culloden Battlefield, Scotland; Mystic Seaport, USA

☐   Value

Value is a term increasingly used in connection with heritage as it competes for funding in increasingly difficult market conditions within the public and private sectors. Traditionally measured in volume and value terms, heritage attractions now need to evidence their contribution in the wider sense of value, through their educational, social and community activities.

The significance of heritage tourism within a destination is difficult to measure and quantify, particularly given the variety of stakeholders and multiple objectives. In recent research conducted on behalf of the Heritage Lottery Fund (2010), it was established that the size of the heritage-tourism sector in the UK, by expenditure, is in excess of £12.4 billion a year. "Heritage is the mainstay of the UK tourism economy, with the breadth, beauty and cultural importance of Britain's heritage being the most important factors behind the 10 million holiday trips made by overseas visitors to the UK each year" (HLF, 2010, p.7). The popularity of heritage within the UK resident population is also well established, with 53% of the population making a trip to experience the atmosphere of a historic town or city at least once a year, and 42% visiting a museum or gallery.

☐   Management issues and challenges

The effective management of HVAs has been the topic of much academic discussion in recent years, as destinations attempt to develop their individuality within an increasingly competitive environment (Chhabra, 2010; Hughes & Carlsen, 2010; Darlow, Essex & Brayshay, 2012). As established by Leask (2010), key challenges facing visitor attractions (including the majority of HVAs) in the external environment include increasing competition from other leisure services and visitor expectations, the decreasing availability of public funding and an increasing need to evidence value and diversify their product offering. Challenges in the internal environment include the lack of rigorous market and management data on which to base decisions, changes in the culture and focus of many organisations on concentrating more on income generation, and the need for increasingly advanced staff and management skills.

Consequently, pressure has increased on heritage attractions to operate efficiently and manage their revenues effectively. Attraction managers have responded by developing a broader range of product offerings and revenue streams, operating more sophisticated pricing systems and improving their communication with potential visitors (Benckendorff & Pearce, 2003; Leask, 2010). Hughes and Carlsen (2010, p. 18) explored the factors around balancing an increasingly commercial focus with authenticity and successful business operation. They observe that "heritage conservationists generally view commercialisation as a path to undermining the integrity of the heritage presented, and hence its authenticity, by replacing conservation-driven management with a profit motive". Thus a tension is created between maintaining the resource integrity and the development of heritage products. Unfortunately, research indicates that heritage managers often lack the required skills and understanding of tourism product development to understand aspects such as the connection between management of a site as a heritage asset and its development and promotion for tourism (Ho & McKercher, 2004).

Adapted from Leask (2010), a review of existing literature has identified the following key challenges influencing the management of HVAs:

- Increasing supply within an environment of variable and seasonal demand.
- Increased competition for leisure spend and changes in leisure behaviour.
- Increasing visitor expectations for innovative services and products.
- Lack of rigorous market and management data on which to base decisions.
- Fragmented nature of the sector both geographically and competitively.
- Decreasing sources of public funds with increasing need to evidence 'value'.
- Imbalances within the sector relating to funding, admission charges and support.
- Changes in management priorities and the need to reconcile curatorial and managerial values and ideologies.
- Large number of stakeholders (and conflicting objectives) in many heritage sites.
- Conflict in balancing access with conservation of resources and their authenticity.
- Individual nature of resources requires individual conservation needs.

■ Can revenue management be applied within the attraction sector?

Revenue management (RM) refers to the strategy and tactics used by a number of industries to manage the allocation of their capacity to different willingness to pay end-users over time in order to maximise revenue (Phillips, 2005 *in* Padhi & Aggarwal (2011, p.725). Padhi and Aggarwal (2011) determine that RM is applicable where four conditions exist; the operator offers a fixed quantity of perishable capacity; the end-users book capacity prior to consumption; the operator can manage a set of price options; and the operator can change the choice of price options over time. If used effectively, then RM should benefit all the stakeholders, with service providers receiving increased yield and thus higher revenues, while the end-user has the option of taking advantage of reduced prices at non-peak times. As stated by Transchel and Minner (2009), the essence of revenue management is about combining flexible and dynamic pricing with market segmentation, promotions and capacity allocation.

In relation to the tourism sector, a definition of revenue management often used is a systematic approach to maximising revenue from the sale of intangible tourist services and facilities through pricing, market segmentation and service enhancement (Leask, Fyall & Garrod, 2012). Pullman and Rodgers (2010) outline a range of capacity-estimation approaches relevant to hospitality and tourism organisations that are applicable at different stages, from planning and development through to operations. More usually researched in relation to its use in the airline and hotel sectors, Leask et al. (2012) have identified revenue management as a technique that is particularly suited to services with: (a) fixed capacity; (b) variable demands; and (c) a segmentable market.

All of these characteristics are typical of the general visitor attractions sector and as such would seem to make the sector an ideal candidate for implementation of revenue-management practices (Chiang, Chen & Xu, 2007; Leask, 2010). The recent study by Leask et al. (2012) in relation to the adoption of revenue management by Scottish visitor attractions over a ten-year period, demonstrated that Scottish attractions have moved further toward embracing the strategic practice of revenue management, most clearly in recognition of the link between pricing, value and the visitor experience.

■ Challenges for the adoption of RM in the heritage visitor attraction sector

Leask and Yeoman (1999) and Leask et al. (2002) established that HVAs do, to some extent, meet the core necessary conditions required for the implementation of Revenue Management techniques. The necessary ingredients identified included the ability to segment the market on the basis of willingness to pay, the ability to predict periods of high and low demand, knowledge of pricing structures, access to information technology to support revenue management systems and a process of establishing a balance of conservation and revenue generation activities (Leask & Yeoman, 1999). In addition to the external and internal factors influencing the management of visitor attractions in general (shown in Table 9.1), particular challenges and opportunities may influence the extent of adoption of revenue management techniques at HVAs relate to the contextual issues raised earlier (Hughes & Carlsen, 2010; Leask, 2010). These include the following.

☐ ## Variety of stakeholders

Multiple stakeholders and managing dual priorities (and potentially conflicting objectives) can present challenges for HVA managers (Donohoe, 2012). Policy documents and academic literature indicate difficulties in balancing the multiple measures in response to changing market conditions and changes in the business environment. As identified by Ryan and Silvanto (2009), the complexity and challenge associated with the variety of stakeholders can create difficulties in the adoption of RM practices. For example, in the case of World Heritage sites, multiple stakeholders are involved at a variety of scales (global to local), with the often limited collaboration and conflicting management control resulting in a multiplicity of goals, measures and outcomes.

Recognition of the importance of visitors as stakeholders is often overlooked in the focus on management of the heritage resource. Ho and McKercher (2004) indicated that while visitors are the core element of cultural tourism, the focus of heritage managers is often on the development of the physical attributes of the resources and overlooks the visitor experience. If it is ultimately the visitor experience that attracts the visitor to visit the HVA, then this is critical in the implementation of RM in terms of market segmentation and determining pricing policies. Likewise the potential contribution of members and volunteers can often be overlooked in the management process (Holmes, 2008).

9

☐ ## Conflict in balancing access with conservation of the resources and authenticity

There is a concern related to increasing number of visitors and their potential to overburden resources and associated infrastructure, ultimately threatening the managing agency's ability to deliver on its conservation priorities (Dearden & Rollins, 2008). As stated by Fyall and Garrod (1998), marketing strategies that emphasize attracting mass tourists and the adoption of commercial values contradict established rules of conservation. This has resulted in increased complexity, uncertainty and conflict in the management of heritage sites – where preservation has historically been the fundamental priority.

One tenet of RM is the ability to balance supply and demand at a site. In HVAs this becomes a key point in the sustainable management of the resource but may fail to take account of the potential missed opportunities in selling a perishable product. Many heritage sites have high fixed costs but are only open to the public for fixed periods of the year to allow for conservation work to take place in quieter periods of the year. The very individual nature of the resource that attracts the visitors can create very individual and costly associated conservation needs.

☐ ## Development of a commercial imperative

The heritage sector has historically relied extensively on public sector support and government policies that support free access to heritage sites for local residents and educational groups. This has instilled an expectation of a 'right to free access' to heritage that is increasingly difficult to sustain in many destinations. Declining public funds have resulted in greater development of commercial activities and revenue streams within the heritage sector, often in conflict with established visitor markets and management attitudes. It has been claimed that increasing commercialisation degrades cultural heritage integrity and authenticity, reducing its appeal and thus potentially reducing success as a tourism product (McKercher & du Cros, 2002). However it has been seen that places with a "strong commercial focus appeared to be successful in terms of achieving and sustaining profitable operation over time" (Hughes & Carlsen, 2010, p.30), which may help to resolve some of these concerns.

An associated issue in relation to the adoption of more marketing focussed activity relates to the marketing of heritage as a commodity. Swarbrooke (1994) argues that commodification can lead to visitors seeing the sites as one-dimensional or trivial stereotypes designed to entertain rather than as complex and sensitive places with important historical value.

One positive point that research has shown is that visitors to heritage sites have been found to be willing to contribute financially, via admission charges and donations, towards the development of quality visitor experiences (Aas et al., 2005; Apostolakis & Jaffry, 2005; and Reynisdottir, Song & Agrusa, 2008).

☐ ## Lack of reliable market intelligence

Hughes and Carlsen (2010) state the overestimating of market demand for a particular cultural heritage experience may often be an issue during the development stage for heritage businesses. This is often due to the lack of reliable and consistent data that HVA managers have access to, or a lack of research skills (Cameron & Gatewood, 2004). This lack of data on which to base forecasting and planning decisions can compromise the opportunities for revenue management activities such as variable pricing, capacity forecasting and market segmentation (Leask et al., 2012). That said, there is evidence of established use of pricing knowledge, capacity forecasting and tools such as pre-booking currently in use in many HVAs (Leask et al., 2012).

Therefore it can be seen that various challenges do exist that might create some difficulties in the adoption of revenue management at HVAs. However, it has also been argued that many HVAs already use aspects of revenue management practice (variable pricing, market segmentation and supply and demand management) and that conditions exist that should encourage its further adoption.

■ Case study: National Trust for Scotland (NTS)

☐ Profile

The NTS manages and cares for approximately 130 properties and 76,000 hectares of countryside within Scotland, with around 50 of these properties charging for admission. It is a membership-based conservation organisation, with approximately 310,000 members at present (NTS, 2010).

☐ Revenue management priorities

Membership and admission charges

The Trust is heavily reliant on support from its members, who fund in the region of a quarter (£10 million) of its annual income from membership subscriptions, and also by the 2500 volunteers, without whom it is said that the organisation would not be able to function. Properties operated by the NTS receive around 1.5 million visitors each year, with around two-thirds of visitors being Trust members. Membership gives free access to NTS historic properties plus reciprocal arrangement for free visits to properties belonging to the National Trust for England, Wales and Northern Ireland.

NTS has experienced some difficult financial and operational circumstances in recent years, which led to a major strategic review being undertaken in 2010 (NTS, 2010). Much of the NTS's focus has always been, and continues to be, on increasing its membership roll. The Trust has made a strategic decision to keep general admissions prices relatively high, in order to encourage visitors to recognise the value of purchasing a membership.

Development of priority properties

Around 20 of the Trust's own properties are considered to be 'priority properties', which attract the greatest numbers of visitors. However, only around 5–10 of these priority properties actually generate any significant profit for the Trust (I. Gardner, personal communication, January 19, 2010). Recent product developments include the multi-million pound, flagship visitor centres at its Culloden Battlefield property and at the Burns National Heritage Park in Ayrshire; a 'Go Ape' tree trail at Crathes Castle and a bungee jump at Killiecrankie. Work is ongoing to redevelop the Bannockburn Heritage Centre in preparation for 2014.

Revenue generation

Given the difficult financial circumstances that the NTS has been experiencing, there has also been growing pressure on the organisation and its respective properties to increase the amount of revenue it can generate. Hindered by the high fixed costs of the care of properties and fixed capacity constraints, in addition to

9

a previously curatorial management focus, the organisation has had to respond carefully. Redevelopment of the website to showcase the various revenue streams has been undertaken, demonstrating the expanded range of the events programme, accommodation provision and retail activities more prominently.

☐ Revenue management activities

Market segmentation

Membership remains the key focus of the NTS market strategy. After experiments with offering a broad range of membership types, these have recently been streamlined to target specifically the family market and long-term membership (I. Gardner, personal communication, January 19, 2010). Developments such as the recently revised website, new product development, sponsorship from commercial companies such as Cadbury's for the Easter-egg trails and adoption of multimedia interpretation are all indicators of the Trust's recognition of the need to respond to and communicate with potential visitors and to engage with new and retain existing members. As an organisation, the focus remains on membership; however in recent years there has been substantial development of new revenue streams, including accommodation rentals, cruises, online retailing, events and filming in addition to the existing catering and retail outlets.

Pricing

As previously mentioned, prices are set to emphasise the value offered by taking up membership. Redevelopment of the website has enabled greater ease of access and communication of membership and payment options. As many other visitor attractions, the Trust has sought to capitalise on the added income that accepting various media vouchers can generate for them, especially now that the extra income they generate is fed back into the finances of the actual property at which they were redeemed. The Trust participates in collaborative deals such as the Homecoming Pass, the Great British Heritage Pass and the Tesco Clubcard scheme, as well as local opportunities for collaborative pricing and marketing activity. In addition, the Trust has embraced the idea of partnership working, as they believe that it can vastly increase the range of opportunities open to them while also, and perhaps even more importantly, enabling them to share any associated risks and costs (I. Gardner, personal communication, January 19, 2010). The key messages they aim to communicate are that membership of the NTS offers value for money and a contribution to the nation's legacy.

☐ Supply and demand management

As identified by Barber, Taylor and Deale (2010), the use of consumer lifestyle data can be effective in developing enhanced revenue opportunities. In the past

10 years it can be seen that the NTS has worked towards building a much clearer picture of their visitors and members, not least through the establishment of a research panel comprising 4000 of its members. This, alongside greater tracking and monitoring of marketing activity effectiveness, demonstrates a move towards greater informed decision-making. A critical point noted by the NTS is that not all of the portfolio must be treated in the same way and that individual sites should be developed as appropriate. This has allowed the variety of new product development at sites such as Killiecrankie Bungee Jump to go ahead.

The NTS makes active use of many of the key features of revenue management as demonstrated above. The organisation has an established history of this activity, but has adopted further use in recent years, predominantly in response to changing market conditions. While this more commercial approach may conflict with established working practice, it may also provide the solution to balancing the sustainable management of supply and demand at the properties in the care of the NTS.

■ Summary

- Barriers to the adoption of RM in HVAs have been identified as being a lack of reliable data on which to base decisions, a lack of commercial imperative and restrictions including high fixed costs and fixed capacity. However, there is a requirement for managers at HVAs to improve the management of sites and organisations in order for them to compete for visitors and funding support in increasingly competitive environments.

- As evidenced by the literature review and case study discussed, revenue management is a potential tool for HVA managers to use in the effective management of their site. Requirements for the use of revenue management included the ability for the business to offer variable pricing, undertake market segmentation and manage supply and demand for the property.

- Within the confines of available resources and skills, all of the above could potentially be used within the heritage tourism sector. Indeed, some aspects make this sector particularly suitable as visitors have been shown to be willing to pay and participate in support for heritage. Therefore the opportunities for the innovative use of existing resources to target new markets, to develop premium products to expand the visitor spend and to take advantage of new product development opportunities are clearly available.

- Opportunities for further pricing development might be sourced from other tourism sectors, such as airlines, or sectors such as retailing, or to change existing practices by instigating admission charges at public sites, as often exist for other leisure services, in order to alleviate congestion, meet funding shortfalls and tackle pricing imbalances within the sector.

9

- Mechanisms to assist in the future adoption of RM in HVAs include; the development of supporting IT to allow for back office systems to support business; the gathering and accessibility of reliable data to inform decision-making; the more flexible and innovative use of heritage resources; and the sharing of best practice.

- HVAs need to focus on identifying the individuality of their resource and visitor experience and the developing RM systems to capture the diverse range of visitors that might be willing to pay to visit.

- Recent trends in diversification at HVAs can be developed to offer new opportunities to engage with new audiences or to extend the engagement with established visitor markets.

References

Aas, C., Ladkin, A. & Fletcher, J. (2005). Stakeholder collaboration and heritage management. *Annals of Tourism Research*, **32**(1): 28–48.

Apostolakis, A. & Jaffry S (2005). A choice modelling application for Greek heritage attractions. *Journal of Travel Research*, **43**(3): 309–318.

Barber, N., Taylor, D. & Deale, C. (2010). Wine packaging: marketing towards consumer lifestyle to build brand equity and increased revenue. *International Journal of Revenue Management*, **4**(3/4): 215–237.

Benckendorff, P. & Pearce, P. (2003). Australian tourist attractions: the links between organisational characteristics and planning. *Journal of Travel Research*, **42**: 24–35.

Boyd, S. (2000). Heritage tourism in Northern Ireland: opportunity under peace. *Current Issues in Tourism*, **3**(2): 150–174.

Cameron, C. & Gatewood, J. (2004). Seeking numinous experiences in the unremembered past. *Ethnology*, **42**(1): 55-71.

Chhabra, D. (2010). Back to the past: a sub-segment of Generation Y's perceptions of authenticity. *Journal of Sustainable Tourism*, 18(6): 793-809.

Chiang, W., Chen, J. & Xu, X. (2007). An overview of research on revenue management: current issues and future research. *International Journal of Revenue Management*, **1**(1): 9–126.

Darlow, S., Essex, S. & Brayshay, M. (2012). Sustainable heritage management practices at visited heritage sites in Devon and Cornwall. *Journal of Heritage Tourism*, 7(3): 219-237.

Dearden, P. & Rollins, R. (eds) (2008). *Parks and Protected Areas in Canada: Planning and Management* .Toronto: Oxford University Press 3rd edition.

Donohoe, H. (2012). Sustainable heritage tourism marketing and Canada's Rideau Canal world heritage site. *Journal of Sustainable Tourism*, **20**(1): 121-142.

Fyall, A. & Garrod, B. (1998) Heritage tourism: at what price? *Managing Leisure,* **3**(4): 213-228.

Heritage Lottery Fund (2010). *Investing in Success: Heritage and the UK Tourism Economy*. London: Visit Britain.

Holmes, K. (2008). Changing attitudes towards volunteering and the implications for tourist attractions. Council for Australian University Tourism and Hospitality Education (CAUTHE) conference.

Ho, P. S.Y. & McKercher, B. (2004). Managing heritage resources as tourism products. *Asia Pacific Journal of Tourism Research*, **9**(3): 255–265.

Hu, W. & Wall, G. (2005). Environmental management, environmental image and the competitive tourist attraction. *Journal of Sustainable Tourism*, **13**(6): 617–635.

Hughes, M. & Carlsen, J. (2010). The business of cultural heritage tourism: critical success factors. *Journal of Heritage Tourism*, **5**(1): 17-32.

Kaufman, T. & Weaver, P. (2006). Heritage tourism: A question of age. *Asia Pacific Journal of Tourism Research* , **11**(2) 136–145.

Leask, A. (2010). Progress in visitor attraction research: towards more effective management. *Tourism Management*, **31**(2): 155–166.

Leask, A., Fyall, A. & Garrod, B. (2002). Heritage visitor attractions: managing revenue in the new Millennium. *International Journal of Heritage Studies*, **8**(3): 247–265.

Leask, A., Fyall, A. & Garrod, B. (2012). Managing revenue in Scottish visitor attractions. *Current Issues in Tourism* (in press).

Leask, A. & Yeoman, I. (1999). The development of core concepts of yield management. *International Journal of Heritage Studies*, **5**(2): 96–110.

Lennon, J. & Graham, M. (2001). Commercial development and competitive environment: the museum sector in Scotland. *International Journal of Tourism Research*, **3**(4): 265–281.

Loulanki, T. & Loulanki, V. (2011). The sustainable integration of cultural heritage and tourism: a meta-study. *Journal of Sustainable Tourism*, **9**(7): 837-862.

McKercher, B. & du Cros, H. (2002). *Cultural Tourism: The Partnership Between Tourism and Cultural Heritage Management*. New York: The Hawthorn Hospitality Press.

NTS. (2010). Fit for purpose: Report of the strategic review of the National Trust for Scotland. Retrieved April 7, 2011, from http://www.nts.org.uk/site/docs/news/ microsoft_word_-_report_january__strategic_review_final000001.pdf

Padhi, S. & Aggarwal, V. (2011). Competitive revenue management for fixing quota and price of hotel commodities under uncertainty. *International Journal of Hospitality Management*, **30**(3), 725-734.

Pullman, M. & Rodgers, S. (2010). Capacity management for hospitality and tourism: a review of current approaches. *International Journal of Hospitality Management*, **29**(1): 177–187.

Reynisdottir, M., Song, H. & Agrusa, J. (2008). Willingness to pay entrance fees to natural attractions: an Icelandic study. *Tourism Management*, **29**(6): 1076–1083.

9

Ryan, J. & Silvanto, S. (2009). The World Heritage Site list: the making and management of a brand. *Place Branding and Public Diplomacy*, **5**(4): 290-300.

Swarbrooke, J. (1994). The future of the past: heritage tourism in the 21st century. In: A. V. Seaton (Ed.), *Tourism: The State of the Art*. Chichester: John Wiley & Sons, 222-229.

Transchel, S. & Minner, S. (2009). The impact of dynamic pricing on the economic order decision. *European Journal of Operational Research*, **198**(3): 773–789.

10 Theme Parks Revenue Management

Ady Milman and Kelly Kaak

Learning outcomes

After reading this chapter, you should be able to:

- Describe the global theme park industry.
- Identify sources of income in the theme park industry.
- Provide an overview of contemporary revenue strategies in the theme park industry.
- Provide a look ahead – how can creative revenue management techniques be utilised to increase revenues in the theme park industry?
- Understand and apply: pay-as-you-go admission pricing strategies; pay-one-price admission pricing strategies; consumer segmentation-based admission pricing strategies; theme park physical design as a revenue strategy; extending the length of stay at theme parks as a revenue strategy; convenience and the bundling of services at theme parks as a revenue strategy.

■ Introduction

Revenue management is a collection of techniques that focus on maximising revenues, and has been credited for income improvement in several segments of the hospitality industry (Cross, 1997). In many service industries, capacity of supply is often fixed while demand is volatile. Therefore, it is challenging for service companies to achieve a balance between supply and demand (Peng, Xiao & Li, 2012). Theme parks are characterised by high capital investment, high operational fixed costs and, to some extent, high operational variable cost. Additionally, demand for the theme park product varies according to time of the year, day of the week and time of the day. Thus, the industry has the potential of benefiting from the adoption of creative revenue management strategies.

To achieve success with revenue management techniques, firms must be willing to constantly reconsider their product offering, their pricing structures, and their general business processes (Cross, 1997). In the U.S. hospitality and tourism industry, revenue management began in the airline industry following the 1978 deregulation, and then spread to lodging and other industry sectors. However, to date, many theme parks have not fully utilised the benefits of revenue management (Berman, 2005), even though there are opportunities to apply this strategy in the industry (Heo & Lee, 2009).

■ The global theme park industry

Theme parks are a relatively new concept of tourist attraction and often attempt to create a fantasy atmosphere of another place and time. Theming is reflected through architecture, landscaping, costumed personnel, rides, shows, food services, merchandising and other environmental attributes that impact the guest's experience (Milman, 2010). Disneyland's opening in 1955 in Anaheim, California is often referred to by both scholars and industry experts as the genesis of the theme park industry (Price, 1999). Walt Disney wanted his park to stress cleanliness, to have a single point of entry, and to contain numerous themed sections around which all attractions, entertainment and retail activities were coordinated. Much emphasis was placed on isolating the outside world from the fantasy world presented in the parks and to provide an environment where families could be entertained together (Price, 1999).

Other theme park attributes referred to in the literature include: the pay-one-price admission fee, annual attendance revenue in excess of US$ one million, corporate ownership, specific design traits such as elaborate landscaping, architecture that entertains, as well as a mix of activities that includes large-scale rides, retail opportunities and live entertainment (Kyriazi, 1976; Lyon, 1987; Carlson & Popelka, 1988; Adams, 1991; Gottdiener, 1997; Williams, 1998). While the contemporary theme park industry was originally introduced in North America, in recent decades, the theme park industry has expanded globally. In 2011, over 196 million people visited the top 25 worldwide parks, a 3.8 percent increase over the 2010 figure (TEA/ AECOM, 2012). While the economic, social and political impact of these entertainment complexes is sometimes overlooked, it is interesting to note that in 2011 the number of visitors to the world's top 25 theme parks was slightly higher than the number of international tourists that visited Spain, China, Italy, and the United Kingdom combined (World Tourism Organisation, 2012).

■ Sources of income in the theme park industry

Revenues for the theme park industry are generated from a variety of sources, but primarily from the admission price. Admission price represents between 49 to 60 percent of overall theme park revenues (Vogel, 2010; Mintel, 2011). The number of guest admissions also represents the volume from which other sources of revenue are derived like food and beverage, merchandise and games.

Guest spending on food and beverage accounts for approximately 14 to 17 percent of theme park revenues; merchandise sales (souvenirs, sundries, etc.) accounts for 6 to 10 percent of revenues (Vogel, 2010; Mintel, 2011) and guest spending on games accounts for another 4 percent of the total revenues (Vogel, 2010). Parking fees, concession charges, and sponsorship funds from external advertisers make up the remainder of the revenue sources for a typical theme park (First Research, 2012) (Figure 10.1).

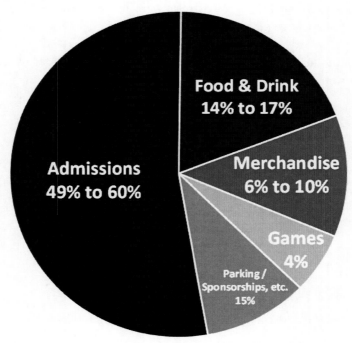

10

Figure 10.1: Approximate sources of theme park revenues

Source**:** Vogel, 2010; Mintel, 2011, & First Research, 2012

Since the bulk of theme park revenue is derived from admission receipts, theme parks have devised a variety of admission pricing options in order to generate as much revenue as possible from a variety of market segments.

■ Contemporary revenue management strategies in the theme park industry

☐ Admission pricing

Pay-as-you-go admission pricing strategy

When Walt Disney planned Disneyland, he insisted on a single physical entrance, as opposed to the multiple entrance gates positioned by many amusement parks at that time. His goal was to control the story that would be revealed as guests experienced the extensively themed environment (Price, 1999). Controlled access via a single entrance gate would also enable the park management to determine accurate daily and hourly guest counts. This information could be utilized to enhance operational efficiency and to devise strategies for maximising revenues.

Disneyland initially used an admission pricing system that was adopted from the amusement parks that were present in Coney Island, New York at that time. A nominal entrance price was charged, and then tickets were purchased to pay for individual rides, shows and other attractions. Disneyland's innovation was to segment the tickets into denominations of varying priced face values from 'A' to 'E', according to the perceived value of the guest's experience (Figure 10.2).

Figure 10.2: Disneyland 'E' Ticket, circa late 1970s

Source: MiceChat.com: http://micechat.com/blogs/samland/3479-e-ticket.html

A number of U.S. parks like Pacific Ocean Park in California, Pleasure Island near Boston, or Freedomland in New York City (Adams, 1991) rushed in to capitalise on Disneyland's success. They also adopted the practice of charging a token fee to gain access to the park and then sold graduated tickets, based on the guests' perceived value of their experience. This admission strategy is referred to as the 'pay-as-you-go' method. It allowed park patrons to pay for only those attractions they had an interest in visiting.

Yet, many of these post-Disneyland parks struggled to survive due to poor marketing strategies, short operating seasons or the development of attractions that failed to appeal to a wide audience. Strategic mistakes among these early parks drove their management teams to develop and implement innovative admission schemes such as the pay-one-price admission strategy (detailed below) that were intended to maximise revenues from their often dwindling attendance bases.

Pay-as-you-go admission pricing strategy benefited guests were required to pay only for those attractions they wanted to experience. From the parks' revenue management perspective, popular attractions could be re-priced to reflect actual demand. However, the pay-as-you-go admission pricing strategy required guests to continuously interrupt their experience to purchase more tickets, and as a result they were less likely to spend on food and merchandise.

Pay-one-price admission pricing strategy

The pay-one-price admission strategy was developed as an alternative to the pay-as-you-go method. Rather than separately pricing every theme park ride or attraction and consequently dedicating staff to selling and collecting tickets, the pay-one-price method offered a simplified ticketing option. The strategy was developed as a competitive method to reinvigorate declining attendance at early non-Disney theme parks.

10

Box 10.1: Pacific Ocean Park's development of the pay-one-price admission strategy

Pacific Ocean Park was the first traditional amusement park to transform itself into a modern theme park. Opened in 1958 at the Santa Monica, California, its initial marketing plan was to capitalize on the overflow from Disneyland. Its first-year attendance reached 1.2 million but then fell to 800,000 on the following year (Adams, 1991).

An innovative strategy was developed where the old pay-as-you-go ticket pricing policy for each attraction was replaced with an all-inclusive $1.50 pay-one-price admission policy. During the 1960 inaugural season of the new pricing policy, attendance increased to 2.0 million (Anon, 1962). The new pricing scheme was incorporated into their marketing efforts and the term 'P.O.P.' became synonymous for both Pacific Ocean Park and Pay-One-Price (Onosko, 1978). This new pricing strategy was soon adopted by other theme parks.

A single, all-inclusive admission was charged at the gate that was more expensive than the pay-as-you-go entrance ticket. From the guests' perspective, the pay-one-price admission pricing strategy provided an opportunity to have a major spending only at the park's entrance, however, the system discourages visits by those patrons who do not desire to use many of the park's attractions. From the parks' management perspective, the system created an operational environment that reduced the need to dedicate staff to sell and collect tickets.

Figure 10.3: Advertisement for pay one price admission at Pacific Ocean Park, circa 1961
Source: PacificOceanPark.Tripod.com: http://pacificoceanpark.tripod.com/

Consumer segmentation-based admission pricing strategies

As the pay-one-price structure took hold in the industry, pricing options were developed according to the age of the guest (e.g. standard adult admission, toddlers, youth, or senior pricing); the number of days of admission (e.g. one-day, multiple consecutive days, annual or seasonal passes) and group sales discounts.

Over time, theme parks have evolved admission pricing strategies that are highly sophisticated, offering varieties of ticketing options that appeal to or entice multiple market segments. These include afternoon or late evening admission discounts, point of sale discounts like online reduced-price tickets; transportation and accommodation package pricing, or pricing based on the geographical origin of the guests. Some theme parks also adopted advance-purchase pricing, with similar rules instituted by other segments of the hospitality and tourism industries.

■ Theme park physical design

Increasing the length of stay at a theme park is a fundamental strategy employed by all park operators; the longer guests stay, the higher will be the expenditure per person per visit (known as 'per caps' in the industry). While the admission charge is often based on the amount that covers most parks' operating costs, the in-park additional discretionary spending generates profits. Therefore, theme park layout designers have attempted to craft sufficient attractions and diversions to keep guests in the park long enough so they could purchase more food and beverage, buy more souvenirs, or play more games of skill. Consequently, creative design of the park's pathways, architecture and landscaping not only help to create a fantasy environment, but also prevent the infringement of the outside world into the theme park world and by so doing encourage guests to stay longer.

Randal Duell, one of the most influential theme park designers, was credited with the 'Duell Loop' spatial design concept as a means to increase revenue (Onosko, 1978). The design calls for a single main walkway that circles through the park passing each attraction. Such a format makes it difficult for guests to selectively pick attractions from the theme park's portfolio. As guests make their way through a park, they become increasingly committed to continue through the loop rather than returning to the entrance gate. After a few hours in the park, patrons are near the back of the park and find it too inconvenient to leave the park.

Physical design to enhance revenues also includes the strategy of positioning merchandise and food points of sale at locations where guests exit attractions, shows, entertainment, and other activities. Many theme parks not only place fixed retail outlets, but sometimes strategically position portable outlets like vending carts that can be moved from place to place, according to the scheduled attractions and activities offered in the park.

Extending the length of stay at destination theme parks

The development of U.S. destination theme parks during the 1970s, and later in other locations around the world, resulted in revenue strategies aimed at increasing the number of days that visitors spend at destination parks. These destination theme parks are essentially resorts that attract the majority of their guests from the tourist market and include accommodation facilities, themed restaurants, shopping, nighttime entertainment, water parks, and other recreational facilities in addition to their theme parks.

As destination theme park resorts expanded into other parts of the globe, similar initiatives have been adopted as park operators seek to preserve or increase their market share. For example, Tokyo Disney Resort includes two theme parks, three Disney-themed resorts, six non-Disney hotels and a shopping complex. Similarly, Alton Towers in Staffordshire, England, offers additional amenities like two hotels, a water park, a spa, and a conference center. Universal Studios Singapore is located within Resorts World Sentosa, an integrated resort that features a casino, oceanarium and four hotels.

Box 10.2: Walt Disney World Resort's RM strategy: The evolution of *Magic Your Way* pricing

In the 1980s, increasing the length of stay at the Walt Disney World meant keeping guests for more days on the Disney property. Since the early 1970s, Walt Disney World was the primary destination of a typical Central Florida vacation, but was losing tourists to the increasing ancillary attractions that emerged during the decades following the opening of Disney's Magic Kingdom. With the opening of Epcot in 1982, one-day, two-day and three-day park admission tickets were introduced, priced to entice guests to spend multiple days in the Disney parks and enjoy Disney's resort amenities.

However, adding more theme parks to a destination resort does not necessarily ensure that tourists' length of stay will increase. Striving to maintain its position as the market leader, Walt Disney World opened in 1998 its fourth theme park, Disney's Animal Kingdom; however, the park's success came at the expense of attendance at the other three Disney theme parks – the Magic Kingdom, Epcot and Hollywood Studios. The Walt Disney Company realized that building additional theme parks would only cannibalize existing parks (Koenig, 2007); therefore, new marketing and revenue management strategies had to be devised to ensure the company's dominance in the heavily-saturated Central Florida theme park market.

Beginning in 2005, Walt Disney World resort implemented a ticket pricing plan that linked the potential discounts with the guests' length of stay. The *Magic Your Way* program increased the cost for a one-day admission ticket but then progressively reduced the ticket cost for subsequent days. For example, the 2005 cost of a one-day theme park ticket was $60 but a seven-day ticket could be purchased for $199 – making the daily admission price just over $28 (Blank, 2004). In addition to the price incentives, the *Magic Your Way* pricing strategy empowered guests to tailor their vacation experience through a menu of 30 ticket options and add-ons.

In response to the success of Walt Disney World's new pricing strategy, Universal Orlando Resort began offering an Internet special ticket that allowed purchasers to spend a week at its two parks for a slight premium over the cost of a single-day ticket. Another length-of-stay strategy was adopted by Central Florida's major non-Disney competitors (Universal Studios, SeaWorld and Busch Gardens), who formed an alliance to sell an 'Orlando FlexTicket' that provided unlimited entrance to the member parks for up to two weeks (Frommer, 2006).

■ Capitalising on convenience and bundling services

☐ Increasing revenue through online advance ticketing

The arrival of online ticket sales technology has provided theme parks with the opportunity to sell admission tickets prior to the actual visit. The incentive was that pre-ordering and purchasing tickets online locks the guest into visiting the park sometimes in the near future. To induce demand, many parks provided online-only special promotions and discounts offered on single-day, multi-day and annual passes to those guests willing to print their tickets at home. Online ticket sales also enabled many theme parks to offer installment plans to pay for these tickets as a means of alleviating the financial burden on potential guests (De Lisser, 2004).

☐ Increasing revenue through enhanced convenience

As vacations have become shorter (Fleischer & Rivlin, 2009), patrons have become more time-constrained. Consequently, many theme parks have implemented some form of queue line management system. Disney parks introduced the *Fast Pass*, where guests manually made a reservation by inserting their park ticket into a device at the entrance of specified high-demand attractions and then receive a paper ticket that provides them with a reservation time at some point during the visiting day. This system allowed the guests to bypass the usual queue line and is offered for no additional charge. Disney's management recognized that guests waiting in queue lines were not able to spend as much time making purchases in the park. Thus, offering their guests the opportunity to avoid time in lines resulted in increased in-park spending (Dickson, Ford & Laval, 2005).

Rival Universal Studios adopted a similar system known as the *Express Pass*, but this convenience comes at an additional price. The price of this convenience varies based on the daily park attendance, which impacts rides and attraction wait times. On slow days, the service is not viewed by the guests as being worth the cost, but on the busiest days the cost of the convenience is perceived to be more beneficial and comes close to the actual cost of an admission ticket (Anon, 2011). Regional parks such as Six Flags and Legoland Windsor in England have also implemented such systems purchased from off-the-shelf providers like Lo-Q that integrates virtual queue systems in amusement and theme parks and other attractions (Lo-Q, 2012).

Furthermore, many parks have adjusted their pricing strategy by bundling additional products and services to their basic admission price rather than increasing the price of their tickets. In addition to adding the convenience of reducing

10

wait time, some theme park added features like free parking, all-you-can-eat food for the day, and admission to special seasonal events.

Box 10.3: Bundling services at Holiday World

Holiday World is an independent theme park located in rural Indiana, USA. Most of the park's guests must drive an hour or more from home or stay overnight to be able to spend a full day at the park. To entice visitors to this remote location, many amenities are included free with the purchase of an admission ticket.

In 2000, the park adopted a revenue management program that included offering free soft drinks to customers. While most park observers believed that this practice would reduce per capita spending on food and beverage, in fact, the reverse took place as per caps increased. Park management attributed the increase in revenue to guests who extended their length of stay in the park and spent their perceived savings by purchasing additional food and beverage (Zoltak, 2004).

■ Revenue management strategies in the theme park industry: A look ahead

Some scholars argue that the theme park industry has not fully recognized the potential benefits associated with the adoption of creative revenue management techniques (Berman, 2005; Heo & Lee, 2009). Prior to implementing traditional revenue management techniques, a number of assumptions about the enterprise must be made to ensure their applicability. First, the park must have a system to collect and store historical data on prices, inventory, demand, and guests' consumption characteristics (Cross, 1997). Second, theme parks must have the ability to segment customers according to their willingness to pay for a particular service at a point in time (Cross, 1997). Third, theme parks must be able to develop, maintain, implement and respond to forecasts of demand, inventory availability, and market share.

While many theme parks may have the ability to meet these assumptions, the industry has several unique characteristics that may make the implementation of conventional revenue management strategies a challenge. For example, a theme park's capacity is much more flexible than airlines' or hotels' capacity (Heo & Lee, 2009). Theme parks do not strive each day to achieve full capacity, and it is typically reached only on the busiest days of the year.

Another characteristic that impedes the implementation of classical revenue management techniques at theme parks is that guests do not make reservations in advance (Heo & Lee, 2009). While more and more theme parks offer online tickets purchased prior to the day of admission, no effort is currently made to capture the exact date the guest plans to actually visit the park.

Nonetheless, throughout the industry, there are a few examples of slowly introduced innovative revenue management strategies. The following examples of revenue management best practices can be a foundation for a new era of industry-wide practice.

☐ Seasonal pricing: adjusting prices based on demand

Admission ticket cost could be set in accordance with dynamic pricing principles, where the price is adjusted based on demand. A higher price is charged on anticipated busy days than on slower days (Sisario, 2011). Due to the variability of demand for theme park visits, admission prices could be adjusted based on the season of the year, the day of the week, and even the time of the day (Heo & Lee, 2009). Such a system, for example, has been implemented at the Dutch theme park Slagharen (Editorial, *Park World*, 2010), which offers a pricing calendar that changes according to anticipated consumer demand.

☐ Enhanced customer segmentation

Different admission prices could be introduced according to the visitors' market segment characteristics. Recognising these differences, prices can be set to maximise revenues for the park. To determine if viable segments exist, current and potential customers must be analyzed according to their potential receptiveness to segmentation options.

Many theme parks around the world have introduced differentiated pricing based on the guest's demographic characteristics like age, height, family size, residence status (local resident, tourist, international visitor), occupation (military personnel, students or the unemployed) or membership in a specific organisation like unions, automobile clubs, or credit cards companies (Klar & Lewison, 2011). Additional differentiated pricing is based on the guests' consumption characteristics, such as their desire to experience a specific ride or an attraction, their preferred length of visit to the park, or their wish to experience reduced queue line waits.

Finally, pricing can also be differentiated according to guests' purchasing behavior like advance or at-the-gate purchases, the willingness to buy a set-day-ticket, special promotions with limitations, the motivation to buy multiple tickets for a lower per-ticket price (e.g. group rate or a family plan), or the readiness to commit to repeat visits over time for a lower per-unit price (Harris & Peacock, 1995).

10

☐   ## Take advantage of advance sales: planning for profits based on an awareness of demand

Historically, little effort has been made to promote capacity through the use of advance sales of theme park tickets. Revenue can be increased through various promotional methods to stimulate the advance sale of admission tickets for days when attendance is expected to be low. Due to the discretionary nature of a theme park visit, providing incentives to visit on specified dates could appeal to numerous market segments and could shift attendance patterns from busy periods to slower times.

In addition to price fluctuations, advance sales for slow periods can use incentive packages to redirect demand. For example, free parking with a pre-paid admission in an off-peak month or a free meal plan for those committing to visit during a traditionally slow period (Swarbrooke, 2002).

Other benefits associated with advance sales, especially online, include the opportunity to solicit ticket upgrades and packages such as preferred parking near the entrance gate or near-by hotel accommodation. This strategy capitalizes on the fact that it is easier to make such pitches online than when competing with other distractions encountered at the front gate of the park. Online sales also enable the capture of email addresses from which a customer database can be developed and used for future marketing efforts. One of the greatest benefits that comes from advance sales is that it leaves the guest with more cash on hand, which is likely to be spent in the park (Brown, 2010).

■   # Summary

- Throughout the development of the theme park industry, parks have adopted numerous, and often innovative, revenue strategies to maximise profits and protect market share. Few of these strategies have utilised classical revenue management techniques. However, considering the ever-increasing level of competition for guests' revenues coupled with the maturing of the theme park industry in many industrialized nations, theme parks must be more willing to experiment and embrace sophisticated revenue management strategies.

- A change in the revenue management paradigm that existed for many decades in the global theme park industry is required. These suggested changes are not independent and rely on the economic, social and political environment where the park is located, and competition of other theme parks in the area and other entertainment alternatives.

- Other external factors that may impact on the adoption of revenue management techniques include changes in technology, demographic composition, and consumers' tastes and preferences, and management willingness to adopt those innovative revenue management techniques.

References

Adams, J. A. (1991). *The American amusement park industry: A history of technology and thrills*. Boston, Massachusetts, USA: Twayne Publishers.

Anon (1962). An advertiser learns: Match the campaign to the subject, *Printer's Ink*, May 11, 1962.

Anon (2011). Implicit Time/Implicit Space; Amusement Park Rides I Space and Time in Revenue Management. Blogs.Cornell.edu weblog, March 27, 2011 by yab24. http://blogs.cornell.edu/revenuemanagement11/2011/03/27/amusement-park-rides/

Berman, B. (2005). Applying yield management pricing to your service business. *Business Horizons*, 48(2): 169-179.

Blank, D. (2004). Disney expands ticket choices. *The New York Times*, December 12, 5.2.

Brown, S. (2010). The future of attractions ticketing. *Funworld*, January, 2010. http://www.iaapa.org/includes/layout/print.asp?/industry/funworld/2010/jan/departments/

Carlson, R. & Popelka, E. (1988). *Directory of Theme & Amusement Parks: A State-by-State Listing of Outstanding Entertainment and Family Enjoyment Areas*. Babylon, NY: Pilot Books, Pilot Industries, Inc.

Cross, R. (1997). *Revenue Management: Hard-Core Tactics for Market Domination*. New York: Broadway Books.

De Lisser, E. (2004). Cheap thrills: A new twist in theme-park pricing; to offset weak traffic, attractions roll out range of discount programs. *Wall Street Journal*, June 24, 2004, D. 1.

Dickson, D; Ford, R.C; and Laval, B. (2005). Managing real and virtual waits in hospitality and service organisations. *Cornell Hotel and Restaurant Administration Quarterly*, **46**(1): 52-68.

Editorial: (2010) Slagharen – the price is right! *Park World Online*, December 29, 2010. http://www.parkworld-online.com/news/fullstory.php/aid/1885/Slagharen_-_the_price_is_right!.html

First Research (2012). Amusement parks & arcades - quarterly update 8/6/2012. Austin, United States, Austin: Hoover's Inc. Retrieved from: http://ezproxy.lib.ucf.edu/login?url=http://search.proquest.com/docview/1032525515?accountid=10003

Fleischer, A. & Rivlin, J. (2009). Quality, quantity and duration decisions in household demand for vacations. *Tourism Economics*, **15**(3): 513-530.

Frommer, A. (2006). On a budget; in Orlando, don't skip the other parks; earmark a few Disney days, then venture off-site. Universal, SeaWorld and the Space Center beckon. *Los Angeles Times*, December 3, 2006, L. 12.

Gottdiener, M. (1997). *The Theming of America: Dreams, Visions, and Commercial Spaces*. Boulder, CO: Westview Press.

10

Harris, F.H. & Peacock, P. (1995). Hold my place, please: yield management improves capacity-allocation guesswork. *Marketing Management*, **4**(2): 34-46.

Heo, C.Y. & Lee, S. (2009). Application of revenue management practices to the theme park industry. *International Journal of Hospitality Management*, **28**(3): 446-453.

Klar, A. & Lewison M. (2011). Dynamic pricing for the attractions industry. A presentation made at the International Association of Amusement Parks and Attractions Expo, November 16, 2011, Orlando, Florida.

Koenig, D. (2007). Realityland: True-Life Adventures at Walt Disney World. Irvine, California, USA: Bonaventure Press.

Kyriazi, G. (1976). *The Great American Amusement Parks: A Pictorial History*. Secaucus, NJ: Castle Books.

Lo-Q (2012). Retrieved on 11/17/2012 from: http://www.lo-q.com/

Lyon, R. (1987). Theme parks in the USA: growth, markets and future prospects. *Travel & Tourism Analyst*, **9**: 31-43.

Milman, A. (2010). The global theme park and attraction industry. *Worldwide Hospitality & Tourism Themes* (WHATT). **2**(3): 220-237.

Mintel Research. (2011). Theme park sales on a roller coaster ride. *Mintel Oxygen Reports*, July 12, 2011. Retrieved on 11/17/2012 from: http://www.mintel.com/press-centre/press-releases/729/theme-park-sales-on-a-roller-coaster-ride

Onosko, T. (1978). *Fun Land U.S.A: The Complete Guidebook to 100 Major Amusement and Theme Parks All Across the Country*. New York, NY: Ballantine Books.

Peng, G., Xiao, B. & Li, J. (2012). Unconstraining methods in revenue management systems: research overview and prospects. *Advances in Operations Research*, 1-23.

Price, H. (1999). *Walt's Revolution by the Numbers*. Orlando, Florida: Ripley Entertainment Inc.

Sisario, B. (2011). Ticketmaster plans to use a variable pricing policy. *The New York Times*, April 18, 2011.

Swarbrooke, J. (2002). *The Development and Management of Visitor Attractions*. Woburn, Massachusetts, USA: Reed Educational and Professional Publishing Ltd.

TEA / AECOM. (2012). 2011 *Theme Index: Global Attractions Attendance Report*. Retrieved on 11/8/2012 from: http://www.aecom.com/deployedfiles/Internet/Capabilities/Economics/_documents/Theme%20Index%202011.pdf

Vogel, H.L. (2010). *Entertainment Industry Economics: A Guide for Financial Analysis*. New York: Cambridge University Press.

Williams, S. (1998). *Tourism Geography*. New York, NY: Routledge.

World Tourism Organisation (2012). *Tourism Highlights 2012 Edition*. Retrieved on 11/8/2012 from: http://dtxtq4w60xqpw.cloudfront.net/sites/all/files/docpdf/unwtohighlights12enhr_1.pdf

Zoltak, J. (2004). Put your hands together for Tivoli Park, Gardaland and Holiday World. *Amusement Business*, **116**(28): 16-17.

11 Revenue Management in the Cruising Industry

David Selby

Learning outcomes

After reading this chapter, you should be able to:

- Understand the key revenue management levers at play in the cruising industry.
- Appreciate the factors that are unique to the sector, in particular itinerary planning.
- See how pricing of cabin grades plays a key role in revenue management.

Introduction

Cruising has been going from strength to strength. The Passenger Shipping Association (PSA, 2012) in its recent *Cruise Review* states that 1.7m of us in the UK went ocean cruising in 2011 - up nearly 60% in five years - with demand for new ships increasing. 18 are to be built between October 2012 and October 2016, valued at $11.6 billion (seatrade-insider, 2012) with increasingly sophisticated innovations being incorporated on board. These include giant outdoor movie screens, rock climbing walls, bowling alleys, zip-wires and surf machines, to mention but a few, and ensure that there is something for everyone in an increasingly diverse product offering for guests of all ages and attitudes. Cruising continues to grow in all parts of the world, with total passengers expected to reach the 20 million mark by the end of 2012 (European Cruise Council, 2012).

However, 2012 has been one of the most challenging years on record and in terms of revenue management, could not have got off to a worse start for the industry. On the night of Friday 6th January – at the beginning of one of the busiest periods in a year for bookings - the cruise ship Costa Concordia partially sank after being inflicted with a 70m gash in its port side hull, during a 7 day Western Mediterranean cruise. The incident had a specific and significant impact on the cruising sector not only in Italy where Costa is based, but throughout Europe and the rest of the world. The industry at large quickly got together to communicate the positive safety record of cruise ships, but with the ship remaining on its side for months, and with recordings of conversations between the coastguard and a captain that appeared to be in shock, it has continued to prove to be one of the public relations challenges of 2012.

In addition, with increasing pressures on fuel and other operating costs, the current recession, and incidents such as Costa Concordia, many cruise lines are facing tougher challenges to succeed in achieving required or expected profits. This is underlined by the Royal Caribbean Cruise Lines 2nd Quarter results, which saw last year's second quarter profits of $93.5 million wiped out as it reported a loss of $3.6 million for the same three months this year, as summarised in the UK's *Travel Weekly* on July 27th 2012 (travelweekly, 2012a). This was reported on the same day and in the same source as All Leisure Group's (owner of Swan Hellenic and Voyages of Discovery) winter half-year losses increasing from £4.2m to £11.2m from the previous year (travelweekly, 2012b). Therefore, managing the revenue line is more critical than ever.

Like other types of holiday offering, such as hotel beds and aircraft seats, excellent revenue management is about understanding behaviours of customers in order to maximise income at the point of departure before the asset becomes 'perishable' (i.e. the ship has departed!). It is not just about charging high ticket prices, because cruise lines are keen for passengers to repeat purchase.

However, the major difference between a hotel and a cruise ship as a holiday option is that a cruise ship can move! A cruise line can take a view as to whether it wishes to continue operating in a particular region, or whether it redeploys a ship – either for all or part of a season – to a different region. In addition, the revenues that many cruise lines achieve on board, or through shore excursions are particularly important in the revenue equation. Therefore, consideration has been given to factors in relation to ships' operations, and not just pricing and sales/distribution issues. As a result, factors influencing revenue management have been divided into two categories with an additional final comment on the implications of the increasing size of new-build ships:

- Shipboard revenue drivers.
    - ☐ Itineraries and itinerary planning.
    - ☐ On board revenues.
    - ☐ Shore excursions.
    - ☐ Tipping and service charges.

- Head office revenue drivers.
  - ☐ Revenue and sales planning.
  - ☐ Ticket pricing and cabin supplements. Discounting versus value adds.
  - ☐ Inventory management.
  - ☐ Distribution channels.

■ Shipboard revenue drivers

☐ Itineraries

An itinerary – a planned journey that a cruise ship, passengers and crew undertake – has to satisfy a range of criteria. Not only does it have to visit places that will appeal to passengers who are encouraged to buy the cruise, but has to satisfy a number of economic and operational criteria from a cruise line perspective. Even before the itinerary detail is considered, one must consider the overall sale-ability of the itinerary and the suitability of the home port (where passengers embark). For example:

- Does the cruise combine a mix of key destinations that will entice customers to buy the cruise paying good prices in the first place, with other less well known ports of call that might also 'surprise and delight' along the way?

- Does the home port have: good communication/transport links to train/air; good parking facilities for passengers to drive to and leave their car cheaply and securely; give support to the cruise line that facilitates the smooth movement of thousands of people on and off a ship in a short space of time?

Once the general parameters are considered, then more detail is examined

Key drivers in itinerary planning

Once the main ports have been identified to help sell the cruise initially, further ports that allow a ship to keep to the 'shortest path' without too much deviation can be considered. There are four key drivers in itinerary planning, and in particular whether a port can be included in an itinerary. Generally speaking, there is a trade-off between one driver and another:

- **Shore Excursions (SX):** Does the itinerary allow for sufficient daylight time to maximise the opportunities for shore-excursion revenue?

- **Port Costs (PC):** Do the ports visited have both customer and cruise line friendly facilities, and are the charges reasonable?

- **On-board revenues (OBR):** Does the itinerary allow enough time at sea, so that the cruise line can maximise the on-board revenues from all ships' facilities (e.g. bar, casino, duty-free shopping - shops can only be open when the ship is sailing)

■ **Fuel (F):** Does it allow for moderate (rather than too fast or too slow) speeds to conserve fuel?

From a snapshot revenue management point of view, one can argue that if the difference between shore excursion revenue SX - and the total port cost added to the cost of fuel while staying in port PC (i.e. which provides electricity for the air-conditioning, lighting etc.), is greater than the difference between on-board revenues made – OBR – minus the cost of fuel for steaming during the same period F, then the case for calling at a port is a good one.

A successful port call from a revenue management point of view is if (SX-PC)> (OBR-F).

Box 11.1: AIDA Short Cruise from Germany to Norway and Denmark

AIDA is a German cruise line which currently operates 9 ships and has a further 3 on order between 2013 and 2016. It commenced operations in 1996 and is the leading German cruise line. It is part of the massive Carnival Corporation which has about 40% of the world market and owns such brands as P&O, Cunard, Princess Cruises, Carnival Cruise Lines, Costa Cruises and a number of others. AIDA vessels call at over 170 ports. During the summer, the AIDA ships sail in the North Sea, the Baltic Sea, the Mediterranean, the Black Sea and New England and Canada. During the winter, the ships sail in the Caribbean, Central and South America, the Canary Islands, the Mediterranean, the Far East, the Arabian Gulf and the Red Sea.

During the low summer season (May, June, September and October), AIDA operates a number of short (4-day) cruises from two different home ports in northern Germany, Kiel and Warnemunde. The example below is a cruise operated by its ship AIDACara in 2012 and has been chosen to illustrate the issues that the itinerary planners have to take into consideration.

Figure 11.1: AIDACara itinerary NE6, from Warnemunde (Germany) to Oslo and Copenhagen

The itinerary plan can be shown in the following illustration.

Date	Port	Arrival	Departure	Distance	Steaming Hours	Speed
				AIDA Short Journey NE6 - Cara		
06/05/2012	Wernemunde		16:00			
07/05/2012	Oslo	22:00		370	28.00	13.21
08/05/2012	Oslo		14:00			
09/05/2012	Copenhagen	11:00	18:00	272	19.00	14.32
10/05/2012	Wernemunde	8:00		108	12.00	9.00
				750		

The chart shows that the ship leaves its homeport at 16.00hr. I have assumed that the ship takes an hour to manoeuvre out of port and an hour to move into port. Therefore, you will see that while the actual time between 1600hr on day 1 and 2200hr on day 2 is 30 hours, in order to calculate the speed between ports, the time used is only 28 hours. The approximate distance is 370 nautical miles and the speed travelled is 13.21 knots, or 13.21 nm per hour. Typically, speeds around 13-14 knots are quite fuel efficient. Anything over 18 knots is usually avoided.

Overall this is a great mini-break appealing to a broad range of AIDA's guest profile:

- By departing at 1600, it allows guests to get acquainted with the ship and relax before dinner.
- There is no early port stop the next morning, so guests can party into the early hours (and purchase drinks/gamble in the on-board casino, for example, generating cruise line revenue).
- There is time for passengers to enjoy the ship's facilities the next day, and take part in the various activities, and time for the shore excursion staff to present not only the ports of call, but also the excursions that guests can purchase.
- Guests have a chance to explore Oslo by night, should they wish, or take a short walk along the front, as well as exploring the city the next morning, before an on-board afternoon 'siesta' perhaps.
- The 1100 call in Copenhagen allows for a lay-in the next day so that guests can party on board once again.

However, there are alternatives:

Both Denmark and Sweden have ports halfway between Warnemunde and Oslo. Aalborg, Denmark's 4th largest city and in the north of the country, is approached by travelling up an attractive Fjord river, whilst due East of Aalborg, Gothenburg in Sweden is a major city, port and capital of its region. By substituting Oslo for these two ports, one achieves the following:

11

06/05/2010	Wernemunde		16:00			
07/05/2010	Aalborg	12:00	18:00	215	18.00	11.94
08/05/2010	Gothenburg	8:00	19:00	90	12.00	7.50
09/05/2010	Copenhagen	8:00	18:00	138	11.00	12.55
10/05/2010	Wernemunde	8:00		108	12.00	9.00
				551		

This is also good as:

- The ship travels only ¾ of the original distance saving approx. 200 miles on fuel per itinerary.
- The ship travels at slower speeds, thereby making extra fuel savings.
- Guests get to see an extra port, and perhaps pay for more shore excursions.
- There is a whole day at Copenhagen, allowing for greater shore excursion revenues than before.

Only AIDA knows whether this would be a good alternative or not, due to the knowledge it has in relation to its own on board revenues, the fuel efficiencies of its ships and what it can negotiate on port costs. However, from a guest point of view, new and different ports are always good to keep the overall programme fresh, and it is likely that this particular alternative will appeal to a slightly older demographic, as there is a greater destination focus and more 'earlier to bed' to make the most of it.

On board revenues

On board revenue is the name given to the income generated from services on board a cruise ship. By sailing on the high seas (i.e. in international waters), a cruise ship is exempt from paying taxes to any particular country on certain services, which is why one typically sees the on-board shops and casinos only open when the ship is at sea. Typically revenues are generated from:

- Drinks sales from bars.
- Tax free shops.
- Casino.
- Spa.
- Ship-board photographer.
- Entertainment (e.g. bingo).

It is likely that a cruise with passengers on a Mediterranean itinerary is likely to generate more on-board revenue than, say, a cruise that visits north of the Arctic Circle and so itinerary planners need to be sure that the ticket revenue gained from the latter needs to be greater, to achieve expected yearly profits. One also needs to think about the stock on board. More hot mulled wines will be sold on the latter, as opposed to cold beers in the former.

More and more these days, cruise lines are starting to introduce inclusive drinks packages, similar to those in resort hotels, in order to improve the revenue line. There is a possible trade off however, as if guests are encouraged to stay on board to drink to maximise the value of their package, they are likely to purchase fewer shore excursions.

☐ Shore excursions

The sales of shore excursions remain one of the most profitable sources of revenue for the cruise lines. Cruise lines that create itineraries that can include a full day at a big city, or at range of big cities, will ensure a profitable cruise from an on board perspective. A two week 'Baltic Capitals' cruise for example, can include direct calls at capital cities of six countries – Finland, Norway, Sweden, Denmark, Estonia, Latvia - as well as allowing visits to both Berlin and St. Petersburg. This is very popular with US citizens looking to visit as many countries as possible in one trip.

One of the most popular cities in the Mediterranean is Rome. Look on any cruise line website, and it would be difficult to find a day trip for less than £100 per person. As a result, more and more guests are deciding to 'do their own thing' and make independent visits to the sites. This can work out to be a great experience, however it is wise not to be late back to the ship – it won't wait!

☐ Tipping and service charges

This can be a very thorny issue with passengers. It was not so long ago that passengers on-board were given an envelope, and they put in what they thought was the correct amount for good service from waiters, housekeeping staff and so on. Many cruise lines have now decided that 'for guests' convenience' the gratuity will be added to the guests' on-board account, to be paid for at the end of the cruise. Some will even invite guests to pre-pay for tips at the same time as paying the final balance for the cruise itself. Typically this can be around 6 euros per person per day, so for a couple on a 2 week cruise, it is an extra £135 on top of the total holiday cost – ouch! Whilst it is possible to queue at the front desk to have the amount reduced, or even taken off completely, it is an unpleasant experience. Some cruise lines include gratuities in the price of the cruise, as they believe it is a good selling point, which will encourage more passengers to book with them instead of competitors.

11

■ Head office revenue drivers

Once an itinerary has been planned and costed out, revenue assumptions incorporated, ticket pricing and margin evaluation complete, the cruise brochures can be printed, loaded on to websites, and product training for travel agents can begin in earnest. Brochure launch is an exciting time for cruise lines, agents and customers alike. Loyalty to cruise lines is high, and the expectation of new itineraries in ports of call is high. However, a cruise will commercially succeed or not based on the prices that a cruise line achieves in its ticket sales – assuming that the ship will be 100% full, for which of course, is what cruise lines typically aim.

□ Revenue and sales planning

Have a revenue management strategy! It sounds simple – but it is absolutely essential to the successful management of revenue. If there is no plan at the outset as to how revenue is going to be achieved, then it is highly likely that failure will occur. The revenue management process will have started long before the brochures go on sale. The team of revenue managers should have a plan of how many cruises it will sell:

- **By channel** (i.e. through travel agents, via internet, direct through the cruise line call centre etc.).
- **By booking day** available between day 1 of sale and departure.
- **By duration** – this is important for 'butterfly' cruises. There will be demand for a 14 night combinations, but it is likely that more margin will be made from selling 2x7 night cruises than 1x14 night cruise.
- **By source market** (i.e. country one is selling to). Some cruise lines sell into more than one country, so in addition to above, there may be sales and marketing offices in different countries charged with selling allocations, all being coordinated from one central headquarters. Responsibility will be taken centrally to ensure the ship sails full, and there may be cabins allocated and returned between source markets. There are no prizes for empty cabins.

It is likely that the general market and economic conditions will have to be taken into account. In a tough market, it might be appropriate to give up margin in order to get early sales, in the expectation that with fewer cabins left to sell, one can achieve good late sales prices. If the market is strong, it might be appropriate to start with particularly high prices in the expectation that the ship will still sell out on a particular departure, without having to heavily discount.

It is essential to measure the rate of sale of cruises on a day to day basis. If the rate of sale drops, revenue managers need to decide whether to introduce special offers to improve sales performance. Normally of course, there is a trade-off between rate of sale, and margin per passenger.

☐   Pricing and supplements

Look through a selection of cruise lines' brochures and one can see an array of different cabin types, each carrying different supplements. Table 11.1 below offers indications on how different cruise lines shape their pricing policies to manage revenue.

Table 11.1: A comparison of UK cruise ships cabin configuration and lead prices

Cruise Line and duration of cruise	P&O (7)	Thomson (8)	Fred Olsen (8)	P&O (7)	Cruise and Maritime Voyages (7)
Ship	Ocenea	Thomson Spirit	Balmoral	Azura	Marco Polo
Passenger Cabins	957	627	744	1557	425
Number of cabin types	13	9	21	26	15
Lead price (Cheapest)	£779	£899	£1,579	£1,059	£611
Lead price per day	£111	£112	£197	£151	£87
Price for suite	£,499	£1,539	£3,079	£3,549	£1,903
No. of lead price cabins	103	102	61	54	16
%age at lead price	11%	16%	8%	3%	4%

Prices and cabin numbers are taken from brochures, based on a cruise departing in August 2012, from the UK to Norwegian Fjords

Cruise ships have different cabin types to help cruise lines drive revenue. Typically these can be inside cabins (no view of the sea), or outside cabins (with a port hole or larger window), and many cabins these days have their own private balcony. Depending on their size, some may be said to be 'standard' whilst others may be called 'superior'. Clearly a superior outside cabin will attract a larger premium than a standard inside cabin. Then there are deluxe cabins and suites that are even more expensive.

It is the lowest (most basic) grade of cabin that advertised prices are based upon (i.e. 'Prices from £xxx') and other grades of cabin are charged at a supplement to this advertised or lead price. The difference between the lead price and that charged for the highest grade cabins can be substantial and so the revenue managers responsible for managing pricing and occupancy must be quick to spot if cabins are not selling and take remedial pricing action.

If one takes Thomson Cruises, its policy is to have more lead-type cabins available at the lead price and rely less on cabin supplements. The highest price for a cabin is less than twice the lead price. Cruise and Maritime Voyages price differently. The Marco Polo has an exceptionally low lead price, but high supplement revenue. The highest price is more than three times the lead price. The overall revenue the two cruise lines achieve is similar.

11

'Savings' versus 'prices from'

Fred Olsen has brochure prices starting at £197 per person per night in this example, with just 8% of cruises at that price, the rest at a supplement. This would suggest that its brochure prices are uncompetitive, and that revenue is generated through offering discounted deals through travel agents, with a "Save yyy% on brochure prices…" There are rules regarding the length of time that holidays are on sale at original prices before discounting can commence, but the savings messages can look attractive. Thomson tends to use a 'Prices from…' message, as it is generally able to maintain a healthy level of lead price cabins.

There are creative ways to sell the next grade of cabin. 'Free cabin upgrades' are common, where an outside cabin might be priced at the same level as an inside cabin for a limited period.

☐ Managing inventory

The management of inventory is about ensuring not only that the overall price levels are sensible to ensure a rate of sale that is not too fast or too slow, but also a number of other factors:

- Ensuring that the price relationship between the cabin types is sensible. It is not a good idea to sell the standard type cabins first leaving all the higher grade cabins left to the end in the late sales market.

- Ensuring that all cabins on the ship are actually loaded onto the selling system to be sold.

- Ensuring that if allocations of cabins are moved across the selling systems (or if all on one system, budgeted correctly) of different source markets, that they are accounted for. There are no prizes for empty cabins when the ship departs.

- To ensure that if an allocation of cabins is released to a tour operator to sell as part of its own holiday package, any unused cabins are returned in good time to re-sell before departure.

- That if the cruise is sold as part of a fly-cruise offering, the number of cabins left to sell ties in with the number of seats available. This might sound simple, but if more families of four travel than are expected seats would become scarce, as families will more often stay in one cabin, yet still take four seats – the same number two couples occupying two cabins would do.

- Monitoring the performance of certain 'cruise and stay' combinations through the season. For example during the low season, demand for weekly cruises may be higher relative to cruise and stay packages, where in the peak summer months, a two-week 'cruise and stay' is likely to be more popular.

☐ ## Distribution channels

There is nothing that is unique to cruising concerning distribution channels. Like other travel and accommodation options, cruises are sold through travel agents, direct through call centres and through cruise line websites. The use of websites to update future passengers on operational issues, for example if there is a delay returning to home port because of bad weather, is becoming more common. Social media is becoming more popular – e.g. Royal Caribbean Cruise Lines 'Port-folio' which gives information on shore side options at different ports.

However, the cruise line product is more complicated to set up and sell than an aircraft going from A to B. The number of different cabin types have been mentioned, fly-cruising and cruise-and–stay, but as cruising is still relatively new for much of the population, the amount of information that needs to be communicated is relatively huge. Therefore, product training to travel agents – which may not be given by revenue managers – is all part of the revenue management process. Ship visits also form a vital element in getting the product message across.

■ # Long-term drivers

Pinpointing revenue management drivers would not be complete without considering the long-term decision making criteria. Ships take a considerable time to build, are very expensive and investment appraisals need to show long-term returns. It is not a coincidence that the size of ships has grown. Whether a ship has 300 or 3,000 passengers it requires the same number of captains – one – and the overall costs of staff, fuel and equipment on a per passenger basis are lower on a larger ship. The larger the ship, the more facilities it has and as a result the more revenue generating opportunities there are too – it's a double win!

However, environmental issues have put further pressures on cost. New regulations on the chemical content of marine fuel are putting costs up significantly and there is scrutiny on how ships deal with the handling of waste. Whilst the cruise industry has a very good record on emissions and waste, they will continue to innovate through new technology.

The largest ship today is Royal Caribbean's Allure of the Seas. At just over 225,000 tonnes, it can carry over 6,000 passengers and has a crew of over 2,160. That's a lot of ship to explore in a week. For some however, the large ships are becoming too impersonal. Many passengers still prefer small to medium sized ships and it appears that there will be a market for these vessels, as long as they continue to be sufficiently cost efficient to operate. The diversity of cruising and cruise ships will continue to ensure that it will remain a growth industry for many years to come.

11

■ Summary

- ■ Revenue management techniques are based on a mix of marketing approaches based on detailed customer analysis, effective segmentation and pricing policy.

- ■ Although 2012 has been a challenging year for cruising, demand continues to increase so ensuring the longer-term prosperity of the industry.

- ■ Cruising as an industry offers considerable opportunity for the further development of revenue management practice with its variety of innovative onboard and shore-based products and experiences.

- ■ With the increasing use of the Internet for searching, selecting and purchasing cruises, cruising is maturing as a web-based product and all the opportunities that delivers with regard to revenue management practice.

References

PSA. (2012). The Cruise Review. Passenger Shipping Association, February 2012. http://www.the-psa.co.uk/downloads/PSA%20Cruise%20Review%20published%202012.pdf (accessed October, 2012).

Seatrade-insider. (2012). http://www.seatrade-insider.com/Orderbook.html (accessed October, 2012).

European Cruise Council (2012). European Cruise Council Report 2012. http://www.europeancruisecouncil.com/content/ECC%20Report%202011%202012.pdf (accessed October 2012).

Travelweekly (2012a). http://www.travelweekly.co.uk/Articles/2012/07/27/41225/royal-caribbean-profits-hit-by-heavy-discounting.html (accessed October 2012).

Travelweekly (2012b) http://www.travelweekly.co.uk/Articles/2012/07/27/41224/all-leisure-group-winter-losses-deepen.html (accessed October 2012).

12 Revenue Management in Hotels and Airlines: A Critique

Paul Whitelaw

Learning outcomes

After reading this chapter, you should be able to:

- Critique the application of revenue management in the hospitality and airline industries.
- Understand the above within the specific context of the role of the firm and its operation in a competitive environment.

■ Introduction

The preceding and subsequent chapters of this text provide a well rounded and insightful description of the underlying theory and application of revenue management. The various sections on theory as well as the case studies provide both academic and practitioner insight into the workings of revenue management. In this section we will critique revenue management in the hospitality and airline industry. This critique will be offered from a number of different perspectives. However, each perspective will address some aspect of the role of the firm and its operation in a competitive environment.

■ Revenue management in competitive environments

The underlying philosophy of revenue management and its subsequent technological advances focus on generating revenue in a competitive environment. It is, as previously identified, merely a context-specific application of demand and supply analysis that has taken advantage of substantial and rapid developments in statistics, mathematics, forecasting, psychology and operations research, supported by corresponding advances in computing and information technology. Whilst not changing the fundamental aim of the business, which is to sell perishable inventory (hotel rooms and airline seats) in a volatile market, revenue management does embrace a range of management practices. Nearly twenty-five years ago, Kimes (1989) discussed the basics of yield management. However, it was in a subsequent paper (Kimes, 1994, p.14) that she explicitly described yield management (as it was known then) as basically selling "the right inventory unit to the right customer at the right time for the right price". As such, revenue management can be seen as merely a function of inventory management, market segmentation and distribution and price setting. This approach has operated since time immemorial in the hospitality and tourism industry with high rates in the high season and low rates in the low season. However, the advent of information and communication technologies (ICT) has created some significant paradigm shifts in the way businesses go about pursuing revenue. The adoption of increasingly powerful and sophisticated ICT brings various areas of management interest such as distribution channels, market segmentation and price setting into the orbit of revenue management. Therefore, this discussion will address these elements as they apply to revenue management, and not as discrete management practices in their own right.

Revenue management has expanded to mean much more than altering rates in response to demand. The development of pricing conditions such as the booking horizon, prepayments, and cancellation terms have been integral to the development of revenue management. Similarly, inventory control has also supported the development of revenue management. In addition, distribution channel management via the use of online third party vendors as well as direct sales from own websites have played a key role in the establishment of revenue management. Finally, as will be discussed later in this chapter, increasingly sophisticated consumer research methods, especially in terms of decision making preferences, price sensitivity and demand elasticity analysis, have driven the increasing sophistication of revenue management as a vitally important management practice (Cross, Higbie & Cross, 2009).

■ Revenue management: hospitality versus airlines

Given that the hospitality industry adopted revenue management from the airline industry, it is not surprising that there are several aspects of revenue management that are common to both industries. Most notably, the sale of highly perishable product that has high capital and fixed costs and a low variable per unit cost in comparison to per unit selling price. Further, both industries have enjoyed exploiting the emergent information and computing technologies that have facilitated both revenue management and disintermediation in the form of customer driven online booking and secure online prepayments. However, there are a number of aspects wherein there are significant differences between the two industries that shape some of the front line operations and practices in a revenue management environment (Talluri & van Ryzin, 2004).

Firstly, the most notable is that the airline product (a seat on a leg of a journey) is much more discrete than a hotel room. Apart from additional revenue opportunities, knowledge about the airline seat and leg required is known at the time of booking. In contrast, a hotel room can be booked for one or more nights. However, the length of stay proves to be much more uncertain with guests regularly extending or shortening their booking on very short notice. Secondly, the airlines are able to marshal their passengers before boarding, when decisions about the consequence of overbookings can be made with all parties present. In contrast, with guests arriving randomly throughout the afternoon and evening, the hotel manager must make decisions about the consequence of overbookings before the guests arrive. These differences have given rise to slightly different priorities in the development of revenue management systems in the hotel and airline industry (Cross et al., 2009). None the less, both industries have pursued the use of ICT to engender higher levels of market knowledge, customer engagement and proactive decision making. It is also worth noting that the airlines now calling it "revenue and price optimisation" (Lieberman, 2010, p.4).

12

■ Revenue management and business practice

As noted, revenue management has evolved from a simple approach to demand based pricing to a very sophisticated management philosophy that embraces several disciplinary perspectives and advanced digital systems and procedures. As a consequence, the adoption of revenue management has had, and will continue to have, a profound impact in several key operational areas including:

- Sales and distribution.
- Customer engagement.

■ The product, pricing and inventory management.

■ Knowledge management, information systems, planning and forecasting.

■ Staffing.

☐ **Sales and distribution**

The three most significant changes wrought by the advent of revenue management on sales and distribution are: the shift from sales staff being 'order takers' to 'deal negotiators'; the commodification and complexification of the product; and the emergence of the 'rooms auction'.

Historically, most hotel and airline reservation and sales staff accepted or rejected reservations based solely on availability of a room or seat type, and performance success was determined typically in terms or occupancy or average rate achieved. However, revenue management metrics shifted the focus from units sold or average selling price to one of total revenue maximisation thus placing a new onus on reservations and sales staff. The advent of constrained allotments of rooms or seats at different rates (despite being the same room or seat) coupled with the new focus on revenue maximisation forced the sales and reservation staff to develop a new, much more commercial approach to dealing with their clients as they sold essentially the same seat or room at differing prices.

The advent of revenue management made rooms and seats both commodities and complex products at the same time. In terms of the explicit focus on price, revenue management commodified both seats and rooms, with instances of prospective customers surfing the web for best prices becoming commonplace. At the same time, the proliferation of different rate brackets, and the terms and conditions attached to those brackets, complicated the transaction. In particular, the customisation of purchase conditions to meet specific market segments effectively multiplied the number of products on offer, despite the product ostensibly being the same seat or room. This created a new dynamic in the market with consumers empowered by the ability to shop around on line looking for the best price, but also somewhat disempowered by the confusing array of purchase conditions attached to the different prices.

Finally, revenue management has facilitated the emergence of the 'rooms auction' as characterised by Kimes (1994), wherein guest demand pushes up the price of rooms as happens in a dynamic auction. As a result, purchasers can become much more engaged in the purchase process by monitoring the market looking for the window at which their preferred booking is offered at the cheapest price. Some, under certain circumstance, can even book, then quickly cancel if they see a similar seat or room on offer at a lower price.

Each of these elements suggests that the sales function is radically altered by the application of revenue management. Beyond the sales function, revenue management has also had an impact upon distribution, especially in terms of the role of third party on line vendors. Vinod (2010) provides a detailed overview of the role of market agents and aggregators in revenue management in the airline industry and alludes to the challenges of ensuring the open and unencumbered flow of rate information around the market. In a not dissimilar vein, O'Connor and Murphy (2008) investigated the most appropriate strategies to employ when dealing with third party vendors under various market conditions. In particular, both the airline and hotel industry we caught off guard in the early days of ICT driven revenue management wherein they abdicated responsibility of the Internet distribution channel to third parties (Thomas, 2012). All of this work clearly indicates that revenue management has impacted on both the sales and distribution functions in the hotel and airline industry, and shows how hotels and airlines have developed specific strategies to deal with these situations.

☐ Customer engagement

One of the most significant areas in which revenue management has had an impact is in the way hotels and airlines engage with their customers. There are three areas that warrant consideration: perceptions of equity and fairness, the role of contracts and groups, and finally, the future of revenue management driven customer relationship management.

In the first instance, several authors have sought to address the issues of equity and fairness in revenue management (Kimes, 1994; Selmi, 2010; Xuan, 2012). What is most intriguing is that while most consumers seem comfortable with the variations in price seen with airlines, there is still considerable reluctance with regards to hotel pricing using revenue management principles. Leiberman (2011) and others have argued that the market will eventually get used to the dynamic pricing environment of revenue management, and that the critical issue is one of transparency. In fact, McMahon-Beattie (2011, p.46) argued that it is not the pricing *per se*, but "rather, it is consumers' level of knowledge of the 'rules' in which variable pricing operates may well cause trust/distrust". That said, Selmi (2010) found that both French and Tunisian hotel guests did not appreciate dynamic pricing in a revenue management setting.

Contracted rates for large corporate clients and groups (be they conference or package groups) can also create challenges in a revenue management environment. According to Xuan (2012), hotels need to carefully communicate to their key clients the impact of revenue management on contract rates. Von Martens and Hilbert (2011) argues that if businesses wish to have long term, loyalty- and value-driven relationships with their key accounts, then they should adopt a pricing system

12

that reflect this ambition. In fact, Cross et al. (2009, p.76), suggest that "customer-centric revenue management could mean that during peak periods, inventory is set aside as a part of the forecasting and optimization process to accommodate certain loyal customer segments through preferential overbooking policies or room upgrades". In contrast, if the business wants a short term, transaction-by-transaction relationship, then an explicitly revenue management approach, based on current demand for each transaction is most appropriate.

The future of revenue management will be discussed subsequently. However, given this focus on customer engagement, it is worth noting that a key element in the future of revenue management is the role of customer relationship management (CRM) (Milla & Shoemaker, 2008). Whilst this approach was driven by the need to gain more and more detailed information on customers to fine tune product and price offers, there is a strong argument that this approach should facilitate strong lines of communication between the customer and hotel and airline in order to make pricing policies fully communicated, transparent, and understood and accepted.

The product, pricing and inventory management

As noted, the early iterations of yield management focussed simply on adjusting prices in response to demand patterns. More sophisticated approaches to revenue management have addressed issues related to the product, to pricing and to inventory management in a much more sophisticated and nuanced way than before. Much of this has been facilitated and amplified by the increasing sophistication of ICT and especially their proprietary websites.

One of the key changes brought by revenue management is the use of 'rate fencing' wherein rates are modified, not necessarily because of the product sold, but because of the nature of the customer, the distribution channel employed, or more frequently, the terms and conditions of the sale. In this setting, hotels and airlines offered a limited number of units (seats or rooms) at a discounted rate to those guests who book long in advance and pre-pay. The terms and conditions attached to these price differentials have effectively created a series of variations on the basic product of a hotel room or airplane seat.

Recently developed allocation algorithms have also provided a new approach to inventory management. Historically, the hotel or airline would allocate a given number of rooms or seats to a specified rate level and when the allocation was sold, the rate was withdrawn from the market. New approaches seek to identify market potential (units to be sold) at a series of price points within the total inventory available. A goal seeking algorithm is applied to these volumes and prices to dynamically adjust not just the number of units available for sale, but also the price at which they are for sale (Martinez, Borja, & Jimenez, 2011).

In the early days of both the Internet and revenue management many hotels and airlines abdicated responsibility for online distribution to third parties, especially in the areas of selling heavily discounted and stressed inventory. As a result of this, much of the bad press about revenue management was in fact misattributed criticism of distribution channel policy (Cross et al., 2009). Recognising that they control inventory, and thus should control the selling environment, many hotels and airlines have recently seized back control in this area. Such control has allowed the industry to more aggressively manage rate and upsell their product. Thomas (2012, p.131) noted that many websites now pursue product differentiation strategies rather than focusing solely on price by "providing its customers with diverse information, from local attractions to high quality digital photography-video tours and multiple language options". The use of fencing and purchase conditions strategies, coupled with the integration of revenue management, inventory management and distribution channel management has clearly indicated that the hotel and airline industries have emerged from the last 25 years of revenue management as highly sophisticated marketers.

☐ Knowledge management, information systems, planning and forecasting

Perhaps the most significant change brought about by the implementation of revenue management is the rapid adoption of information and computer technologies and their ongoing impact on revenue management. This impact has occurred in refining existing revenue management practice, developing new approaches within revenue management, and developing ICT based marketing approaches, such as customer relationship management (Milla & Shoemaker, 2008), to further support revenue management (Guadix, Cortés, Onieva, & Muñuzuri, 2010). There are a few dimensions in this worth noting.

Whitelaw (2008) raised the issue of ICT and its role in addressing three key managerial challenges; operational, managerial and strategic. In the first, the technology facilitated the conduct of business such as using computerised property management system (PMS) to check people in and out of a hotel, or allocate seats on a plane. At the managerial level the technology provides a range of fairly standard reporting functions such as operational statistics (rooms sold, seats sold) and financial results (revenue, expenses and so on) to support operational level decision making. At the strategic level the technology transforms fundamental business processes by both automating key functions such as self check-in and by using newly emerging marketing activities such as 'analytics' to provide new insights into the way to do business (Abdelghany & Abdelghany, 2009; Bodea & Ferguson, 2012; Cross & Dixit, 2005; Davenport, Harris & Morison, 2010; Garrow, 2012). For example, using advanced analytics to generate the high

12

level strategic insights needed in an advanced revenue management environment. In this instance, the focus is on the strategic perspective, and in particular the data collecting, analysis and decision making systems (i.e. analytics) employed in an advanced revenue management environment.

Authors such as Iyengar and Suri (2012) argue that the data provided in the new analytics environment can support advanced evaluations such as Customer Lifetime Value (CLV) analysis and Customer Profitability Analysis (CPA) which will greatly enhance long term decision making and profitability (Cross, Higbie & Cross, 2011). At the same time, Zakhary, Atiya and El-Shishiny (2011) recommend the use of Monte Carlo simulations (amongst other analytical techniques) in the forecasting of demand. Lieberman (2010) has argued that online tracking software can be used to better understand the competitive dynamic of the market, and thus improve pricing strategies.

According to Vinod (2008, p.27), "in an effort to get closer to the consumer, airlines are investing in data mining, business intelligence and advanced data analytics to understand customer traits, behaviours and preferences in order to improve customer retention, acquire new customers and maximise the revenue-generation potential from the customer base. The renewed focus on customer loyalty and the customer experience are key areas of investment for airlines to differentiate themselves". The term customer-centric revenue management was coined by Cross and Dixit (2005) and it is likely that this may emerge as the most apt description of this approach to revenue management.

☐ Staffing

Given the aforementioned significant and far reaching developments in revenue management, it is not surprising that it has had and will continue to have an impact on staffing in both hotels and airlines. There are three key areas: existing staff, new staff and team processes. As previously noted, the change in approach to selling rooms places new demands on front line sales staff. SpringerLink (2006) observed that incentives, as part of a broad employment package, can help encourage existing staff to embrace revenue management. Furthermore, the advanced theoretical disciplines and sophisticated computer systems place considerable demand on the recruitment and ongoing development of a highly skilled, creative and communicative technical and management team that is appropriately rewarded. John McEwan, director of revenue strategy for Vail Resorts, observed "we look for people with strong educational backgrounds in economics and hospitality. We also look for people who are very good analytically and who have good people skills. The ideal person is a combination of all those pieces — and they're hard to find". Cross et al. (2009, p.63). Shabbir et al. (2011) noted the importance of employing highly creative people to help drive revenue management.

Finally, the all embracing aspects of revenue management indicate that decision making needs to be much more collaborative, involving colleagues from almost all areas of the hotel or airline. Many hotel chains now have revenue management meetings which are attended by representatives from sales, catering, convention and other service areas, as well as rooms, marketing and finance (Cross et al., 2009).

■ Into the future: some key considerations

There can be no doubt that competitive pressures as well as technological and theoretical advances will continue to drive the deployment and sophistication of revenue management, but there is considerable debate as to the trajectory of this development. Okumus (2004) argued that the development is unlikely to be smooth and linear. The evidence to date suggests that the lines between revenue management, distribution channels, customer relationship management and inventory management will become increasingly blurred. This suggests that the revenue management team will play an increasingly important and central role in hotel and airline operations. From an internal perspective, it is likely that whole of transaction, whole of business and whole of customer analysis will contribute to decisions about which bookings to accept and at which price (Iyengar & Suri, 2012). From an external perspective, market surveillance software will be employed to track competitor offerings in order to better understand the state of the market (Lieberman, 2010). One area that will be of ongoing academic interest is the relationship between overbooking and prepayments via credit card at the time of booking. Overbooking was a key element of early revenue management (Lieberman, 2010). However, given that a customer books and pays in advance (often with strict conditions, little flexibility and few options for refund), it would be a brave organisation that systematically overbooked in an increasingly litigious society.

At this stage it is worth pausing and reflecting on the benefits of revenue management that have been enjoyed by its various stakeholders. This review will focus on the hotel and airline industries, the ancillary service industries, academics, staff and finally the customer.

□ The industry

As discussed by Cross and his colleagues (Cross et al., 2009), the development and deployment of revenue management has been disrupted and distorted by the impact of severe external shocks, such as the recessions in the early 1980s, and the early 1990s and perhaps most significantly by the immediate aftershocks of the September 11 terrorist attacks. The uncertain and underperforming state

12

of the market at these times challenged advocates of revenue management. In many instances the general poor state of the market was conflated with teething problems in moving across to a revenue management approach. As such, there was often an undue focus on discounting to rate and demand insensitive market segments, which not surprisingly reduced selling prices without stimulating demand. However, according to several authors (Hendler & Hendler, 2004; Jain & Bowman, 2005) gains in profit in the range of three to seven percent are feasible. However, some authors (Lieberman, 2010; Metters, Queenan, Ferguson, Harrison, Higbie, Ward & Duggasani, 2008) have claimed increases in the vicinity of 15 percent.

☐ Suppliers and vendors and the academy

Since the advent of yield management in the early 1980s, a veritable industry of computer, mathematical and management consultants has sprung up to advocate, develop, implement and operate revenue management systems (Vinod, 2010). Also, universities around the globe now offer specialist programs in revenue management and a raft of associations (such as INFORMS), conferences (such as AGIFORS) and journals (such as the *Journal of Revenue and Pricing Management*) have emerged to support this academic community.

☐ The staff

Despite the pressures placed on front-line customer service and sales staff, revenue management has created the need for a cadre of highly educated and thus well paid technicians and managers to run the revenue management systems. Whilst a small property will have one or two revenue management technicians, larger properties are known to have revenue management teams of more than a dozen, while some chains have revenue management departments of more than 100 staff in head office (Cross et al., 2009).

☐ The customer

Given that revenue management is solely focussed on generating more revenue in total and per available unit for the hotel or airline, one can reasonably argue that the one stakeholder who loses is the customer, given that it is the customer who is paying this extra revenue. However, it can also be argued that the demand inducing pricing strategies of revenue management make consumption of air travel and hotel rooms affordable for some market segments who could not pay traditional, stable rates.

Furthermore, it can be argued that as a service industry, both airline travel and hotel accommodation are not essential services and thus consumers have the discretion not to purchase if they deem the price too high. None the less, the stronger focus on price, revenue and profitability by all stakeholders has the potential to harden the relationship between the airline and passenger and the hotel and guest.

■ Summary

- The advent of revenue management has had a significant impact on the hospitality and air travel industries, especially in the distribution, selling and pricing of hotel rooms and airline seats.

- The advance of revenue management, coupled with advent of ICT has changed the way the industries manage, sell and price inventory, and engage with their customers. Despite disquiet about the loss of customer engagement, the decline of value added selling, and quality based pricing, revenue management has forced the industry to become more competitive, more efficient and more focussed on profitability. At a sector wide level, this has improved market efficiency and thus must be seen as a good thing.

- All parties can identify several direct benefits from revenue management, although the benefits for the customer are less clear cut. It is possible that this strong focus on price, revenue and profitability has eroded some of the romance in the experience of air travel and hotel accommodation. However, rather than seek to put the genie back in the bottle, both the hospitality and airline industries need to better develop and harness these technologies to rebuild communication, trust and engagement with their customers.

References

Abdelghany, A. & Abdelghany, K. (2009). *Modelling Applications in the Airline Industry*. Burlington, VT: Ashgate Publishing Company.

Bodea, T. & Ferguson, M. (2012). *Pricing Segmentation and Analytics*. New York, NY: businessexpert Press.

Cross, R. G. & Dixit, A. (2005). Customer-centric pricing: the surprising secret for profitability. *Business Horizons,* **48**(6): 483-491. doi: 10.1016/j.bushor.2005.04.005

Cross, R. G., Higbie, J. A. & Cross, D. Q. (2009). Revenue management's renaissance: a rebirth of the art and science of profitable revenue generation. *Cornell Hospitality Quarterly,* **50**(1): 26.

Cross, R. G., Higbie, J. A., & Cross, Z. N. (2011). Milestones in the application of analytical pricing and revenue management. *Journal of Revenue and Pricing Management,* **10**(1): 8-18.

Davenport, T. H., Harris, J. G. & Morison, R. (2010). *Analytics at Work: Smarter Decisions, Better Results*. Boston, MA: Harvard Business School.

12

Garrow, L. A. (2010). *Discrete Choice Modelling and Air Travel Demand*. Farnham, Surrey, England: Ashgate Publishing Limited.

Guadix, J., Cortés, P., Onieva, L. & Muñuzuri, J. (2010). Technology revenue management system for customer groups in hotels. *Journal of Business Research*, **63**(5): 519-527.

Hendler, R. & Hendler, F. (2004). Revenue management in fabulous Las Vegas: combining customer relationship management and revenue management to maximise profitability. *Journal of Revenue and Pricing Management*, **3**(1): 73-79.

Iyengar, A. & Suri, K. (2012). Customer profitability analysis an avant garde approach to revenue optimisation in hotels. *International Journal of Revenue Management*, **6**(1): 127-143.

Jain, S. & Bowman, H. B. (2005). Measuring the gain attributable to revenue management. *Journal of Revenue and Pricing Management*, **4**(1): 83-94. doi: 10.1057/palgrave.rpm.5170131

Kimes, S. E. (1989). The basics of yield management. *The Cornell Hotel and Restaurant Administration Quarterly*, **30**(3): 14-19.

Kimes, S. E. (1994). Perceived fairness of yield management. *Cornell Hotel and Restaurant Administration Quarterly*, **35**(1): 22-24.

Lieberman, W. H. (2010). Revenue Management in the Travel Industry *Wiley Encyclopedia of Operations Research and Management Science* (pp. 1-17): John Wiley & Sons, Inc.

Lieberman, W. H. (2011). From yield management to price optimization: lessons learned. *Journal of Revenue & Pricing Management*, **10**(1): 40-43. doi: 10.1057/rpm.2010.44

Martinez, M. E. A., Borja, M. A. G. & Jimenez, J. A. M. (2011). Yield management as a pricing mechanism. *Review of Business Information Systems (RBIS)*, **15**(5): 51-60.

McMahon-Beattie, U. (2011). Trust, fairness and justice in revenue management: creating value for the consumer. *Journal of Revenue and Pricing Management*, **10**(1): 44-46.

Metters, R., Queenan, C., Ferguson, M., Harrison, L., Higbie, J., Ward, S. & Duggasani, A. (2008). The "killer application" of revenue management: Harrah's Cherokee Casino & Hotel. *Interfaces*, **38**(3): 161-175.

Milla, S. & Shoemaker, S. (2008). Three decades of revenue management: what's next? *Journal of Revenue and Pricing Management*, **7**(1): 5. doi: 10.1057/palgrave.rpm.5160127

O'Connor, P. & Murphy, J. (2008). Hotel yield management practices across multiple electronic distribution channels. *Information Technology & Tourism*, **10**(2): 161-172.

Okumus, F. (2004). Implementation of yield management practices in service organisations: empirical findings from a major hotel group. *The Service Industries Journal*, **24**(6): 65-89.

Selmi, N. (2010). Effects of culture and service sector on customers' perceptions of the practice of yield management. *International Journal of Marketing Studies,* **2**(1): 245-253.

Shabbir, M. S., Shamim, A., Kaleem, A. & Shahbaz, M. (2011). Creativity: a driving force behind yield management. *International Journal of Economics and Business Research,* **3**(4): 459-467.

SpringerLink (Online service). (2006). The spread of yield management practices the need for systematic approches (pp. xvi, 153 p.).

Talluri, K. T. & van Ryzin, G. J. (2004). The Theory and Practice of Revenue Management. Springer: New York.

Thomas, A. M. (2012). International hotel revenue management: Web-performance effectiveness modelling – research comparative. *Journal of Hospitality and Tourism Technology,* **3**(2): 121-137.

Vinod, B. (2008). The continuing evolution: customer-centric revenue management. *Journal of Revenue & Pricing Management,* **7**(1): 27-39.

Vinod, B. (2010). The complexities and challenges of the airline fare management process and alignment with revenue management. *Journal of Revenue and Pricing Management,* **9**(1/2): 137-151.

von Martens, T. & Hilbert, A. (2011). Customer-value-based revenue management. *Journal of Revenue and Pricing Management,* **10**(1): 87-98.

Whitelaw, P. A. (2008). ICT and Hospitality Operations. In P. Jones (Ed.), *Handbook of Hospitality Operations and Information Management* (pp. 167-184). London.

Xuan L. W. (2012). The impact of revenue management on hotel key account relationship development. *International Journal of Contemporary Hospitality Management,* **24**(3): 358-380.

Zakhary, A., Atiya, A. F., El-Shishiny, H. & Gayar, N. E. (2011). Forecasting hotel arrivals and occupancy using Monte Carlo simulation. *Journal of Revenue & Pricing Management,* **10**(4): 344-366.

12

13 Car Rental Revenue Management

David Cretin and Emanuel Scuto

Learning outcomes

After reading this chapter, you should be able to:

- Understand the world of the car rental industry from the revenue management perspective.
- Understand the different segments of customers in the industry.
- Be familiar with the constraints of optimisation in the industry.
- Have a comprehensive vision of the specific approaches to revenue management at the corporate and franchisee levels.

■ Introduction

In both leisure and business travel, car rental is one of the components of the transport phase albeit not the main driver. Over the past 10 years, with the widespread use of revenue management, the big global players such as Europcar, Avis and Hertz, have begun to integrate optimisation techniques from the airline and hotel industries. However, significant differences in the characteristics of supply and demand provide sector-specific constraints. As such, the specific characteristics of the sector and its peculiarities that make its revenue management complex will be illustrated, as will different applications at station, corporate and franchisee levels within the same network.

■ Sector overview

Business line car rental has specific characteristics related to its history and the development of sales on the Internet over the last ten years. Several market segments coexist.

☐ Market segments

There is a need to distinguish three major families with very different behaviours: direct, indirect and business segments.

Direct market segment

The 'Direct' (or B2C) market is defined as an individual customer reserving directly through a rental company without going through an intermediary, or one with special conditions granted to certain partnerships (e.g. train companies, airlines, hotels). One of the important features of this market segment is the dynamic price defined by the rental company and submitted to the arbitration of the yield. These market segments are often privileged and protected by landlords (rental companies) because they contribute most to the margins. They therefore require precise follow up by the pricing and revenue management teams. Usually landlords create market sub-segments based on the rental period to refine offerings and better meet the needs of this clientele.

Indirect market segment

Under the terminology 'Indirect' (or B2B2C) are grouped transactions through an intermediary: Broker and Tour Operator (TO). Landlords contract with them because they are sometimes or often better known than the company itself and, thanks to powerful marketing, are able to operate varied means of communication to reach various type of clientele. In return, these intermediaries are paid via the granting of a very low negotiated rate, impacting strongly on the margin of the renter.

For a few years now, and through the development of dynamic pricing and the visibility that is offered through the Web, the TO/Broker prices have been linked to the public pricing of the owner. They fluctuate during the year according to traditional yield rules (seasonality, utilisation ratio, events, etc.). These intermediates are no longer paid through a net fares model but via commissions (the so-called 'retail model') whose levels are set by negotiation. Like direct markets, and depending on their capacity, landlords do not hesitate to conduct sales and stimulate demand through promotions on these markets.

13

Business market segment

Business (or B2B) market segments have in common a contract engaging both parties: to provide vehicles responding to the need of the corporate clients, with the same quality of service throughout the network of the lessee in return for a fixed and guaranteed price to be applied during a contractual period with little or no seasonal variation. This price is governed by a number of criteria such as volume of rental days, share of total business give to the main landlord, the rental period, the type of rental station requested by customer and the network coverage (national and/or local contracts). In return, the client company undertakes not to book its vehicles through other car rental company referenced in the contract.

We can distinguish three main categories of business customers: clients renting for very short durations of 1 to 4 days; those renting on a monthly basis (30 days and more); assistance companies using the car fleet of the landlords to ensure their members a means of substitution in case of accident or breakdown of their own vehicle (like Axa assistance in France, Adac in Germany, AAA in USA). Figure 13.1 below illustrates the proportion of each of the two main typologies of customer activities in volume, revenue and margins. The job of the revenue manager in the car rental industry is to fine tune the levers of action to generate maximum volume to guarantee covering the minimum revenue to compensate the fleet holding costs.

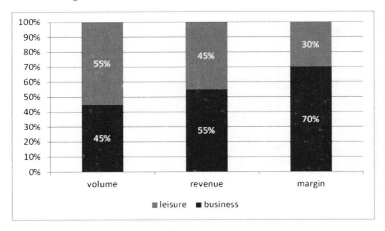

Figure 13.1: Proportion of Key Performance Index (KPI) per types of clients

☐   Consumer behaviour

The customer purchasing behaviour is impacted by various factors influencing the rental approach. First, the objective of the move (business, weekend or holiday) generating long or short road trips, then the rental location where the car will be picked up and finally the rental duration.

Type of consumption

Customers prefer two modes of booking: travel agencies or the phone for corporate clients and intermediaries for leisure customers. The strong development of the Internet in the world of travel has generated an explosion of car hire sites run by consolidators or brokers: they negotiate very low price levels in exchange for a high volume of rental days guaranteed. These European players are Holiday Autos, Auto-Escape, and Ebookers, without forgetting the most important of them, the American Auto Europe.

These brokers flourished hugely through the 1990's on a weakness left by landlords, who were not interested in commercial rental activity, but with the margin over the purchase and resale of the fleet. Since the arrival and expansion of the Internet, brokers have taken an important place in the world of vehicle hire to such a degree that a broker can be both a customer and a competitor in some countries. Very often, a rental company promotes its brand on its own market and simultaneously sells through an intermediary which becomes its own competitor.

■ Revenue characteristics of the car rental industry

☐ Is capacity too flexible?

Car rental yield specificity resides in the management of its inventory, its stock or its capabilities (based on the various terminology found). Unlike all other sectors of activity in which the yield applies (which is also a parameter definition of the yield), this parameter is not stable for several reasons.

Fluctuation of volume

During the year, depending on the evolution of demand, volume can fluctuate significantly. In traditional travel sectors, yieldable capacity does not move in the hotel, very little in the air (change of aircraft type) or train industry (adding a block train or train duplex-2 floors in the French high speed train). In car rental, purchases and sales of vehicles are made throughout the year. Delivery of new vehicles is concentrated at the beginning of high season to serve the additional demand. In Figure 13.2, the fleet almost varies from single to double between the beginning of the year, months of high season in the destinations of the Caribbean and the period between the months of September and October corresponding to low season. Fleet adjustments enable the maximization of utilisation.

13

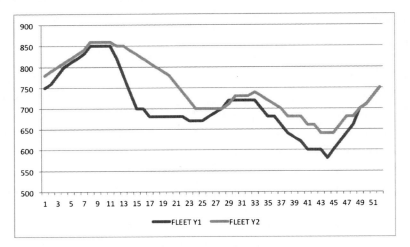

Figure 13.2: Compared evolution of daily available fleet over two years

Vehicles move depending on customers' routes

Most vehicle bookings are made with return to the station of departure. However, some clients choose to bring their rental back in a different agency than the original one, generating a so-called 'one way'. Where the returning station is located in the same city (i.e. departing from a city airport, back at the downtown station in the same city), the impact on available capacity is low. However, when a vehicle is returned several hundred kilometers away, the impact on the logistic organisation is much stronger. This can be exacerbated when this situation occurs in high season or when the client brings the vehicle into a station that was not mentioned on the initial lease at the time of departure. Therefore, the following client booked is not able to get the confirmed vehicle because it is not available as originally planned.

In the case of a fairly popular vehicle type (economic or compact category), finding an alternative for the client does not pose too many problems (subject to stock availability). In the case of a less popular type, or a specific vehicle, or one that is not present at all in the station in which the following client planned to retrieve it, the commercial inconvenience can be highly problematic. This phenomenon is accentuated by a North to South flow (residential to vacation areas) during summer or winter vacations.

The lessor vehicles break down or are damaged

With a recent or even new fleet, the risks of failure are limited. But when demand is strong, the risk of accidents is proportionally higher. Suddenly, a vehicle booked and blocked for a client may be unavailable for a long period.

Delayed delivery of vehicles

A delayed delivery of vehicles ordered by the landlord from the car manufacturers can cause much stress in the system as a new transfer is required to bring them closer to the most demanded location sites.

Imponderables

In late 2008, Europcar France ordered 500 vehicles from the Spanish manufacturer Seat. Assembled in Spain, these vehicles were delivered and stored on the logistics platform of la Bourboule (Pyrénées, France) waiting to be distributed to the rental location of the South of the France. In June, a huge thunderstorm accompanied by hail heavily damaged windscreens and roofs of the vehicles making them unusable.

Assistance and car replacement

Unless car drivers have personally experienced car damage, they tend to know very little about car assistance underwritten by the vehicle manufacturer to an outsourced professional (e.g. Axa Assistance) which itself has subcontracted the car replacement to a rental car company, (often one of the 3 big operators: Avis, Hertz or Europcar). These assistance companies are big customers for rental companies and therefore get advantageous tariff conditions associated with highly specific contractual clauses that imprison landlords in a near-zero margin and very strong operational constraints in the replacement vehicle availability. Let's take the example a car breaking down during a rental. Volkswagen or Toyota assistance manages a replacement car via the assistance company. Even during normal conditions or in the off-peak season, managing this request can be difficult. However, it can become a logistical nightmare when the driver is German and the car broke down on a French motorway on the way back from Spain to Dusseldorf in Germany. The car manufacturer/assistance company will book a replacement car for the driver to be able to continue his journey back home. From the car rental company point of view, this rental has to be honoured even though the French car will end up in Germany. What then happens to the regular driver who booked his weekly rental and got the confirmation for the car that has been delivered to the German driver on behalf of the assistance company? Operationally speaking, an alternative has to be found via a free upgrade if a car exists ('a downgrade' in the yield management terminology as some revenue is missing). Who, however, pays for the landlord's revenue loss?

Vehicle orders

For an outsider, it seems obvious that a car manufacturer wants to sell the maximum number of vehicles. Yet despite a difficult economic environment and industrial overcapacity, major manufacturers may not accept all orders. This

13

situation impacts the car rental companies as they do not have a perfect mix of fleet matching the needs expressed by clients (unconstrained demand in revenue management application) especially regarding small car groups like minis and economies. To understand this situation, it is necessary to integrate two points:

- On a particular vehicle, the manufacturer will be able to generate an average of 7 profits throughout the car life cycle: the original sale, the financing potentially attached to it adding insurance and maintenance, resale profit on the second hand market, etc.

- The vast majority of rental vehicles purchase is done on the basis of a monthly rent for a period of 4 to 8 months: this commercial policy is called 'buy back'. At the end of the contract, the car rental company returns all the cars to the dealership, which sells them on the second hand market as 'first hand deals'.

So, on low margin cars like mini or economy models, the manufacturer does not want to take the risk of getting back a large proportion of small vehicles. They aim to maintain the market at an acceptable price and margin level and therefore will limit the number of orders brought by the purchaser and will constraint the fleet mix to push the bigger, higher margin cars.

☐ Variable capacity: an advantage?

As described above, stock variability-induced problems need to be taken into account by the revenue manager. In some instances, however, such cases can become a competitive weapon. In the months when demand is lower than foreseen, it is the duty of the revenue manager to propose either temporary decreases in the fleet or propose transfers of vehicles from a sub region to a region under demand pressure.

☐ Problematic costs

Who bears the cost of non-use between two locations? An oriented business-type location such as key international airport hubs are under intense demand pressure from Monday to Thursday with a significant lack of vehicles for short rental durations. However, weekend parking is full resulting in additional costs arising from transfers to feed leisure hubs often located in the city centre or near railway areas. Of course, theses transfers require to be done again on Sunday nights or Monday mornings to be able to serve customers coming during week-days at the airport.

In contrast, there is a complementarity between certain business type agencies and other leisure hubs in some areas. In Europe, around the Alps, some airport agencies are open only during the winter season and remain closed during low season months. Indeed, due to their particular location, they have an advantage of maximising utilisation of the fleet in a few months. However, transfer costs and downtime associated with the transport of the vehicle must always be included in the contribution calculation. Another example: the airports in resort areas that are fed by low-cost airlines only during summer periods and sometimes not every day (Easyjet, Ryannair, Transavia, etc). The selling prices have to integrate these transfers, non-utilisation and depreciation costs while remaining price competitive on the market.

AVIS

Find Rental Cars > Types of Rentals > Weekend

Weekend Car Rental

Looking for something fun to do this weekend? At Avis, weekend rental means more fun and bigger savings.

- Convenient local and airport locations
- Special low rates for weekend rentals
- Wide selection of vehicles, from Compacts to Luxury to Minivans
- 24 Hour Roadside Assistance — Day or night, Avis is at your call in an emergency. Simply dial our hotline at 1-800-354-2847 for prompt assistance

☐ No decremental stock

Although maybe hard to believe, most car rental operating systems do not support the concept of decremental stock at time of reservation. In any business property, when a product is booked or purchased, it is deducted from the original stock which becomes a 'left-to-sell'. Yet in most companies, this notion of 'dynamic stock' is completely unknown. Unless a specific operational information system is available for a small window in the future, the vast majority of reservations in the booking engine (web, call centre) are deducted automatically. For the generic vehicles (mini, economic, compact), the reconciliation between booking and available stock for a given date is managed by the Distribution or Logistic Department: this daily operation is called fleet point. According to the tensions in demand, the fleet point gives a clear situation of between 3 and 7 days before the date of departure of the vehicles.

With or without this fleet point, matching future stock availability with demand patterns is usually done from 30 to 14 days before departure, which significantly impacts the yield management daily job. Price settings and fluctuation through reservation lifetimes is complex and the number of parameters to be taken into account does not help the revenue manager in his search for reliable information. Due to the strong technical constraints and the lack of visibility on available stock, all rental companies have developed mechanisms pricing offsets.

13

■ Franchisees and franchisors on the same territory

Like the hotel industry, the majority of the volume of activity for international brands is generated by major corporate countries (Western Europe, North America). International business is done through a network of franchisees. For some European countries, such as France, Spain or Italy, international brands have the specificity of sharing their own country with local franchisees called the 'domestic' franchising network. This specificity of the car rental sector generates specific constraints in terms of revenue management. The similarities and differences of this situation are illustrated below.

☐ Pricing

In a territory, the countries or regions are divided into different tariff zones. Priority areas are defined according to the importance of the volume of business handled. Main cities, international airports and principal railway stations are managed by the franchisor while the franchisee will take care of an operational area more limited in space. On the other hand, the franchisor will define its pricing at the national and regional levels based on global market constraints (framework agreements with partners or large corporate accounts). Conversely, the franchisee has a narrower margin of manoeuvrability because it must apply the rules of pricing coming from the franchisor while trying to focus on its local rates in order to maximise its margin. Located at the end of the chain, it must apply policies contracted for negotiated clients that apply on its agencies, even if the cost of treatment makes little or no contribution. To work around this situation, the franchisee can develop its own web site, generating direct volume of reservations.

☐ Electronic distribution

The tools available to optimise the electronic distribution are very different from those existing in the world of the hospitality. If they are properly interfaced with the central reservation systems (CRS), they are far less efficient in terms of advanced pricing functionalities. Car rental reservations systems are less robust due to the complexity of the rate engine they are linked to. In fact the number of possible combinations required for a single reservation limits the number of rate updates to protect main database of the system. For example, in the central system Greenway of Europcar, should intervene on more than a dozen different settings pages to change a price!

Impacts among the revenue managers are significant to the extent where all the parameters of changes in price may be operated simultaneously and on all dimensions: rental dates, length of rent, car type, agency starting, etc. For example, using the tools, pricing automation is still uncommon, thus preventing interventions on prices several times a day based on reservation fluctuations. These impacts are sensitive to the franchisor but are even more for the franchisee that must systematically pass through the administration of sales to see its price changes become live in the CRS. This additional intermediation generates delays which one can count in days to get a new rate online. These actions must therefore be strongly anticipated to set a new price.

☐ PMS operational system

Each transaction (booking or rental contract) must be entered into the computer system to facilitate tracing the car's movement and allow the billing. These systems are called Greenway at Europcar, Wizard in Opinion, Tas at Hertz. They are very complex and have for the most part been configured between 20 and 30 years ago, a period when the Internet did not exist at all and where very large database technology was simply not used to full potential.

These are heavy systems, adapted to big operations and therefore are of little or no use for franchisees. Local computer providers have therefore moved into the breach and have developed smaller and sometimes more flexible systems. Some gateways have been created to allow communication between the central system of the franchisor and the local franchisee. These exchanges transfer reservations to be downloaded every ten or twenty minutes (so called 'one way' in yield and distribution). When prices and/or availability are concerned (so called 'two ways'), the local system should be in the position to update the main central system with an updated fleet availability and new prices.

☐ Web and partnership marketing

The marketing dimension is the undeniable advantage of a car rental company around its network of franchises that have little or no capacity to invest heavily in the development of a brand and visual identity. The franchisor usually provides a powerful web tool to attract enough traffic. This mode of operation is of course funded through royalties paid by each franchisee via the royalty on every single sale. In addition to these royalties, the franchisee has to pay reservation fees that impact on its margin. For a booking at a negotiated price, for which the franchisee was not involved to fix the booking conditions even if this account generates a fairly high level of operational cost to be served, the money left over for the franchisee is frequently minimal. And, unlike other sectors such as hotels or air transport, it is not possible to optimise negotiated accounts through dynamic pricing or specific inventory techniques.

13

In the same way, managing a large marketing partnership such as a low cost carrier (EasyJet with Europcar or Ryanair with Hertz) can be excessively costly in term of margins as sold prices are always commissionable at each level for the partner. Local partnerships (usually minor) are left to the discretion of the local franchisee with the application of the contractual conditions limited to its trading area only.

Through marketing partnerships with car manufacturers, the means of action are also quite different between the franchisee and the franchisor. A manufacturer can rely on a national rental company to accelerate the discovery of a new model. Test marketing offers can also be made but will be limited to the subsidiary network.

☐ Fleet and logistic

With regard to purchases, agreement frameworks negotiated by the franchisor are rarely implemented by the franchisee on its territory. Indeed, franchisees will develop local partnerships with car dealers and will often get more favourable buying conditions attached with more flexibility in fleet management. As in air transport with the development of code sharing, rental of cars within a network share vehicles more or less smoothly in a 'pool fleet'. From the optimisation standpoint, how does one share revenue directed via a rental on a non-pool vehicle? By facility and by habit, landlords are trying to maximise their income via the increase of their own fleet. Yet as previously described, the vehicles are moving from one station to another within the network and do not always get returned to the same place. To avoid non-pool fleet cars remaining unused for too long, his goalkeeper may be charged a penalty beyond 48 hours while the vehicle is not moving. To encourage the receiving station to return the vehicle as quickly as possible, a financial incentive can be calculated based on the repatriation of a non-pool vehicle to its owner.

Of course, if the detention lasts too long or that the vehicle is not close enough to the owner station, the car be can be retrieved at any time by sending a carrier; a source of additional costs. This operation is profitable only if the demand and the probability of renting the car will compensate the additional costs associated with the vehicle recovery. What about the impact on the margin of such an operation when it comes to serve a negotiated client who has a low contribution? Such are the issues of a fine policy to optimise available capacities!

■ Summary

- The car rental industry is classically seen as simple and low-differentiating with regard to brands. As an illustration, look at the site of Expedia and compare the features and details displayed on the page 'hotel' from those on the 'car hire' page. Connecting on Expedia's extranet (management of rates and inventory for sale module), the hotels have almost full control of information while this module does not exist for the car rental companies. Without complex interface with CRS of the franchisor, there is no display on the Online Travel Agencies!

- The future of revenue management of this industry will be through a greater mastery of the optimisation tools available at the finest level of transactions: the day of rental, the car category, the departing station (and return) and the length of rental. However most brands do not allow such efficiency as compared to what is on offer in the hospitality sector. Powerful tools existed as channel managers (Availpro for example). This would require transversal discussion and exchanges between industries and significant financial investment to develop new rate engines and distribution functionalities similar to the ones existing in hospitality. The revenue manager will also have to work with more transversality with marketing to refine offerings to meet clients' changing behaviours. The client would find a greater variety of offers. Within current environmental city policies, owning a car is becoming more and more difficult and expensive. And renting a car is an inexpensive alternative for maintaining mobility.

13

14 Revenue Management and Customer Relationship Management

Xuan (Lorna) Wang

Learning outcomes

After reading this chapter, you should be able to:

- Understand the impacts of revenue management on customer relationship management.

- Critique the concept of customer relationship management and appreciate the contextual background to the notion of the relational approach to customers.

- Understand the differences between business-to-consumer and business-to-business relationships in order to appreciate the effect revenue management has on customer relationship management in the hotel industry.

Introduction

Revenue management (RM) may have been one of the most examined subjects in hospitality and tourism research but its effect on Customer Relationship Management (CRM) and on organisations' marketing strategies remains a largely overlooked area. The value of customers and customer relationships are widely acknowledged in the field of marketing, which shows that acquiring customers is usually much more expensive than retaining them (Anton, 1996, p.11; Stone, Woodcock & Machtynger, 2000), and a well-developed relationship with customers, especially those strategically important business-to-business key accounts, offers critical benefits and opportunities for profit enhancement to both selling and buying companies (McDonald & Rogers, 1998). However, if the concept of RM is primarily driven by desire for short-term revenue maximisation, the sustainability of the revenue growth is questionable for two reasons. First, current RM practice is revenue-oriented, which emphasises the revenue yield maximisation from relative capacity such as airline seats, hotel rooms and conference spaces rather than profit yield from all possible yielding sources (e.g. customers). Second, to date, RM has been practiced mainly to accommodate the needs of selling organisations to increase their revenue and has taken limited consideration of the relationship needs of their buyers, namely the customers. Hence, if the short-term revenue growth takes place at the cost of customer relationship, the organisations' future financial success will be at risk. On the other hand, RM and CRM could and should complement each other if both practices are focused on the same goal. An integrated approach to RM and CRM could offer greater opportunities for companies to better understand customers' behaviour and their relationship needs. Revenue managers could therefore take proactive, rather than their previously reactive, actions to work with identified preferred customers or customer groups to co-create mutual benefits in a competitive market.

■ Understanding customer relationship management

Customer relationship management (CRM), as an extended partition of relationship marketing, has been studied extensively in the generic management and marketing fields. It is rooted in the relationship marketing theory that has evolved from the short-term transactional-based marketing philosophy to a long term relationship focused marketing paradigm (Hakansson, 1982; Gronroos, 1990). Although relationship marketing and CRM both stress the importance of two-way communication and focus on customer retention (Lockard, 1998), their management priority is found to differ. Relationship marketing emphasises overall customer retention as well as internal relationships with employees, external suppliers and other stakeholders (Berry, 1983; Gronroos, 1996; Gummesson, 1999), whereas CRM focuses on external customers and draws attention to identifying and retaining the profitable customers (Anton, 1996; Buttle, 2004), and improving the profitability of less profitable customers or segments (Ryals, Knox & Maklan, 2000).

Similar to attempting to define RM, it is difficult to make generalisations about the term 'customer relationship management' since the concept is composed of divergent aspects, each of which can be viewed from a different perspective. This is epitomised by the study carried out by Zablah, Bellenger and Johnston (2004,

14

p.476), in which they reviewed more than forty distinct CRM definitions and suggest that there are five dominant perspectives of CRM – process, strategy, philosophy, capability and/or technological tool. Thus, it is necessary to clarify that in the context of this chapter CRM is seen as a theoretical concept, which Hasan (2003, p.16) defines as 'a business philosophy aimed at achieving customer centricity for the company'. More specifically it is about identifying, satisfying, retaining, and maximising the value of a company's best customers (Rigby, Reichheld & Schefter, 2002).

The word 'customer' also requires rigorous explanation as it can refer to very different groups of people – consumers, clients or other stakeholders (Johnston & Clark, 2001). The term 'customer' in the marketing literature generally refers to customers from both a business-to-consumer (B2C) context and a business-to-business (B2B) context (Buttle, 2004). In the B2B cases, the term 'accounts' is often used interchangeably with 'customers' (e.g. key accounts management – KAM, or strategic account management – SAM) to reflect the relational approach to valuable customers that considers the customer as a long-term investment made by the supplier in its own future (McDonald & Rogers, 1998). It is an investment of time and effort, in many cases requiring 'a short-term sacrifice for prospective long-term gains' (Cheverton, 1999, p.8). It is noteworthy, however, that in benefiting from the rapid technological advancement, relationships initiated by existing and prospective customers that are enabled or facilitated by online websites and various social media sites should also draw the attention of CRM; these include consumer-to-business (C2B) and consumer-to-consumer (C2C) relationships. Figure 14.1 below depicts the links between relationship marketing and CRM as well as the four main relationship domains.

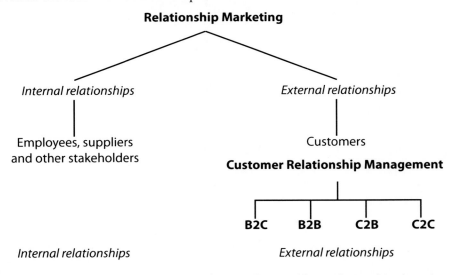

Figure 14.1: The links between relationship marketing, CRM and four relationship domains

The goal of the CRM is explicit; that is, 'to develop more profitable relationships with profitable customers' (Buttle, 2004, p.39). In order to achieve the intended CRM benefits, the high-value customers need to be distinguished to prioritise the relationship investment to provide them with deserved preferential treatments. Although the issues of lacking accountability and measurement of customer value in marketing have been addressed by researchers (Rust, Lemon & Zeithaml, 2001; Sheth and Sharma, 2001), literature in this area remains limited in comparison with the extensive CRM studies. Customer Profitability Analysis (Peck, Payne, Christopher & Clark, 1999) and Customer Lifetime Value analysis (Dwyer, 1989; Jenkinson, 1995) are, to date, two main methods suggested in the literature to assess customer values.

☐ Relationship foundation - trust and commitment

There are two essential yet imperative factors that form a relationship and impact upon the relationship development – trust and commitment (Morgan & Hunt, 1994; Gronroos, 1996; McDonald, Rogers & Woodburn, 2000; Humphries & Wilding, 2003; Buttle, 2004). Morgan and Hunt (1994) explain relationships as a series of transactions, which build an awareness of a shared relationship through trust and commitment. Buyers, therefore, must have confidence in the company's competence and integrity (Bowie & Buttle, 2004) before a trusting relationship can be established, and the *commitment* is reliant on this essential *trust*. From a relationship progression perspective, trust and mutual dependency are considered to be 'two major milestones' that imply the strength of the relationship, where the reference to mutual dependence is used in appreciation of the existence of both parties' commitment (McDonald et al., 2000, p.51).

☐ Relationship development

The dynamic nature of the relationship and the fact that the relationship changes over time have been widely acknowledged (Dwyer, Schurr & Oh, 1987; Buttle, 1996). There are several schools of thought about how relationships grow. Rao and Perry (2002) consider that these can be broadly categorised into two concepts – *stages* theory and *states* theory. The former focuses on 'a progression of change processes through stages' while the latter emphasises 'strategic moves of exchange actors, which occurs in an unstructured and unpredictable manner at any point in time' (Ford, McDowell & Turnbull, 1996; Rao & Perry, 2002, p.603). In the context of the hotel industry, the states theory appears to more appropriately portray the relationship development process (Wang, 2012b). This is because business relationship development does not necessarily follow an orderly progression of phases over time, and the phases do not depend on 'fulfilment of a set of conditions but rather depend on the circumstances/opportunities at a given point in

14

time' (Rao & Perry, 2002, p.604). However, if this proposition is followed – as if the relationship development or termination is based upon changeable situations – then the future of the relationship can be as unpredictable as the unstable business circumstances.

The customer's reaction towards RM practice is a fairly complex subject and is not fully understood by academic research; however, it is evident that RM can affect customer relationships and could cause customer conflicts, even compromising relationship development with strategically important key accounts in a B2B setting (Kimes, 1994; Noone & Griffin, 1999; Wirtz, Kimes, Ho & Patterson, 2003; Wang, 2012b). Wirtz et al. (2003, p.217) draw attention to this neglected area and stress that 'the customers seem to have been relatively forgotten in this [RM] stream of research', even though the notion of customer-oriented relationship marketing has already been embraced by many organisations in the hospitality and tourism industries. This next section discusses the impacts of RM on CRM and examines the areas where possible customer conflicts could occur in B2C and B2B relationship management contexts. The conflict areas investigated include the perceived fairness issue and the effects of different pricing strategies on customers, the implications of inventory control techniques on customers, and the potential management conflicts that need to be overcome in order for an organisation to integrate RM and CRM.

■   RM impacts on customers

The practice of RM has undeniably provided opportunities for many customers to enjoy hospitality and tourism products, which they may not have been able to afford otherwise during periods of high demand. This gives companies the chance to reach wider customer groups, to showcase their products, to establish relationships and ideally to retain the customers. While many of us have benefited from RM practice with a positive value-for-money experience, others may feel they have fallen victim to the revenue-driven practice. There are a number of noticeable reasons for customer resistance to the RM practice. Firstly, the fluctuating price may lead the customers to believe that the practice is unfair. Secondly, the discounted price during low seasons would unavoidably lead to reduction of the reference price. Thirdly, various prices publicised on different distribution channels cause customer confusion about the actual value of the product. The popularity of online booking also reduces the customers' trust in hotel companies, as the online travel companies seem to provide better deals than the hotels' online websites. Furthermore, the inventory control techniques employed by companies such as availability control, length-of-stay restrictions and overbooking could also negatively affect the customer relationships. Lastly, since customers find it more and more difficult to assess the reference price and reference transaction, there is a financial risk attached to customers' future purchase of the product, as they will not be sure whether they are getting a fair deal each time they book, and may therefore lose confidence in the selling company.

☐ The fairness issue and the effects of pricing strategies on customers

Kimes (1994) suggests that customers' perceptions of the 'fairness' of yield management practice lie at the root of the customer conflicts that arise following the implementation of RM. She suggests that customers may perceive the practice as *unfair* if there is a lack of information on transaction and if no rationalised pricing decisions are provided. Understandably, foreseeable benefit from an increase in revenue could easily lead an organisation's operational practices to concentrate on its revenue-maximisation needs, which surpasses the needs of customers. As a result, the adoption of revenue maximisation strategies such as demand-oriented pricing, controlled availability to certain rate and preferred customers only, may lead the customers to feel that they have been taken advantage of and treated unfairly by the hotels, consequently affecting customer satisfaction (Kimes & Wirtz, 2002). The effects of RM strategies on customers are elaborated in the sections below.

The use of a differential pricing strategy may improve the hotels' ability to target both the prevailing market conditions and customer behaviour more effectively and achieve higher revenues from the fixed capacity; however, it may also have negative effects on customers (Kimes, 1994). The differential pricing strategies employed by RM practitioners, typically the demand-based pricing, the multi-tier pricing and the online pricing strategies, have one common objective, which is to maximise revenue. This is exemplified by hotel pricing that is no longer driven by the nature of the product, but more by market demand (Brotherton & Mooney, 1992; Collier & Gregory, 1995). The differential pricing strategies adopted to maximise hotel yield have shifted the main determinant factor for hotel pricing from traditional room-type pricing to the present style of pricing, based on market-demand or/and market segments. The research findings from six hotel groups suggest that pricing was a central part of the marketing strategy in these groups and that the main objective of pricing policy was to maximise revenue (Collier & Gregory, 1995).

Demand-based pricing

Demand-based pricing is often used as a practical tactic by revenue managers to manipulate the market during the predicted low-demand periods in order to avoid lost revenue from otherwise unsold inventory. However, the frequent price fluctuation would also cause customer confusion, as the reference price they

14

know, which is usually informed by market prices and past experience, would be greatly affected (Kimes, 1994). The confusion that customers experience may hinder their future booking behaviour and willingness to pay. Regular guests who used to enjoy their preferential rate privilege may also find the demand-based pricing practice unreasonable if they have to pay more during high-demand seasons. Thus, there are two main areas where demand-based pricing could affect customers. First, in response to market volatility, the constant price fluctuation would make it difficult for customers to predict the reference price. In comparison with traditional straightforward pricing by room type, customers would find it difficult to understand the criteria involved in demand-driven price, particularly if there are different prices listed on different distributional channels during the same period. Second, in association with the fluctuating price, the discounted price during low seasons would unavoidably lead to a reduction in the reference price, which is likely to cause a decrease in the customer's perception of the value of the product. Therefore, if the reasons for the price differences are not justified and effectively communicated to the customers, conflict may arise because the customer may assume that the hotel behaved unfairly, or opportunistically, to gain additional profit.

Multi-tiered pricing

Multi-tiered pricing is another typical pricing strategy employed by RM practitioners, which causes customer conflicts. It refers to the selling of a product at different prices in different markets. Hotel companies have long used a multi-tiered price structure, which is designed to sell essentially the same core product to maximise revenue by offering different levels of discount to attract customers from different market segments. In a similar manner to demand-based pricing, it also aims to maximise the capacity efficiency and to increase revenue. However, instead of discriminating the price by market factors that affect the demand, tiered-pricing differentiates the price by the benefits or restrictions associated with the core product and customer behaviour-related factors. For example, according to different customer groups' behavioural habits, hotels offer comparatively low room rates to the price-sensitive market (e.g. leisure groups) to secure occupancy, and at the same time quote a relatively high rate to the non-price-sensitive or less price-sensitive corporate guests, in order to achieve higher revenue (Coulter, 2001). This can be considered as price discrimination based on market segment (Dorward, 1987) and/or customer behaviour which, if not justified, can lead the higher paying guests to view the practice as unfair (Kimes, 1994).

Some literature refers to the range of factors that are associated with the tiered pricing as 'rate fences', which can be physical (i.e. view from the room, discount on ancillary services) and/or non-physical (i.e. volume of the consumption, transaction and customer characteristics) in nature (Hanks, Cross & Noland, 1992;

Dolan and Simon, 1996). Wirtz et al. (2003, p.221) consider that 'properly designed rate fences allow consumers to self-segment on the basis of service characteristics and willingness to pay, and can help companies restrict lower prices to customers who are willing to accept certain restrictions on their purchase and consumption experiences;' however, as a method to justify increased pricing and the different layers of prices, rate fences could also have a negative effect on customers if they are not logically designed or if the discounts offered in exchange for lower rate are not sufficient. Although the product (hotel room) is essentially the same, accommodation, by offering additional benefits such as a room with a sea view, express check-in/out, use of club lounge, or discounts on other hotel services (i.e. reduction on telephone calls, laundry service and restaurant meals), hotels could charge premium rates for the product package. On the other hand, hotels could also impose restrictions on the lower rate such as non-changeable/refundable booking or minimum length-of-stay to distinguish the product in order to reflect the risk that customers have to take in exchange for special discounts. Hence, if the benefits offered or the restrictions imposed by the company are imbalanced against the relatively high price paid and discount offered, customers may object to such pricing policy as they believe it offers insufficient benefits.

Online pricing strategies and presentation

Many hospitality and tourism firms consider the Internet as an effective channel through which they can sell their products at a comparatively low price in an attempt to maximise revenue. On the one hand the online pricing approach may help the hoteliers to dispose of their unsold rooms at the last minute; on the other hand, they may also cause customer confusion and misperceptions about a hotel's pricing practice. The increasing number of online distribution channels has also shaken the hoteliers' control over their own inventory, due to the fact that the large volume of room nights sold over the Internet has increased the bargaining power of online travel companies to demand the best rate from hotels. Some online travel companies openly promote themselves as places that can deliver the best available rates (BARs). If such a situation continues, this may not only confuse loyal hotel guests about where they could get a better deal in terms of preferential rate, but the hotel's brand value may also depreciate. This would force the hoteliers into a situation where they risk becoming an inventory supplier to the online companies. As a result, hotels could lose their own customers to the online travel intermediaries in the long run.

The last-minute clearing pricing approach could lead the clients to believe that the online travel companies provide better deals or lower prices than the hotel companies do (Enz, 2003; Tso & Law, 2005). Enz (2003) points out that customers are confused by the range of Internet distribution channels for hotel rooms and the pricing practices of these channels. The study by McMahon-Beattie, Palmer and Yeoman (2004) that examines the ongoing relationship between variable pricing and the consumers in an online company also reported similar results. Their findings show that 'customers were disillusioned' on finding out that the company offers discounted prices to new customers but not to the regular ones (McMahon-Beattie et al., 2004, p.163). These authors suggest that the active engagement of variable pricing practices could result in a loss of customers' trust in the selling company, which will inevitably have a knock-on effect on the long-term buyer-seller relationship. Hence, whether the hotel's approach to pricing is logical from both the clients' and the hotel's perspective – or not - appears to be a key factor that affects a trusting relationship.

Industry reports show that much of the customer confusion over online pricing was caused by the changes to the merchant model (Starkov & Price, 2005). Known as 'a wholesale agreement that involves net rates and room allotments with cut-off dates', the concept of the *merchant model* is in fact nothing new, but has long existed in the form of the wholesale model based on tour operators (Starkov & Price, 2005). The hotel industry's increased dependence on the online merchants after the 911 tragedy in 2001, has stimulated the involvement of third-party travel Internet sites (e.g. Expedia, Hotels.com, Travelocity.com and others), as the hoteliers believed that these websites could deliver much needed incremental business. In order to combat the dramatic business decline after 911, many hotels allocated a certain percentage of their room stock to these online merchants at a steeply discounted rate. Yet what caused the customer conflicts appears to be the transparent approach to price of the current merchant model rather than the discounted rate itself. In the past, hotel companies did not allow wholesalers and tour operators to publish the wholesale rate if it was not bundled with other travel services. In other words, previously, wholesale hotel rates were mostly part of a travel product package, and the true room rate was not disclosed to the individual traveller, but the current merchant model allows the customers to view the actual rate being paid.

Lastly, the presentation of online BARs could also affect customer perceptions of fairness. A BAR is commonly recognised as the best available rate on a specific day for transit customers who do not qualify for a negotiated preferential rate such as corporate rate or conference rate. Findings from an early study in this field show that the 'economy brands seem to be the only ones in the [hotel] industry as a whole displaying a logical online pricing strategy' (O'Conner, 2003, p.95). Other more recent studies suggest that customers who are unfamiliar with the BARs find *non-blended rates* are more acceptable and more reasonable than *blended rates* (Rohlfs & Kimes, 2007). Essentially, the former presents a list of room rates (e.g. £100 for the first night, £110 for the second night and £120 for the third night of a three-night room booking), while the latter presents one single daily rate that representing an average of the BARs for the three-night stay (e.g. £110 per night). Noone and Mattila (2009) substantiate the link between price presentation strategies and customers' willingness to book, and suggest that a non-blended rate presentation approach generates a higher willingness-to-book rating than a blended presentation approach. Research findings in this particular area have enhanced our understanding about how to better engage with online bookers, that helps to pave the way for a more customer-centric RM.

☐ Customer conflicts caused by inventory control

Apart from the pricing strategies, inventory control is the other main strategy that is used by RM practitioners to maximise the revenue. Kimes (1989) considers that most hotels use one or more of the three basic approaches. Apart from the pricing and rate control issues discussed above, two other approaches are related to the effective management of the inventory – allocation control and availability control. The former basically means that the hotel can allocate a certain number of rooms to each rate category, subject to booking restrictions for each category; while the latter often refers to the actual restrictions set up, such as minimum length of stay, maximum length of stay or even closed to new arrivals (Kimes, 1994). There are three main techniques widely used to facilitate the allocation and availability control; these are capacity restrictions, length of stay control and overbooking. Each of these techniques and its impact on customer relationships is discussed below.

Capacity restrictions

The capacity restrictions are used to facilitate the allocation and availability control, but they could also result in customer conflicts (Kimes, 1994). This is because the restrictions were set up to prevent loss of revenue due to relatively lower-paying customers during high-demand periods, when the rooms can be sold at a higher rate (i.e. rack rate). In other words, hotels use the restrictions to save the inventory for the high-yield customers, with no regard for regular customers. Thus, Wirtz et al. (2003) argue that as a result of this, regular customers could be turned away during high-demand periods, which may cause irreversible damage to customer loyalty. At an individual guest level, regular visitors may lose their privileged status when the restrictions are applied. For instance, in order to maximise revenue, most hotels separate customers into different segments and charge them different rates based on their different needs and behaviour (Hanks et al., 1992). Once the room allocations for certain business rate categories are used up, then the guest is likely to be offered another higher available 'corporate rate', even if there are rooms available at lower leisure rates. Thus, the capacity restrictions attached to each rate category have, to an extent, taken advantage of predicted customer behaviour.

Undoubtedly, time-precious business travellers are easily targeted by RM practice to increase revenue. Research findings from a study conducted in Hong Kong hotels suggest that 'half of the research sample did have problems of corporate clients complaining that they could not take advantage of discount prices' (Ho & Ingold, 1998). Equally for the price-sensitive leisure travellers, although the leisure rates are usually lower than the corporate rates, the number of rooms allocated to the rate category is also generally less than the corporate rate. Depending on the demand situation, a number of rooms are set aside at lower rates and once these are taken, customers will have to pay more for the next available rate. Thus, restricted or preferred availability restrictions may mean that hotels turn away their regular customers during the high-demand season and hence reduce the effectiveness of preferential rates for regular guests. Effectively, in the eyes of the customers, hotels appear to be using discounted rate as a way to retain their regular customers, when in fact customers benefit little from the rate, since the added capacity restrictions meant that the preferential rates only became available when customers could have found cheaper rates elsewhere such as online booking sites.

Length-of-stay restrictions

Length-of-stay restrictions, which is a common technique used by the revenue management team could also have a negative effect on customers. The concept underlying length-of-stay restrictions is *duration management* which, according to Thompson (2002), is aiming to increase control over the length of time customers are occupying the inventory unit [room], since the customers' staying duration variable constrains or controls the number of rooms available on different days. In order to reduce uncertainty about guests' staying duration and to avoid empty rooms during low-demand days, hotels impose minimum or maximum length-of-stay restrictions (e.g. three days) for certain lower rates. Again, such restrictions have the advantage of allowing hotels to utilise their capacity usage; but they may be at the expense of the customers' interests. Consequently, if a guest booked in under a discounted rate and then decides to checkout early, an early departure fee will often be charged as a penalty. Similarly, if a guest checked-in under the maximum length-of-stay restriction, and wishes to extend their stay, then the discounted rate may not be applied to the extended days. In extreme circumstances, if the hotel is fully booked, there is no question of continuing the discounted rate, and the hotel could even reject a guest's request to extend their stay. Thus, it is easy to see why customer conflicts could arise, if customers are not aware of the reasons behind the length-of-stay restrictions.

Overbooking and overselling

In order to prevent the uncertainties over customer arrivals, and as a consequence of no-shows, many hotel operators and travel companies adopt 'overbooking', which is considered an essential RM technique (Lieberman, 1993). Such a practice may help companies to reduce their number of 'empty but not unsold rooms' on high-demand days, but the risk of damaging customer relationships is high, due to the fact that overbooking often leads to overselling. Overbooking is defined as 'reservation of more rooms by a hotel than are actually available, sometimes deliberately to compensate for anticipated no shows' (Medlik, 1993); however, it is not overbooking that leads to customer dissatisfaction, but 'overselling'. Overselling (when actual arrivals exceed available rooms) can easily lead to the loss of loyal customers, and other consequential negative effects, such as negative word of mouth, which will put a firm's reputation and long-term yield at risk.

The damaging effect of overselling may even result in customers taking legal action against the company concerned. In Europe and the USA, airline overbooking is now regulated by law, which means that airlines must disclose this practice and their compensation policies (e.g. EU Passengers' Rights). In the hotel industry, however, customers' rights tend to be withheld. This is because, to date, no clear regulations have been brought in that force hoteliers to be more transparent in their overbooking practices and to regulate the compensation policy. Thus, in an attempt to compensate for cancellations and no-shows, overbooking is a common practice in the travel and hospitality sectors but customers could interpret such a practice by a company as a shift away from customer care to focus on financial gain. On the other hand, if the oversold situation is well-managed with a generous reward scheme in place to attract air passengers or hotel guests to give up their seat/room voluntarily in advance, the negative relationship impact can be significantly reduced. In fact, in this scenario, customer relationships can be greatly enhanced as most of the time-flexible but price-sensitive customers would willingly compromise their convenience in exchange for what they deemed to be fair compensation.

RM impacts on key account relationships in a B2B context

The RM impact on B2B relationships could be more far-reaching than those in a B2C context, although our understanding is limited due to lack of research in this area. Millman and Wilson (1995) suggest 'key accounts' are the customers in a B2B market identified by the selling companies as of strategic importance. As a natural development of CRM, the purpose of key account management is to achieve maximum sales from the identified key clients (Wnek, 1996). Although it does not explicitly indicate whether it is the sales volume, revenue or profit that this 'sales' is referring to, the yielding source of key account management is clear – it is the identified key clients. Hallberg (1995) suggests that 80:20 rules are useful

14

to rationalise the relationship management priority since for most customer segments one third of the customers produce around two thirds or more of the sales volume. For this reason, the relationship development with the 20 per cent of key accounts becomes crucial for the success of firms.

Recent studies carried out in the hotel industry show that B2B relationship management is not exempt from negative relationship impacts as a result of extensive RM practice. Based on their findings from an international hotel company and its key accounts, Wang and Bowie (2009) have confirmed the long-held assumption that RM can indeed affect B2B relationships. Their findings reveal that, from the company's perspective, revenue managers and account managers acknowledge that RM has positively influenced the process of identifying and analysing key account activities and making contractual decisions. In the light of RM analysis, total revenue generation, total income less displaced business and the client staying profile information are now included in client value assessment in addition to the two traditional measures – profitability and customer lifetime value. From the clients' perspective, however, RM practices were found to have significant negative consequences which damage trust and undermine long-term relationship stability and commitment. Table 14.1 below provides a summary of how RM could both positively and negatively influence key account relationship management.

Table 14.1: Managers' opinions on revenue management and key account relationships

The arguments that revenue management is a positive influence on KA relationships	The arguments that revenue management is a negative influence on KA relationships
RM rationalises the business relationship, in terms of identifying and analysing the value of a KA	RM reduces the trust between key clients and the company because revenue management acts purely in the interests of the company and provides constraints on KA benefits
RM provides a better understanding of genuine customer value of the client instead of using business volume value	RM inhibits long-term relationship development because its objective is to maximise daily revenue, which potentially can destroy relationship value
RM helps to identify market trends and enables the account manager to adopt a proactive selling approach	RM reduces relationship stability since KAs perceive that RM tactics are 'opportunistic', and undermine attempts to develop long-term relationships
RM allows the management to take a proactive selling approach, which provides mutual benefits for both parties - instead of a reactive approach towards market demand	The lack of flexibility in RM systems and management's reluctance to override the system's decision means that KAs often have to pay market rates instead of preferential rates
RM facilitates long-term marketing planning by providing accurate information derived from client behavioural data collected through revenue management system	RM can therefore damage potential longer-term profitability as KAs respond by changing their buying behaviour, because of companies' opportunistic behaviour

Source: Table IV in Wang & Bowie (2009). Reproduced with kind permission of Emerald Group Publishing Limited

The crucial importance of 'trust' in B2B relationships should also be stressed. McDonald et al. (2000, p.67) suggest that the key account managers must watch out for any opportunistic behaviour on the part of anyone in their own companies, which might breach that trust. They remark:

> "It is critical that all those involved with the relationship in any respect are aware of the way in which the particular customer should be treated in order to ensure that any action or decision will build and not undermine the position of trust achieved. Care must be taken to avoid acting inappropriately, inadvertently as well as deliberately."

Understandably, based upon the entrusted relationship foundation companies can focus on the long-term future and can adopt a more proactive rather than reactive approach to business development. Overall, by focusing solely on the efficient use of the company's capacity resources, considerable financial costs may be incurred following the loss of tomorrow's customers (McCaskey, 1998). In order to prevent customer conflicts and damaging customer relationships, revenue managers must take customers' perceptions of fairness and any adverse effects of RM practice into consideration to minimise the impact of unconstructive or negative relationships. At the same time, information derived from RM analysis should be utilised to determine strategic CRM and, more broadly, marketing management decisions. Thus, there is a clear need identified for the integration of RM and CRM within the hospitality and tourism industry.

■ Summary

- In spite of RM being one of the most researched areas in hospitality operations management, lack of conceptual development at the interface between RM and CRM remains. Although our understanding about customer perception towards RM has been greatly enhanced in recent years, along with our knowledge of what is deemed as fair or unfair practice, the existing literature offers insufficient guidance on how to incorporate CRM with RM at the strategic level, as two complementary management practices, to gain competitive advantage. Thus the outcome of this chapter echoes the suggestions from other recent RM studies that there is an apparent need for RM and CRM integration (Noone et al., 2003; Mathies and Gudergan, 2007; Milla & Shoemaker, 2008, Von Martens and Hilbert, 2011; Wang, 2012a).

- A number of managerial implications have also emerged.

  ☐ First, although the relational approach to customers is widely embraced in theory, hospitality and tourism organisations are yet to fully commit to CRM in practice. The increasingly challenging business environment requires senior executives to build an overarching management structure to enable a more holistic approach to CRM and RM.

14

☐ Second, in a B2B relationship context, a typical occurrence is that internal disagreement in RM and CRM-related decision-making may arise. The main divergence is that one management group would have more confidence in the relationship's sustainability and value, whereas the other, such as the financial controller or revenue manager, would demand a quick return on investment made into key accounts. It is understandable that managers who are under pressure to meet financial targets are less comfortable with losing control over the investment or taking risks. On the other hand, such an occurrence could be prevented if the key account managers understand the revenue manager's reluctance and address the finance constituency issues in contract proposals. Thus staff cross-functional training issues cannot be undermined to enhance mutual understanding between RM and CRM practitioners.

☐ Third, in order to achieve sustained financial success, revenue managers should adopt a *proactive* rather than a *reactive* approach towards total revenue generation from both capacity and fruitful customer relationships. Based on information derived from analysis of customer behaviour, profitability and lifetime value, an organisation could make more informed decisions about its market or client mix and review its distribution strategies in order to secure the desired regular businesses particularly in volatile market conditions.

☐ Lastly, the C2B and C2C relationships that are initiated by customers and enabled by the rapid development of social digital media are equally, if not more, important than in managing B2C and B2B relationships. As an emerging challenge for revenue managers in the hospitality and tourism industry, the issue of managing rate integrity and parity across all communication channels with customers cannot be overlooked.

■ It is important to emphasis that customer relationship management is not merely about what the company could *offer to* customers but an interactive and continuing process that companies *develop with* customers in order to gain long-term success. It is anticipated that the notion of RM and CRM integration within the hospitality and tourism industry will generate much research interest for years to come. Therefore it is hoped that this chapter will serve as a stimulus for future, extended, RM and CRM research.

References

Anton, J. (1996). *Customer Relationship Management: Making Hard Decision with Soft Number.* New Jersey: Prentice-Hall.

Berry, L. (1983). *Relationship Marketing: in Emerging Perspectives on Services Marketing.* Chicago: American Marketing Association.

Bowie, D. & Buttle, F. (2004). *Hospitality Marketing: An Introduction.* Oxford: Butterworth-Heinemann.

Brotherton, B. & Mooney, S. (1992). Yield Management - progress and prospects. *International Journal of Hospitality Management,* **11**: 23-32.

Buttle, F. (1996). *Relationship Marketing: Theory and Practice.* London: Paul Chapman Publishing Ltd.

Buttle, F. (2004). *Customer Relationship Management - Concepts and Tool.* Oxford: Elsevier Butterworth-Heinemann.

Cheverton, P. (1999). *Key Account Management: The Route to Profitable Key Supplier Status.* London: Kogan Page.

Collier, P. & Gregory, A. (1995). The practice of management accounting in hotel groups. In P. Harris (Eds.), *Accounting and Finance for the International Hospitality Industry,* (pp. 137-159). Oxford: Butterworth-Heinemann.

Coulter, K.S. (2001). Decreasing price sensitivity involving physical product inventory: a yield management application. *Journal of Product and Brand Management,* **10**: 301-315.

Dolan, R. J. & Simon, H. (1996). *Power Pricing.* New York: The Free Press.

Dorward, N. (1987). *The Pricing Decision: Economic Theory and Business Practice.* London: Harper & Row.

Dwyer, R., Schurr, P. & Oh, S. (1987). Developing buyer and seller relationships. *Journal of Marketing,* **51**: 11-27.

Dwyer, R. (1989). Customer lifetime valuation to support marketing decision making. *Journal of Direct Marketing,* **3**: 8-15.

Enz, C.A. (2003). Hotel pricing in a networked world. *Cornell Hotel and Restaurant Administration Quarterly,* February, pp. 4-5.

Ford, D., McDowell, R. & Turnbull, P. (1996). In *1996 Research Conference Proceedings,* Centre for Relationship Marketing, Roberto C. Goizueta School, Emory University, Atlanta, GA, 59-67.

Gronroos, C. (1990). *Service Management and Marketing, Managing the Moments of Truth in Service Competition.* Lexington: Lexington Books.

Gronroos, C. (1996). Relationship marketing: strategic and tactical implications. *Management Decision,* **34**: 5-14.

Gummesson, E. (1999). *Total Relationship Marketing.* Oxford: Butterworth-Heinemann.

Hakansson, H. (1982). *International Marketing and Purchasing of Industrial Goods.* New York: Wiley.

14

Hallberg, G. (1995). *All Customers are not Created Equal.* New York: Wiley.

Hanks, R.D., Cross, R.G. & Noland, R.P. (1992). Discounting in the Hotel Industry: A New Approach. *Cornell Hotel and Restaurant Administration Quarterly*, 5-23.

Hasan, M. (2003). Ensure success of CRM with a change in mindset. *Marketing Management*, **37**(8): 16.

Ho, R. & Ingold, A. (1998). Yield management in Hong Kong Hotel: a comprehensive study. In *3rd Annual International Yield Management Conference: Applying the Value Concept to Yield Management.* Northern Ireland, September, 49-68.

Humphries, A. & Wilding, R. (2003). Sustained monopolistic business relationships: an interdisciplinary case. *British Journal of Management,* **14**: 323-338.

Jenkinson, A. (1995). *Valuing your Customers: From Quality Information to Quality Relationship.* London: McGraw Hill.

Johnston, R. & Clark, G. (2001). *Service Operations Management.* London: Prentice Hall.

Kimes, S.E. (1989). The basics of yield management. *Cornell Hotel and Restaurant Administration Quarterly,* **30**: 14-19.

Kimes, S.E. (1994). Perceived fairness of yield management: applying yield-management principles to rate structures is complicated by what consumers perceive as unfair practices. *Cornell Hotel and Restaurant Administration Quarterly,* **35**(1): 22-29.

Kimes, S.E. & Wirtz, J. (2002). Perceived fairness of demand-based pricing for restaurants. *Cornell Hotel and Restaurant Administration Quarterly,* **43**(1): 31-37.

Lieberman, W.H. (1993). Debunking the myths of yield management. *Cornell Hotel and Restaurant Administration Quarterly,* **34**: 34-38.

Lockard, M. (1998). Test your retention IQ. *Target Marketing,* **21**(3): 32-41.

Mathies, C. & Gudergan, S. (2007). Revenue management and customer centric marketing – How do they influence travellers' choices? *Journal of Revenue and Pricing Management,* **6**(4): 331-346.

McCaskey, D. (1998). Yield management vs. relationship marketing, in *3rd Annual International Yield Management Conference.* Northern Ireland, September, 138-161.

McDonald, M. & Rogers, B. (1998). *Key Account Management: Learning from Supplier and Customer Perspectives.* Oxford: Butterworth Heinemann.

McDonald, M., Rogers, B. & Woodburn, D. (2000). *Key Customers - How to Manage Them Profitably.* Oxford: Butterworth-Heinemann.

McMahon-Beattie, U., Palmer, A. & Yeoman, I. (2004). To trust or not to trust: variable pricing and the customer. In I. Yeoman & U. McMahon-Beattie (Eds.), *Revenue Management and Pricing: Case Studies and Applications,* (pp. 157-165). London: Thomson.

Medlik, S. (1993). *Dictionary of Travel, Tourism and Hospitality.* Oxford: Butterworth-Heinemann.

Milla, S. & Shoemaker, S. (2008). Three decades of revenue management: what's next? *Journal of Pricing and Revenue Management,* **7**: 110-114.

Millman, T. & Wilson, K. (1995). From key account selling to key account management. *Journal of Marketing Practice: Applied Marketing Science,* **1**(1): 9-21.

Morgan, R. & Hunt, S. (1994). The commitment - trust theory of relationship marketing. *Journal of Marketing,* 20-38.

Noone, B. & Griffin, P. (1999). Managing the long-term profit yield from market segments in a hotel environment: a case study on the implementation of customer profitability analysis. *International Journal of Hospitality Management,* **18**(2): 111-128.

Noone, B.M. & Mattila, A.S. (2009). Hotel revenue management and the Internet: the effect of price presentation strategies on customers' willingness to book. *International Journal of Hospitality Management,* **28**(2): 272-279.

Noone, B.M., Kimes, S.E. & Renaghan, L.M. (2003). Integrating customer relationship management and revenue management: a hotel perspective. *Journal of Revenue and Pricing Management,* **2**(1): 7–22.

O'Connor, P. (2003). On-line pricing: an analysis of hotel-company practices. *Cornell Hotel and Restaurant Administration Quarterly,* February.

Peck, H., Payne, A., Christopher, M. & Clark, M. (1999). *Relationship Marketing: Strategy and Implementation.* Oxford: Butterworth-Heinemann.

Rao, S. & Perry, C. (2002). Thinking about relationship marketing: where are we now? *Journal of business & Industrial Marketing,* **17**: 598-614.

Rigby, D., Reichheld, F.F. & Schefter, P. (2002). Avoid the four perils of CRM. *Harvard Business Review,* **80**(2): 101-108.

Rohlfs, K.V. & Kimes, S. E. (2007) Customer perceptions of best available hotel rates. *Cornell Hotel and Restaurant Administration Quarterly,* **48**(2): pp.151-162.

Rust, R.T. Lemon, K.N. & Zeithaml, V.A. (2001). Where should the next marketing dollar go? *Marketing Management,* **10**(3): 24-28.

Ryals, L., Knox, S.D. & Maklan, S. (2000). *Customer Relationship Management.* London: Prentice Hall.

Sheth, J.N. & Sharma, A. (2001). Efficacy of financial measures of marketing: it depends on markets and marketing strategies. *Journal of Targeting, Analysis and Measurement for Marketing,* **9**(4): 341-356.

Starkov, M. & Price, J. (2005). The End of the Merchant Model as We Know it. Retrieved April 5, 2005, from hotel-online website: http://www.hotel-online.com/news/PR2005_1st/Mar05_MerchantModel.html.

Stone, M., Woodcock, N. & Machtynger, L. (2000). *Customer Relationship Marketing: Get to Know Your Customers and Win Their Loyalty.* (2nd Ed.), London: Kogan Page Ltd.

Thompson, G.M. (2002). Optimizing a restaurants seating capacity: use dedicated or combinable tables? *The Cornell Hotel and Restaurant Administration Quarterly,* **43**(4): 48-57.

14

Tso, A. & Law, R. (2005). Analysing the online pricing practices of hotels in Hong Kong. *International Journal of Hospitality Management*, **24**: 301-307.

Von Martens, T. & Hilbert, A. (2011). Customer-value-based revenue management. *Journal of Revenue and Pricing Management*, **10**: 87-98.

Wang, X.L. (2012a). Relationship or revenue: potential management conflicts between customer relationship management and hotel revenue management. *International Journal of Hospitality Management*, **31**(3): 864-874.

Wang, X. L. (2012b). The impact of revenue management on hotel key account relationship development. *International Journal of Contemporary Hospitality Management*, **24**(3): 358-380.

Wang, X.L. & Bowie, D. (2009). Revenue management: the impact on business-to-business relationships. *Journal of Services Marketing*, **23**(1): 31-41.

Wirtz, J., Kimes, S., Ho, J. & Patterson, P. (2003). Revenue management: resolving potential customer conflicts. *Journal of Revenue and Pricing Management*, **2**(3): 216–226.

Wnek, N. (1996). Cultivating your garden: the increased importance of key account management as a business discipline. *Marketing Business*, June, 41.

Zablah, A.R., Bellenger, D.N. & Johnston, W.J. (2004). An evaluation of divergent perspectives on customer relationship management: towards a common understanding of an emerging phenomenon. *Industrial Marketing Management*, **33**(6): 475-489.

15 Staff Empowerment and Revenue Management

Frederic Toitot

Learning outcomes

After reading this chapter, you should be able to:

- Appreciate how hotel companies are able to recruit the best talents in revenue management, train them in the most effective way while ensuring they stay in the company as long as possible.

- Make connections between the efficiency of revenue management policies in a hotel company and the global organisation of that company.

- Understand the importance of the human factor in revenue management and describe the key steps for managing effectively the human resource processes, both at individual and corporate levels.

- Appreciate the development of revenue management practices in properties that cannot afford or are not willing to hire a full time expert.

■ Introduction

Multiple articles and books have described and analysed revenue management (RM) theories from a technical point of view: looking mostly at RM systems and processes. Indeed, thanks to very efficient RM systems (called *RMS*) and clear implementation guidelines, Revenue Management has allowed many industries to develop and optimise their revenues. Today the question is not so much about the effectiveness of the machines or the processes in place, but really about the people driving these machines, that is to say the revenue managers (or yield managers). From a few expert positions in the airline industry in the 80's, the job of revenue manager has boomed across the world, becoming critical in many companies. But it appears that a lot of these companies are struggling to find the *right drivers for the right seats.*

■ Revenue management efficiency versus organisation in the hospitality sector

Hotels and resorts belong to the service industry in which clients have to be welcomed, served, accommodated and taken care of on a daily basis. It is the core of the business, and it will remain so. Historical positions, such as hotel manager, chambermaid, waiter or receptionist will last as long as hotels are in business – despite the fact that technology progress and cost restrictions may threaten some of their current responsibilities, especially in the economy segment. However, in recent years, many hotels belonging to a chain (whether a voluntary or integrated chain) have seen jobs and responsibilities transferred to their head office, or even externalized. We can quote the human resources, accountancy, IT, marketing and reservations. These transfers were the result of a cost rationalisation and effectiveness process.

In parallel, a new kind a job has emerged in the hospitality business, usually in relation with the development of the Internet; the position of revenue manager belongs to that family of new-trendy-fashionable-technology friendly-expert positions.

The good news coming from other pioneering sectors, such as the airline industry, is that the development of revenue management (RM) in the hospitality business has been so successful that it has convinced some industry leaders that their company cannot do without it. It has not, however, always been the case. Some senior managers still do not understand what is at stake with RM, or simply may not consider this management method as really critical for their business. Senior management support is crucial for RM to function effectively. Still viewed as new by many and considered as the 'black box', it is absolutely key that senior management believes in the effectiveness of the method. It means that one of the top priorities of the company should be the development and the implementation of a global RM strategy across all the properties. Then, this managerial vision has to materialise into an appropriate organisation linked to the hotel operations, sales, marketing and pricing teams. An effective organisation has to be set up and agreed across the board. Each model has its strengths and drawbacks but it will anyway have a strong impact on the way RM human resources will be recruited, managed and developed.

Three main models co-exist:

- **Centralisation**: the RM resources are working in the same location, usually a head office (worldwide or regional). This allows an optimal sharing of best practices between experts, the delivery of a common message and more effective management and monitoring of the RM practices.
- **Clusterisation**: the teams work by groups in various locations – usually covering a market place or a country. This option leaves more room for local initiatives, while keeping groups of revenue managers together.
- **Decentralisation**: revenue managers work in the hotels under the responsibility of the hotel manager (they can work for up to 3 or 4 hotels). This gives more responsibility and autonomy to local operations, with an on-site expert close to the market and environment challenges.

The last success factor is linked to the actual responsibilities granted to the revenue managers in the organisation, whichever the model.

Power to the revenue managers: Revenue managers are definitely playing a strategic role in the optimisation of the global revenue of the properties they work for. To maximise their impact and make their recommendations heard and implemented, their positioning in the local organisation has to be clarified and well considered. In a head office or a regional office, the revenue manager must be part of the management committee. In a hotel, he should directly report to the hotel general manager (and not to the rooms division or sales & marketing manager). Failing to do so will lead to a probable dilution of the RM impact and certainly affect the revenue optimisation at the end of the day.

A revenue manager has to be considered as an expert, a decision-maker who can play an active role in the booking pick up, in the forecasting and optimization process. These strategic responsibilities have now to be confronted with the reality of the profiles found on the market, and how hotel groups manage to recruit, ramp up and develop the expertise of their revenue managers.

■ Increasing RM efficiency through the human factor

Revenue management can be approached on three angles:

- The systems and tools at the revenue manager's disposal, from a simple Excel spreadsheet to a complex RMS.
- The processes and methods agreed with the management: actions and tasks to achieve on a recurrent basis.
- The human resources piloting and monitoring the whole RM strategy.

15

As outlined in the previous section, the role and responsibilities of a revenue manager are critical. Therefore no hotel can afford to recruit or position the wrong person in the wrong seat. At the **corporate level**, a revenue management global organisation could be built according to the following steps:

1 Agree on a **RM organisation**.

2 Define the **positions and titles.**

3 Design a **competency referential**, both for personal and technical expected competencies by position.

4 Issue a **compensation & benefits scheme.**

5 Advertize and monitor the **available positions** across the regions.

6 Ensure a good **detection process** by building relationship with schools, working on the pool of internal talents (within the company) and external profiles (competition).

7 Fine tune the **screening and recruitment** process by issuing a recruitment kit.

8 Build and implement an **induction program** for new recruits.

9 Design and implement a **global training program.**

10 Issue an assessment tool for the **annual assessment of Revenue Managers.**

11 Work on the **career paths** to support the Revenue Managers in their development, both within and outside the RM network.

At the **individual level**, every revenue manager mapped in the organisation should be known, assessed and developed (training and career plans), which could be a challenge in a decentralised organisation. In any case, to ensure the success and the professionalism of every revenue manager in the organisation, three steps have to be planned ahead and carried out: the induction process, the on-the-job training and coaching sessions and the career succession plans.

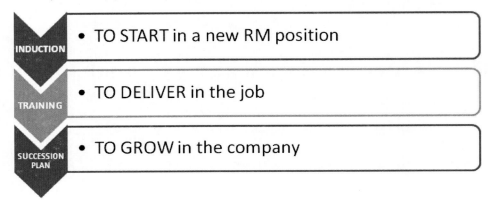

Figure 15.1: Human resources and revenue management

The induction period is that period lasting from a few hours to several weeks during which a new revenue manager needs to be briefed, taught and coached on his new responsibilities and duties. In many cases, companies tend to overlook the importance of that period for a new recruit. The main reasons why hotels or head offices are reluctant to organise induction periods are:

- The costs (training rooms, trainers, renting of material, accommodation, airfares, etc).

- The complexity of organization, in some cases, (lack of participants in one given location to cover for the costs, spoken languages, levels of expertise, etc).

- The lack of support/willingness from the company, coming often from the belief that new employees will learn on the job, by themselves or through the daily contact with colleagues and clients.

A revenue manager will have to learn and integrate a great deal of information when taking a new role and this will not be possible unless some time, resources and support are granted by the company to that effect. The key subjects to cover when starting in a revenue management role are:

- Hotel (or office) integration.

- RM global responsibilities and tasks.

- Operational immersion (other services in the hotel, at the head office, etc).

- RM & pricing hotel strategy.

- Hotel brand(s) strategy.

- Sales, marketing and pricing corporate strategy.

- Knowledge of PMS, CRS, RMS and other systems.

At the end of his induction period, the new revenue manager should be able to start in his new role with a close support and on-request coaching sessions by his manager or colleagues.

■ Training courses in revenue management

Like in most expert positions, the job of revenue manager involves the understanding and mastering of many complex concepts and theories (dynamic forecasting ,for instance) coupled with the operational aspects of the industry the RM is working into (e.g. hospitality, rail, airlines).

This variety and complexity of responsibilities can only be taught, maintained and improved through a comprehensive training program on revenue management. No revenue management network can grow and beat the competition without being trained and coached on a continuous basis. Companies attempting to save some revenue by limiting the training programs are seriously looking at

15

a backlash on the medium and long term, especially on specialties dealing with revenue, technology and market trends such as revenue management. A typical revenue management program could be built on three main levels:

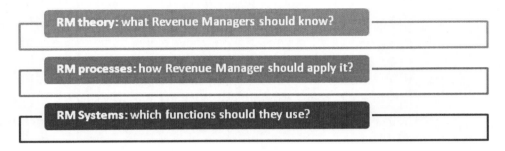

Figure 15.2: Revenue Management Program

The three training levels have absolutely to be linked and 'speak the same language'. For instance, the concepts taught in the 'RM theory' course must be really applicable in the operations. The same could be said of the RM Systems: the functions, tables and figures analyzed during the 'RM Systems' course should be useful and have an actual impact on the daily job of the revenue managers. This is where a majority of companies will struggle. They will find it relatively easy to build a given training course but will find more difficult the linkage of that course with the others already written and deployed in the same field. That situation is aggravated in international and multi-brand hospitality companies as they will have, in addition, to fit in with the local strategies, languages, environment, systems and management style.

It is obvious that the training roll-out strategy usually follows the organisation model of the company (centralised, clusterised or decentralised). It is more comfortable both for the head office and the business units as it is their way of working. On the other hand, business units belonging to a mostly decentralized hotel chain will find it difficult to accept and integrate 'ready-made and non modifiable' training courses coming from headquarters.

☐   Theories and general concepts

The objective of these courses is to teach all 'revenue key players in the organisation' the most important concepts that they are likely to use in their job. This could be approached on several levels, from basic to expert. The final objective is to provide the required knowledge to every impacted collaborator according to his role and responsibilities. The more basic courses could include some exercises on:

- Revenue management added values for the hotels: why is revenue management so important nowadays in this business?

- Revenue management global levers: pricing, overbooking & length of stay controls.
- Inventory control and management of the demand in a constrained capacity mode.
- Introduction to forecasting.
- The more advanced could focus on:
- Total Revenue Management (rooms on other revenue generating outlets).
- Individual & group forecasting.
- Optimization process.

☐ Processes and implementation of a strategy

In terms of training, that part may be the most difficult to deploy as it heavily dependent both on the global knowledge of the network and the good working order of the RM systems. Besides, unlike RM theory and RM systems, it appears that RM processes are very much linked to local cultural habits, procedures and organisation. To be effective, an RM strategy has to be considered as a fine dish produced in a fine restaurant. There must be a talented chef working in a functional kitchen, but there must also be properly written and well thought recipes that will support and guide the staff. An RM global process is like a food recipe. Tasks have to be prioritised and carried out in the correct order, and no step should be overlooked. Hotel managers in general and revenue managers in particular have to be trained on a consistent, perennial and efficient RM process. For instance, we could think of a basic process with the following steps:

1 The quality of the collected data (history and on-the-book) has to be checked and corrected if necessary.

2 The past data has to be analyzed and a global business review has to carried out, in order to detect the trends by segment/season/day of week and the revenue impacting factors.

3 A daily forecast for the coming year must be built both in terms of occupancy and revenue by segment.

4 The pickup of the bookings has to be monitored on a daily basis, and the selling recommendations adapted according to the on-the-book and forecast new situation, both in terms of pricing and availability by rate bucket.

15

☐ Revenue management and distribution systems

Last but not least, revenue managers must be knowledgeable about the tools and the systems that support them in their daily work. Professional revenue management cannot do without a proper system. Indeed, the number and the complexity of the situations are far too numerous to expect a revenue manager to handle them manually. For instance, a revenue manager working in a 100 room hotel with 10 different prices and 10 business segments would potentially have up to 100*10*10*365 = 3,650,000 actions to take every day for the 12 coming months. Training the revenue managers on managing their tools is therefore crucial. However, in most hotels, the RM tool looks like a basic program: a table with formulas and macros that automates the data calculation and display process but with usually a limited data processing capability. In other properties (usually larger, more distributed and/or belonging to a chain) a Revenue Management System (RMS) is installed. The RMS is interfaced with the hotel reservation and inventory systems (PMS and CRS) and has a very powerful data processing capability. It displays history, on the book and forecast graphs and tables with a wide array of options and functions to activate when required. Whatever the quality and the complexity of the tool/system, the key functions have to be taught to revenue managers. It is also important to give them the ability to read, analyze and extract the key information according to the information displayed.

■ Empowering the teams in revenue management

One of the major challenges that hotel companies and independent properties are facing is coping with the increasing impact of revenue management in their operations. Most hotel managers understand nowadays the importance of RM but they often struggle in the effective implementation of an RM culture and RM discipline in their property. For a start, the vast majority of hotels cannot afford to hire a full-time revenue manager, simply because their revenue and activity does not allow it. In this category, we usually find the economy and super economy hotels, the small-capacity hotels (below a 100 rooms) as well as hotels suffering from an adverse economic environment (very low occupancy, bad location, etc). For these properties, the empowerment of key staff members can work very well. By empowerment, we mean the possibility of giving to an employee or a manager some extra responsibilities that are not part of their usual set of responsibilities.

Empowerment is effective if:

■ The staff who are to be empowered are clearly identified and selected according to clear rules (e.g. service they work for, level of seniority, technical knowledge).

■ These collaborators are willing to be empowered and know what the management expects from them.

■ Their knowledge, skills and experience are sufficient to carry on these new responsibilities.

- An incentive and/or rewarding process is set.
- A regular feedback on the performance is given to the empowered staff.
- In hotels with no full time revenue managers, RM and pricing responsibilities could be given to:
- The Hotel General Manager: for setting the global strategy and being eventually responsible for achieving it (communication to the head office and/or owners).
- The Rooms Division/Reservation Manager: for following up the hotel RM strategy on a daily basis (rate levels, pick up of the booking, inventory control, distribution channels, competition).
- The Front Desk Manager: for ensuring that the RM daily recommendations are effectively carried out with the customers (check in, check out process).

It is also key to train the heads of services, such as F&B, banqueting or housekeeping on basic revenue management concepts. First, because they can manage better their department and adapt their staff planning and global organisation according to the forecast, and because they are then able to spread a revenue culture within the hotel, down to the first line staff. This empowerment strategy is working very well too in RM fully-integrated hotels, with the revenue manager acting as a coach or trainer and ensuring that the hotel teams are aware of the RM main concepts and their impact. For instance, a property running at a high occupancy level and practicing some revenue management will certainly have an overbooking strategy. In other words it will sell more rooms than there are in the hotel in order to offset the negative impact of no-shows and late cancellations and reach a final occupancy rate closer to 100%. If the front desk and reservation agents are not trained on the real objective and added value of overbooking, they will naturally tend to avoid getting in this kind of uneasy situation in which the potential of walk out (i.e. a guest with a confirmed reservation who cannot be checked in because of overbooking) is very real. A professional revenue manager should be able to defuse these tricky situations by communicating (daily) and training (regularly) the hotels teams on these practices.

15

■ Summary

■ While most reports and articles focus on revenue management through the technological and business angle, it is becoming obvious that we should not forget the human factor. Not only are good and efficient revenue managers (or acting revenue managers for that matter) indispensable to lead the strategy and monitor the tactics, but they also are the natural expert coaches for the rest of the teams in the hotels.

■ An efficient revenue management organisation in a company is closely linked to the global organisation of that company (centralised/decentralised, by brand/country) but also to the ability of the senior management to recruit, train, develop and empower the right profiles for the right positions.

16 Risk Management as a Tool to Optimise Revenue during Black Swan Events

Kate Varini and Sarah Kamensky

Learning outcomes

After reading this chapter, you should be able to:

- Explore the role of a senior revenue manager.
- Assess forecasting and its effectiveness during periods of heightened uncertainty.
- Appraise the nature of a Black Swan (complex) event.
- Appreciate the value of integrating risk management and revenue management.

■ Introduction

This chapter will explore the interrelationship between revenue management and risk management, specifically in relation to events of low predictability and high consequence. Senior revenue managers implement pricing strategies and distribution channel management. Both practices are influenced by the demand forecast which revenue managers adjust regularly. Their possible risk universe will be scoped and risk prioritization discussed. The chapter is divided into two parts: Part One provides the theoretical underpinning of risk management strategies and its possible integration into revenue management. Part Two explores survey results showing which elements senior revenue managers may already utilise intutitively and how these may be incorporated into a more systematic approach.

■ Theoretical underpinning

Risk management strategies can neutralize or minimise threats and maximise opportunities posed by complex Black Swan events. To this end, risk response, risk process initiation, risk assessment, risk response planning, risk response, recovery, signal detection, communication, and learning can be implemented.

Increasingly leading to profit optimisation, revenue management has evolved from maximising the yield of the core product, to focusing on the total contribution drawn from all revenue opportunities (total revenue management). As both an art and science, revenue management aims to leverage predictable duration and variable prices to manage customer behaviour considering finance, marketing, sales and channel strategies. Revenue managers establish the availability of product ranges for specific market segments by incorporating rate fences (or restrictions) to minimise revenue dilution. These might include booking lead time, preferred inclusions, desire for flexibility (to freely modify, or cancel reservations). Revenue management has evolved from optimising yield (focusing on price and inventory control) to being a more strategic function that integrates finance, marketing and operations functions. The driver of this evolution has primarily been the emergence of the Internet and the buying power it has transferred to the consumer.

Effective strategic revenue management has become critical to the success and longevity of hospitality organisations in both booming economic times and during recessionary periods. Low cost airlines demonstrated how revenue management significantly raises load factors and profits. Aggressive cost management (including cost of acquisition) combined with yield management and customer relationship management has emerged as a highly competitive model that customers responded to positively.

A critical element of a successful revenue management strategy is an accurate forecast as a means to achieve better decision-making by reducing uncertainty. Monitoring and prompt adaptation to fluctuating market conditions further improves performance. The level of forecast accuracy is determined by the level of detail (if compiled manually, then the forecast cannot be detailed), data availability, quality, relevance and the type of uncertainty. Unexpected events can have significant negative impact on forecast accuracy, generating missed opportunities (Taleb, 2007). The identification of patterns and precise relationships can enable accurate forecasts incorporating precise uncertainty levels. As a contrast to predicting the outcome of simple actions like coin flipping or throwing a dice that involve independent events, prediciting human behaviour is more complex. When variables are not independent of one another (as in real life) predictability is low and uncertainty levels cannot be reliably assessed. Statistical models scientifically assess potential losses and opportunities so as to improve decision making without however completely assessing the correctness of decisions (Makridakis & Taleb, 2009a). Paradoxically, although simple models do not always fit well with reality, they have been found to predict the future better than complex or sophisticated statistical models. Also, 'expert judgment' has been proven to be no more accurate than opinions of knowledgeable individuals. In general, averaging either the predictions of several individuals or the forecasts of two or more models improves forecast accuracy. Thus forecasts can be differentiated as those which can be modelled and incorporated into probabilistic predictions that assume normal distribution e.g. everyday events that re-occur, such as the time it takes a person to get to work each morning on *normal* days, also known as subway uncertainty.

Management science is rooted in the belief that order is the predominant force, following the premise that all things can be known. This belief is flawed as basic assumptions surrounding human decision making behaviour (related to cause and effect of human interactions and markets, that humans make rational choices and that all human actions are intentional) are only true within some contexts. This is further exacerbated by the fact that commonly available tools and tech-niques further multiply the instances where these assumptions prove to be untrue. Emergent order, where no director or designer is in control, represent a natural phenomena (rather than the result of poor investigation, inadequate resources, or lack of understanding) which can positively enhance business performance (Kurtz & Snowdon, 2003).

"In the domain of emergent order, the goal to predict (and thereby con-trol) the behavior of systems not yet studied (but similar to those that have been studied) under conditions not yet extant and in time periods not yet experienced" is difficult if not impossible to achieve— but other goals are achievable". Kurtz and Snowdon, (2003, p.3).

Rare and unique events are difficult to model effectively. Within this category are 'Black Swans' which are events/crisis with low predictability and high conse-quence such as a plane crash. Historically, humans have demonstrated a tendency to underestimate the probability of rare events although aware of the risk that these can occur (Makridakis, Hogarth & Gaba, 2009).

An unexpected crisis can have serious consequences on the firm's commercial advantage, reputation and consumer trust. The need for business resilience has risen as a consequence of the increasing complexity of the political, economic, social environment. Black Swan (or complex) events are becoming less and less rare; firms are increasingly faced with dynamic and complex hazards and threats i.e. natural disasters (floods, tsunami, earthquakes), terrorist attacks, and financial crises (Paraskevas, 2012a). Such a surprising, unexpected event could often have been predicted by combining certain small pieces of information (signals or flags)

16

together (Taleb, 2008). Hotels and revenue managers are facing fundamental shifts in the risk landscape but it is difficult for them to define the causes that underpin these changes or how they could respond to them.

Makridakis and Taleb (2009b) suggest the need for contingency plans for classes of events rather than precise plans. Paraskevas (2012b) proposes that firms need to create strategic approaches to manage operational and strategic risk and safeguard the business continuity of operations and employee/customer safety. Being nimble in responding to a Black Swan event can limit potential adverse effects, promote rapid recovery and thus positively impacting bottom-line performance. The assessment of uncertainty needs to be realistic and broad, allowing for what has not been imagined previously, to generate ideas and develop strategies that could neutralize sources of threats (Makridakis et. al. 2009). A possible approach could be to use a collaborative approach and visualisation to facilitating human evaluation of the things that could possibly go right or wrong. The first step is to map out what is different in today's landscape and to determine how to adapt to these differences. Insights gained can then be used to develop appropriate risk-protection strategies. Senior revenue managers are responsible for ensuring that the firm's commercial strategies extract the maximum benefit from the opportunity in the marketplace. While automated systems model and mostly manage subway uncertainty, an effective human interface will enable the effective application of optimization strategies during uncertainty, using a portfolio of responses covering identification, evaluation, elimination or mitigation of risks. Neutralising elements that might threaten assets or the earning capacities of a firm through analysis and proactive action will safeguard commercial advantage, reputation and customers' trust.

Table 16.1: Risk process initiation

Risk identification	Building the 'risk universe' i.e. all of the risks that could have an impact on the organisation's strategy considering the historical review, the current and the creativity view (to detect possible future uncertainties, they may have never happened before). Useful methods include visualisation, scenario painting, rich pictures, appreciative enquiry or story-telling.
Risk analysis	Evaluating the probability and severity of the risks with the 'risk universe'. Likelihood and impact are assessed, especially those considered non controllable. Risk analysis is challenging as risks are uncertain, complex and ambiguous. Analysis has to be documented so that risk monitoring can be done efficiently, together with the identification of possible early warning signals
Risk evaluation (aka risk monitoring)	Prioritising risks possibly by using a heat map, where risks are characterised through their probability and their potential impacts. This identifies the worst threats and the best opportunities. Those risks that are classified as having low predictability should be assigned to a risk category where a risk response could be adapted from a similar known scenario.

Risk process initiation identifies risks in relation to business objectives and levels of risk acceptance. Risk assessment is then deployed using risk identification, risk analysis and risk evaluation (Hillson, 2010).

Response planning (determining risk treatment) involves decisions about what to do about the risk i.e. accept, mitigate, avoid, transfer (AMAT) and/or covert into an opportunity. At this stage it is crucial to determine risk ownership at the first line of defence (Hillson, 2010). Each risk family should judged for tolerability and acceptability; a tolerable (acceptable) risk is one that can be mitigated or transferred, e.g. an event where the consequences are justifiable in terms of costs and possible benefits. Risks can be classified as complex, uncertain and/or ambiguous and the costs/benefits of corresponding antidotes need to be assessed, thus evaluating the treatment option for its effectiveness, efficiency, external side effects, sustainability, fairness, legal implementability, ethical acceptability and public acceptance (Renn, 2009b). A risk response matrix can then be used to consider causes, consequences, caution measures taken to prevent or minimise the impacts, and coping measures taken to deal with the risk (Paraskevas, 2012a). A firm could decide to mitigate or avoid a risk, for example, by outsourcing a critical service (Hillson, 2010).

During the risk response planning, senior management can perform a range of tabletop exercises using simulation, stress tests and/or scenario analysis. Stress tests and scenario analysis are used to cover a variety of factors that can generate exceptional losses or profits in the trading portfolio. Their aim is to give some insights of those events. Stress testing and stress scenarios can be either based on historical events, which might recur in the future or, on future 'imagined' events (Crouhy et al., 2001).

Table 16.2: Risk treatment options (Paraskevas, 2012b)

Avoidance	Impacts and probability might potentially destroy key assets, or when treatment options are not justifiable due to their costs. Avoiding risks can augment the gravity of other risks
Mitigation	Seeks to lower the consequences, or the probability, or decrease the exposure to the risk to ensure business continuity.
Acceptance	Focuses on the effects a risk may have. A company accepts risks if it is within its risk appetite or if the costs of the other options do not justify the expected rewards
Transfer	Aims to share or transfer the risk to another party through insurance, specific contract terms, outsourcing, joint ventures, or partnerships for instance, hedging i.e. buying future or forward contract now for the future to secure a certain price.

Senior revenue managers need to identify events that can affect the achievement of strategic revenue management objectives. The ability to detect early warning signals that may emerge prior to the complex (Black Swan) event can increase commercial advantage. A possible early warning system would need to be a dynamic process where data showing unusual patterns is proactively captured and evaluated to assess potential threats/opportunities on an on-going

16

basis (Paraskevas, 2012b). Signal detection is a complementary mechanism for crisis management. A three step process of signal scanning, capture and transmission for analysis by a response center that will interpret the signals presented. Human factors in influencing interpretation are cultural, structural, psychological and professional and may also be external. Others tactics include impact analysis, damage limitation approaches and learning from past swans (identification of causes and consequences).

Signal scanning to indentify unusual patterns is performed by technical or human detectors, or a combination of the two. Collective intuitions are useful to build a picture of future events (Makridakis and Taleb, 2009b) and those in the front line tend to be able to detect unusual patterns earlier than senior management. An example of firms that use this approach are credit card companies that block consumer credit cards when IT systems detect unusual spending patterns. Signal capture relies on the detector's diagnostic ability in detecting a real signal (over what could be defined as noise) and not missing a signal completely. Seeming disparate signals may be detected in various parts of the organisation and detectors may not know how pass-on the information. A hub (middle manager) is proposed to separate out noise before relaying signals back to decision making center. Pattern recognition is a useful method of detecting signals that a scenario that deviates from the norm may be emerging.

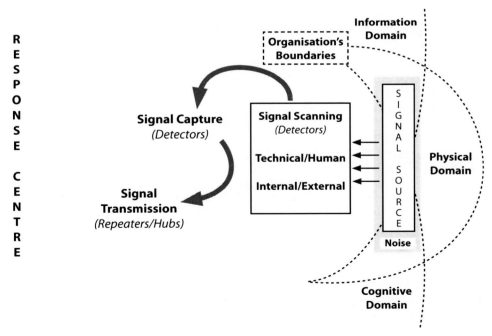

Figure 16.1: The crisis signal detection process. Adapted from Paraskevas (2012a, p.6)

Signal detection alone may not trigger the desired responsive actions. Commonly the interpretation of signals hinders the 'out of the box' interpretation of signals in relation to what will possibly be. Experts will notice signals that non-experts will not, people working inside the organisation will notice things that externals will not and vice versa. Ultimately successful signal detection depends on a collective mind and a shared sense of purpose (Paraskevas, 2012a). Hence the need for senior revenue managers to maintain a revenue management culture within the organisation and thus encourage, for example, the capturing of possible signals in a response center such as a system to detect special events (or exception days where unusual demand is detected). The communication and learning steps as well as the signal detection have also be planned in advance so as to be effective when an event occurs or the whole risk management cycle could be rendered ineffective.

■ Risk and risk management approaches

The next section will explore how senior revenue managers consider risk and the level of acceptance of possible risk management approaches, particularly in relation to possible black swan events.

Examples of risk taken by hotel revenue managers:

- Overselling requires all relevant information pertaining to inventory allocations. When there is a low awareness of third party agreements, the dangers of overselling increases.

- Overbooking aims to enable the property to achieve a sell out night where all inventory units are occupied. Achieving this with no instances of denied customers (walks) is a challenging task which required an accurate prediction of no-show (last minute modifications etc.) levels.

- Loyalty club membership may offer guaranteed availability if bookings are made 72 hours before arrival. Making this promise incurs risk as the hotel may already be in a sold out/overbooked situation at this point in time.

- Group business: how much to accept/decline? As this business is at lower rates, the hotel should only accept the amount of business that would allow forecasted unsold rooms (distressed inventory) to be sold. Also the negotiation process occurs far from the arrival day, hence there is a reliance on the forecast which will have varying degrees of accuracy.

- B2B relationships; the cost of acquisition is higher when business comes in via an intermediary especially during high demand periods when rates are at their highest. Hence the tendency would be to reduce availability during such times. However, this can incur the wrath of partners who may then punish the hotel partner by reducing their visibility/availability during need periods.

16

Table 16.3: Possible elements within the risk universe of senior revenue managers.

e-Commerce

Data analytics is not appropriately developed

Investment is made into direct channels

We allocated too much/too little inventory to intermediaries (cannibalisation or stimulation)?

Customer data ownership, growth in power/ability to leverage economies of scale, dynamically package travel products

What are the risks and opportunities associated with online travel agencies: What are the drivers of their revenue?

How to distinguish displacement vs incremental revenues

Inventory in Tour operator allotment may all come back last minute

Organisation & Systems

The revenue culture is not properly in place, e.g. Operations does not adhere to the revenue manager's recommendations

Perception of commoditization increases

The technology fails (RMS, CRS, GDS, PMS)

Our forecast is wrong (extreme, high, medium vs low demand periods)

We don't develop the right products

Metrics do not adequately measure performance versus opportunity e.g. we only evaluate revenue from core products / not contribution or profit (flow through)

Revenue managers make mistakes: misunderstand data, introduce bias, misread reports or are simply incompetent

Finance develops unrealistic revenue forecasts/budgets

Market segmentation is wrong

Yield Management

Inventory is uploaded incorrectly (too much/too little availability)

What if the length of stay restrictions are too aggressive/conservative?

What is the risk of overbooking (TO allotment, group business, individual) during periods of extreme vs high demand? How can hedging be used to mitigate these risks?

Prices are too high/low (inventory unsold/inventory sold out too quickly: loss of opportunity)

Competitors lower/increase prices

Consumers

Customer data is hacked

Consumer behaviour changes with different channels, e.g. lead time for booking

The growth in mobile devices impacts sales

Consumers perceive price gouging during a crisis (impact on consumer trust and propensity to buy in the future?)

Consumers perceive our products as commodities (impact of frame of reference, price sensitivity)

Global environment

Recession, war, natural disaster etc.

A research study was undertaken to assess how senior (high performing) revenue managers from one large multinational hotel chain perceived risk management strategies and the level to which they implement related strategies. Analysis of the surveys and interview data identified risk categories and that forecasting poses significant challenges. The senior revenue managers are aware of past risks related to technology, products, forecasting, revenue managers, price and distribution as well as group bookings and events. When a complex (Black Swan) event threatens revenue management objectives, senior revenue managers use direct web sales to manipulate demand followed by price after the event. Risk reduction strategies involve business customers and risk transfer might involve major tour operators. Offering value-added features or restricted discounts to local business and repeat customers could reduce the consequences of low demand. To minimise losses if a major (sporting) event is cancelled at the last minute was not considered as a real issue when inventory is prepaid and non-refundable. However, the hotel could offer a special rate or to change the dates, or to redirect the customers to other hotels from the company. Hedging could be used with intermediaries and customers. Senior revenue managers mitigate, transfer and avoid some risks intuitively, but in isolation, rather than via an integrated enterprise risk management approach. They know that they deal with risk on a daily basis and are confronted with voluntary risks such as the use of the internet and involuntary risks such as unstable political or economical situations.

Establishing risk families provide options to categorise and treat risks in a similar way. This was done for the Olympics where three types of risks were identified; system issues, something happening in London, but the hotel is not directly affected, and the third one on something happening in the hotel, ceasing operations. Everybody knows who is doing what in those situations. It can thus be assumed that risk owners have been defined. Risk mitigation or reduction can be either proactive (reduce the likelihood) or reactive (reduce the consequences)

Senior revenue managers face voluntary and involuntary risks in their daily work where commercial assets are menaced by Black Swan events that cannot be actively avoided. To mitigate the consequences, direct web sales and the price should used (with caution). After a Black Swan event online travel agenices that generate the most leisure customers can be a useful source of fresh demand. Risk transfer is already applied through prepayments and deposits. However, hedging could be a useful technique to integrate customers as well as distributors in the transfer of risks. Senior revenue manager do not currently attempt to forecast re-occurring rare events that have the potential to impact revenue significantly or those that have never happened before but that could potentially occur (these are not reflected in hotels forecasts as they cannot easily be predicted by an automated system i.e. the potential that disruptive public demonstrations will occur).

16

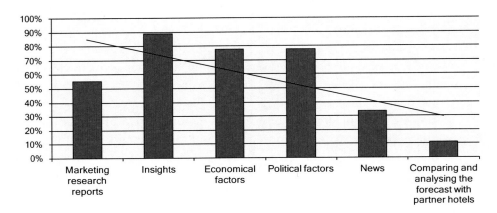

Figure 16.2: Factors used to adjust computer generated demand trends

Note: Expected business not yet visible to the system (i.e. groups that are expected to be confirmed). Senior managers in the sample also report that competitor pricing and availability adjusting rates and forecast accordingly.

☐   Risks posed by Online Travel Agencies (OTA)

Although different for each hotel, in general the majority of bookings are made via electronic channels such as Expedia and Travelocity, hence these are great source of business. However OTA have high commissions attached that can make them less favourable. Most large hotel chains offer a two-way interface enabling real time updates to pricing and availability across all channels. Also, hotels generally have a portfolio of tools (channel managers and direct connectivity through CRS) that allow efficient daily management of related channels.

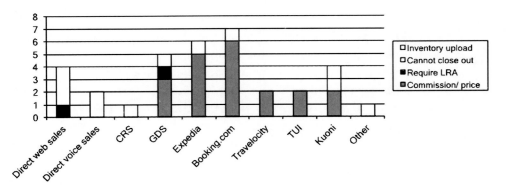

Figure 16.3: Which channels pose most constraints?

☐   Summary of risks identified by surveyed senior revenue managers

(I) Technology

- Systems may cease functioning at the central and property level (CRS, PMS).
- Web and connection to distribution channels suspended.
- Revenue Management system out of service.
- Low speed, no data integrity, no access, no connectivity. Power outage.
- Problems with the interface (PMS platforms not syncronizing correctly with CRS) during high demand events, when the system suddenly receive a huge amount of data.
- Systems that rely on constant use of high speed internet. Inventory between different channels out of balance (PMS shows there is no availability for a specific date, while another channel remains open, or vice versa).
- System speed across networks within global companies is an increasing issue, where file sizes and data requirements are outgrowing the speed on network technology.

Systems are in place to warn when something does not look correct and simple errors such as incorrect pricing are often quickly resolved. Automated tools used to compare pricing are not always able to compare, e.g. a competitor room rate include taxes/no breakfast while for another the rate includes breakfast and for a third competitor, the rate is for room only (excluding taxes). Hence market positioning is not always as simple as it appears; a revenue manager that is not aware of these subtle differences could easily make wrong pricing decisions. There are many tools and systems which are help revenue managers identify market price points and sensitivity on any given day.

(ii) Products

- Incorrect pricing which turns into lost revenue opportunities. Segments not targeted.
- No demand.
- Inventory not available. Promotions that fail to appeal customers.
- A big investment in a hotel facility that will not get used.
- Terms and Conditions not applied correctly.

(iii) Forecasting

- Non materialisation of contracted business.
- Unstable political and economic environment. Social unrest impacting demand.

16

- High volatility of exchange rates.

- Lack of control on business booked due to unclear contractual conditions, especially for MICE.

- Lack of insights when new competitors appear at different price points than expected. Wash factors not predictable for re-occuring events, like fireworks or sports events, that can be cancelled due to weather conditions, etc. Forecasted special events where the global & local political & economical situation must be taken into consideration.

- Demand pattern changes, e.g. during Olympic Games demand was not predictable, even when comparing impacts to recent host cities as is not comparing apples to apples as supply of rooms, can be radically different.

Forecasting is itself a source of risk, both when forecast is too high or too low, as it can result in missed opportunities either way. Hence the need to regularly monitor and evaluate variance to expectations. Strategies should then be adapted to these variances as needed.

(iv) Revenue manager

- Switches to competition with all his/her knowledge of the strategy. Makes deliberate mistake for a fraudulent benefit, inexperienced when trying to spot trends in order to react as efficiently as possible.

- Not qualified for the job. Forgot to restrict dates that the hotel is expected to be fully booked

- Typing error in a rate code, can result to an overpriced or the opposite for a room product.

Revenue managers need to analyse large quantities of data regularly. A right balance between attention to detail and efficient decision making is important (details are important, but looking too much at them can distract you from the things that really matter). Usually a forecast is a team effort, with more than one team contributing to it (Marketing, Sales, Reservations, etc). Every single data must be collected and loaded correctly by the revenue manager in the forecast tool, so the bigger the property, the bigger the risk of making some calculation mistakes.

(v) Pricing

- Competitors entering price war in a market.

- Change in price points for direct competitors missed time for reaction; revenue loss.

- If Comp Set is not closely monitor there is a risk to be out of the market.

(vi) Intermediaries – 'This is really high risk business'

- Increasing fees/commissions that are not accurately forecasted, can significantly impact profit.

- Too many entities are in the middle between the supplier and the end client, complicating the ability of the revenue manager to monitor all intermediaries to ensure the hotel has a preferred status.

- The signing of an exclusivity deal with competition.

- The high cost attached to some online travel agency bookings, given the heavy discounts/rate categories usually booked via this channel.

- Leisure business / low room revenue / poor extra spend/ usually restricted when high demand is forecast.

- As it is important to have preferred placement, regular checking is needed to ensure that the hotel is properly displayed with a good ranking.

- Very important to keep a great relationship with their representatives.

- Each OTA has its own software to manage inventory and prices, but not all are capable of applying all yield settings (e.g. Min/Max length of stay, etc.).

- Tour Operators usually have wholesaler agreements. Very demanding with allotments and closed out dates. Revenue managers need to make sure that their rates are competitive with any other published rate.

- Corporate Travel Agencies generally have a high revenue value but are very costly to acquire given the commission levels attached. The sales manager needs to maintain good relations and get the corporate accounts that book through these intermediaries.

A strong corporate channel may have a significant GDS fee attached to each booking. The extra revenue generated by the guest should compensate for this.

(vii) Groups and events

- **Price** is not the unique element to be negotiated, especially when dealing with large volume. Terms & conditions that are inappropriately negotiated can result in significant losses, e.g. partial or full cancellation, deposits/prepayments, guarantee by organizer and by individual participants.

- **Additional/last minute requests**: sales team needs to be prepared to handle these from a revenue/sales perspective; it is not just an operational question. Should a client request a sudden change in an already contracted item, the team needs to be able to decide what can be offered free of charge and what should be charged (considering where costs are generated). A last minute change in meeting room set-up that requires extra staffing or a late request to provide a meal for 200 persons when there is a lack of personnel may pose significant risk to profit, reputation, satisfaction etc.

16

After a crisis companies' managers see revenue management as an important tool, to manage demand. They would use the following to create demand during and after a crisis.

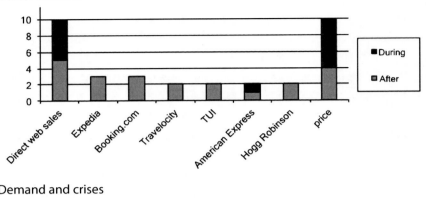

Figure 16.4: Demand and crises

■ During risky events and times of crisis none of the above can really help to create demand. You need find those markets and segments that get a 'benefit' out of this (i.e. security or insurance companies, etc).

■ When marketing directly on the Internet, consider the broader idea of direct sales (be it web, sales team, or any direct sales activity) versus indirect channels/resources.

■ Important to note that marketing directly on the Internet is a key factor for branded/chain hotels, however non-branded/individual hotels are more likely to depend on external sales channels/GDS.

Which stakeholder would be more susceptible towards risk reduction/transfer during or after a crisis, to minimise losses and optimise revenue?

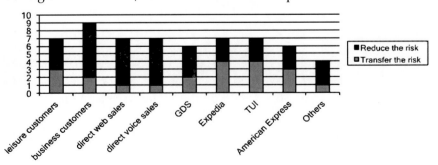

Figure 16.5: Risk reduction

Managers were asked to imagine working in a region where their hotel is situated in the city centre of a capital and civil unrest such as during the Arabic Spring is taking place. Below are the measures they would take to reduce the consequences of low demand and optimise revenue after the crisis has occurred (i.e. in relation to prices, promotion and place):

- Focus on local business as inbound will take longer to recover.
- Price appropriately in the market.
- Ensure correct price positioning with value added products available for sale not necessarily considering rate reduction as no extra revenues will be generated.
- Ensure the hotel is not losing share in its competitive set.
- Open discounted products for as long as possible (with pre-payment, non refundable), trying to tackle local business (since guests from abroad are unlikely to come), trying to promote as much as possible hotel's safety.
- Invest in a strong advertising and promotional campaign with strong promotions in all e-channels to create awareness of the new situation and of the attractive packages.
- Not necessarily drop rates, but create packages with value of money to attract business.
- Target regular guests / database with special offer.
- Find out the accounts that are first to invest money to the city & and be proactive versus competition by signing contracts with them.
- Check competitive destinations about prices, promotions, and be creative and attractive, so as to 'steal' business.
- It is not always about optimising revenue after or during such events, it is also about protecting what you have and not making any panic decision which may damage the business longer term (i.e. drastically dropping rate).
- First need to re-evaluate the demand. If the demand to the city has drastically dropped as a result of the civil unrest then it is unlikely that you are going to be able to do much about it. You have to accept that this is the current situation a think about the longer term.

To reduce the risk of cancellations and minimise losses during and/or after a complex (Black Swan) event, senior revenue managers suggested the following:

For these kind of events the rooms have to be partly or fully paid in advance and no refund is given.	87.5%
Customers who want to cancel are offered a special rate, but no refund is given.	37.5%
Customers who want to cancel are offered to change their reservation for a another date, which is done in collaboration with the airlines	25.0%
Customers who want to cancel are re-directed to the hotels of the company near the new location so that the hotel is loosing revenue, but not the company.	37.5%
Customers who want to cancel are re-directed to the hotels of the company near the new location. The Senior Revenue Manager of both regions agree that a part of the revenue is transferred to the hotels in Brazil.	12.5%

16

The ownership model of the company would also come into play i.e. if the owners of the two hotels were different this would have an impact. With regards to implementing hedging with partners, the managers suggested they would agree rates for a two year contract valid as of today so to have a win-win situation. The hotel gets the volume as of now when they agree a rate for two years. This agreement will be made through several intermediaries, such as Business Travel Agents (AMEX, Carlson, etc), GDS channels etc. When implementing hedging with customers the managers suggested they would be more flexible with fenced rates e.g. allow guests that have booked non refundable advance purchase rates to change the dates and/or create a Package (like loyalty package), where you guarantee rate and availability for one year one, prepaid and non refundable. It was suggested that the customer mind set might only be ready to accept generally accepted practices that address such a risk, i.e. prepayment, deposits, cancellation policies.

■ Summary

- Hotels are increasingly exposed to crisis scenarios that pose both threats and opportunities. Hence there is a need to assess the risk universe to develop contingency approaches to possible complex (Black Swan) events. Revenue managers use forecasts to control inventory and price to manage and create demand.

- Risks have two components: danger and opportunity. A Black Swan is a complex event with severe consequences that is very hard to predict. Within the risk management cycle, identified risks are evaluated in terms of probability, their impacts, and their priority as well as the early warning signals that arise.

- Complex events occur more and more frequently due to a number of different elements, such as wider and more dynamic consumer access to local and global information, the growth of emerging economies and the general increase in consumer power. Complex events present both threats and opportunities for the organisation. Risk management is an ongoing process and communication, learning and signal detection are needed throughout the process.

- Senior revenue managers face significant risk and already use risk management strategies in a reactive way. It is recommended that the risk management cycle is integrated more systematically with their operational cycle so as to be more efficient in applying the treatment options. Also, regional senior revenue managers should define their risk universe *together*, with a view to making less isolated decisions, sharing ideas for action to applied across the enterprise. While avoidance of Black Swan events is unlikely, proactive identification of mitigation strategies to complex event types could significantly enhance commercial advantage. No matter which treatment is implemented, the outcomes should be observed to make sure that they have the intended effects as new risks may emerge from the treatment, hence signal detection and the resulting timely communication is critical. A risk learning centre could facilitate the communication of the learning phase; failures and achievements could be used as information for other parts of the organisation. Vicarious learning could also be used to evaluate what went wrong and what went well by sharing experiences. Observing how an organisation manages a Black Swan event can help others avoid the same mistakes and implement actions that went well in their own risk strategy.

References

Crouhy, M., Galai, D., Mark, R. (2001). *Risk Management*. New York: McGraw-Hill.

Hillson, D. (2010). *Exploiting Future Uncertainty - Creating Value from Risk*. Surrey: Gower Publishing Ltd.

Kurtz, C.F. & Snowdon, D. J. (2003) The new dynamics of strategy: sense-making in a complex and complicated world. *IBM Systems Journal*, **42**(3).

Makridakis, S., Hogarth, R.M. & Gaba, A. (2009). Forecasting and uncertainty in the economic and business world. *International Journal of Forecasting*, **25**(4): 794-812.

Makridakis, S. & Taleb, N. (2009a). Decision making and planning under low levels of predictability. *International Journal of Forecasting*, **25**(4): 716-733.

Makridakis, S. & Taleb, N. (2009b). Living in a world of low levels of predictability. *International Journal of Forecasting*, **25**(4): pp.840-844.

Paraskevas, A. (2012a). Mitroff's five stages of crisis management. In: Golson J.G., Penuel, K.B., Statler, R., Hagen, R. (Eds.). *Encyclopedia of Crisis Management*. New York: Sage Ltd.

Paraskevas, A. (2012b) "Risk Treatment". In: Golson J.G., Penuel, K.B., Statler, R., Hagen, R. (eds.). *Encyclopedia of Crisis Management*. New York: Sage Ltd.

Renn, O. (2009a). The Risk Handling Chain". In: Bouder, F., Slavin, D., Löfstedt, R. (Eds.). *The Tolerability of Risk - A New Framework for Risk Management*. London: Earthscan, pp.21–74.

Renn, O. (2009b). Components of the Risk Governance Framework". In: Bouder, F., Slavin, D., Löfstedt, R. (Eds.). *The Tolerability of Risk - A New Framework for Risk Management*. London: Earthscan, pp.1-20.

Taleb, N. (2008) *The Black Swan – The Impact of the Highly Improbable*. London: Penguin Books Ltd.

16

17 Timeshare Revenue Management

Amy Gregory

Learning outcomes

After reading this chapter, you should be able to:

- Understand the concept of timeshare/vacation ownership and be able to discern between the timeshare product that is purchased and the timeshare product that is used, including the various usage options a timeshare owner may have.
- Be familiar with the inventory management techniques required to support owner usage of the timeshare product.
- Recognise why the available supply of timeshare inventory is more dynamic than traditional lodging products.
- Comprehend how the timeshare industry analyses customer data to generate the most cost-effective customers to generate the greatest long term revenues.
- Understand how inventory allocation among various customer segments may impact the ongoing profitability of a timeshare resort.
- Apply revenue management measures and terms specific to the timeshare industry.

■ Introduction

This chapter addresses revenue management within the timeshare industry with a focus on the unique aspects of forecasting demand, inventory allocation, and evaluation of revenue management efforts in an environment of dynamic supply. The chapter demonstrates how the timeshare industry is using revenue management techniques in their revenue and inventory management processes that go beyond traditional inventory management strategies by targeting, analysing and selecting the most profitable customers and allocating rooms' inventory according to anticipated returns from the particular market segment in order to generate the greatest long term profitability for the business.

Current literature suggests that the emphasis of revenue management practices is evolving. Traditional inventory-centric practices of revenue management concentrated on the inventory and its optimization. Recent thinking advocates that a more customer-centric view, one that focuses efforts on the analysis of customer data to yield insights into the most valuable customers to sell to, may result in greater profitability for business enterprises (Cross, Higbie and Cross, 2009). Unlike typical lodging products, the timeshare product is sold to consumers for their ongoing use, and a relatively small portion of the inventory is rented, as in a traditional lodging establishment. Nonetheless, inventory is managed and allocated according to market segment and the needs of the greater enterprise including use by the consumers who own the product, marketing for the purpose of selling the timeshare product, and rental to offset the cost of developer-owned or managed inventory.

The timeshare industry is a large, global industry with more than 5,300 resorts in over 100 countries; accounting for worldwide economic impacts exceeding $115 billion (USD) annually. While most consumers and students may be aware of the timeshare sales and marketing components of the industry, many are less aware of the unique operational aspects of timeshare resorts, including a rental component generating annual rental revenues in excess of $2 billion (USD) worldwide. These rental revenues account for approximately 15% of the annual revenues produced by the industry, and many expect these numbers to increase as the timeshare product continues to evolve (ARDA, 2012a).

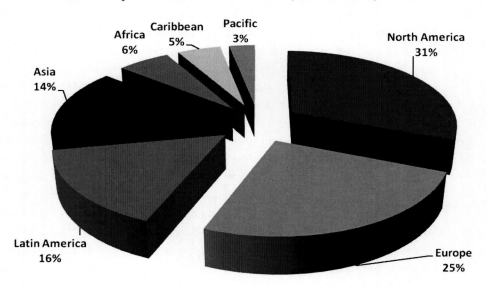

Figure 17.1: Worldwide Timeshare Resort Distribution. ARDA (2012b)

17

■ The business of timeshare companies

Many individuals believe that the timeshare industry is just about sales. In fact, the timeshare industry is established on three primary business components, with some of the larger companies including a fourth. You may hear the businesses of timeshare referred to as a 3-legged stool. Each of those legs is attributed to a component of the business: real estate development and sales; consumer financing and resort management; the larger timeshare companies may also have a fourth leg, a mortgage bank.

From its inception, the timeshare industry was about real estate development and sales. This component of the business includes resort feasibility, planning, construction, development, sales and marketing, as well as all of the components of a business to support that such as accounting, corporate finance, legal, human resources, etc. Think of this component of the business as everything that is involved in identifying a resort location, buying the land and/or existing infrastructure, defining what will be sold (intervals, points, fractions, etc.), getting all of the necessary funding to construct the inventory, hire staff and begin sales, preparing/filing legal documentation, marketing, sales, contract processing, etc. This is the first component of the timeshare business.

Once the timeshare resorts are built, someone has to manage them. A homeowners' association is formed to oversee the ongoing management, general upkeep and running of the resort. The association hires a management company that is responsible for the inventory management, including reservations systems, and property management for the resort. Unlike hotels, timeshare properties are sold off, generally in weekly intervals, to individual consumers who then collectively own the timeshare resort. Each owner pays dues to the homeowners' association which uses those funds to run the resort, i.e., pay the electricity and water bills, replace furnishings when things break or wear out, maintain the pool, grounds, and landscaping, staff the resort with a General Manager, front office staff, housekeepers, maintenance engineer. So, in addition to the general operations of the resort, much like a hotel is managed and operated, timeshare resorts must also maintain and manage a homeowners' association. This is the second component of the larger timeshare business. The third and fourth components of the industry are best described together. Both have to do with financing: consumer financing and investor financing. Most timeshare companies offer some form of consumer financing, the third leg of the stool. Because you cannot go to a bank and take out a loan for a timeshare, as you can for the purchase of a car or a home, timeshare companies offer financing to consumers. Many of the timeshare companies have expanded their business model by engaging investors through the sale and purchase of consumer loans originated within the timeshare company. This is a very profitable component of the business for those companies adept enough to engage in this segment of the business. This is the fourth leg of the stool and is typically representative of the larger timeshare companies.

■ The timeshare product

The timeshare product has been defined as a legal form of real estate ownership either in the form of deeded ownership, where the purchaser actually receives title to the property, or in the form of a right to use, where the purchaser has the legal right to occupy the property for an established period of time. The purchaser pays for the time that they use upfront as a one-time purchase and shares the responsibilities for their owned increment of time as well as the common areas and shared amenities of the property. Annual dues (maintenance fees) are paid by each owner in order to operate and maintain the property. The property that is owned or accessed is typically in one week increments (or point equivalents that allow the owner to break their stays up into nightly increments) in two bedroom/ two bathroom condominium units, often referred to as villas in the industry, in a resort-like setting.

Timeshare resorts typically include services and amenities one would expect to find in a resort hotel. For example, there is a front desk that offers check-in/ check-out functions providing room assignments to the owners and distributing/ collecting keys to the villas, a housekeeping staff that is responsible for daily or mid-week maid service, if requested, and a full cleaning of the villas before/after owners arrive or depart, concierge service to provide information on local events and activities off the resort property, and a maintenance team that is responsible for the upkeep of the units, grounds, and amenities. In addition to the services provided, there are also amenities available at timeshare resorts that are comparable to a resort hotel. For example, it is not uncommon for a timeshare property to have a swimming pool, tennis court, golf course, fitness facilities, game room, full service restaurant/snack bar/pool bar, as well as a convenience store. In most cases, the ongoing operations of the resort are overseen by a General Manager who has responsibility for the property; just as a General Manager in a traditional hotel would.

Regardless of whether a timeshare owner owns a week-based or a points-based product, the usage options each year are roughly the same:

■ *Occupy*: timeshare owners can choose to occupy a unit in their home resort or within their system of resorts. They may also allow another friend or family member to occupy the villa as a guest if the timeshare owner does not plan to use it in any given year. It is the timeshare resort management company's

17

responsibility to ensure that inventory is available each year for the timeshare owners to occupy according to their purchase contract.

■ *Exchange*: timeshare owners may choose to explore a resort destination that is not a part of the original system of resorts that they purchased into. For example, an owner purchasing with Disney may choose to vacation in Spain one year. If Disney doesn't have a resort in Spain, the timeshare owner would give (or deposit) their week, or points-based equivalent, with one of the timeshare exchange companies in order to stay in a resort in Spain. The process of exchange means that the owner relinquishes the right to occupy the timeshare that they purchased in exchange the right to occupy somewhere else. The timeshare resort management company must make inventory available to the exchange company that is equivalent to what the owner purchased.

■ *Trade*: if a timeshare owner has purchased from one of the larger lodging companies, these may offer the opportunity for the owners to trade their timeshare week for an alternative pre-packaged vacation experience, such as a cruise or safari, or an allotment of points in the company's hotel program, i.e. Marriott Rewards, Hilton Honors, Starwood Preferred Guest, etc. The process of trading means that the owner relinquishes the right to occupy the timeshare that they purchased in exchange for another vacation experience provided by their management company. If a timeshare owner chooses to trade their week for an alternative vacation experience, the timeshare resort management company typically rents the week that the timeshare owner owns in order to generate revenue to offset the cost of the alternative vacation experience given to the timeshare owner.

■ *List for rent*: if a timeshare owner chooses not to use their timeshare vacation in any given year, they may opt to list the inventory for rent. Developers and management companies closely manage these programs in order to maintain the appropriate pricing in the market place for both the rented product, as well as the larger product – the owned timeshare week that the individual purchased. As a result, if a timeshare owner would like to list their unit for rent, they likely deal directly with the management company who will handle the transaction for a fee or percentage of the rental proceeds. These rentals look very much like traditional hotel resort rentals, however, the distribution channels for these units may be constrained to maintain price integrity, and ultimately the value of the owned timeshare product. As a result, it is unlikely that consumers will find many timeshare properties for rent through wholesalers, online travel agencies, or other third party sources. It is important that the rental price of the product is aligned with the purchase price of the owned timeshare product in order to maintain the value of the timeshare product for sale.

■ Unique characteristics of revenue management in the timeshare industry

☐ Dynamic supply

Physical capacity

Unlike traditional hotels which are constructed in single phases and opened all at once, timeshare resorts are typically built in phases bringing on several units for occupancy according to the sales pace, with subsequent phases being delivered in future years. A timeshare property may open with 25 units (3,100 timeshare weeks; 9,100 annual room nights) in its first year of operation, bring on 25 units each year over the next several years, and ultimately stabilize with 125 units (6,500 timeshare weeks; 45,500 annual room nights); an average midsize timeshare property. It is important to note that more than 1/3 of the timeshare resorts in the United States are classified as large with 275 units (14,300 timeshare weeks; 100,100 annual room nights) on average. Further, several 'mega resorts' with more than 1,000 units (52,000 timeshare weeks; 364,000 annual room nights) are typical in the most popular resort destinations such as Orlando, Florida.

Resort occupancy

Recall from the beginning of the chapter, that unlike a hotel, a timeshare resort is sold off in its entirety to individual buyers/owners who then have the right to use their timeshare, generally on a weekly basis for the term of ownership, which may be in perpetuity. As a result, the timeshare management company is responsible for ensuring each of the owners has access to the product that they own. These owners may choose to occupy, exchange, trade, or rent during their annual use period. It is the management companies' responsibility to allocate inventory accordingly. However, because the inventory is owned by the individual consumers, the management company may not have the right to utilize the inventory unless the owner has given them the right to do so. As such, an owner may choose not to utilize their allocated time and the inventory may go completely unutilised. As a result, it is important that the timeshare inventory management companies know how their owners intend to use the product so the inventory can be optimised rather than go unused. Even a smaller percentage of rental revenues earned as a commission for the management company is better than inventory that perishes and opportunity that is lost.

Because of the owned nature of the timeshare product, occupancies at timeshare resorts are generally much higher than typical hotels and resorts. Figure 17.2 provides a comparison of occupancy rates across hotels, resorts and timeshare properties in the United States from 2010 to 2012. The higher timeshare resort

17

occupancy rates are directly related to the owned nature of the timeshare product. Timeshare resort developers, unlike hotel developers, sell their inventory rather than rent it. The management company must allocate inventory for use according to ownership, and can only consider inventory for rent if it has been relinquished by the unit owner to the management company in exchange for something else, i.e., rental proceeds or an alternate vacation experience.

As such, it is important to distinguish between resort occupancy and rental occupancy in the timeshare industry. Resort occupancy is comparable to the traditional revenue management calculation: total room nights occupied/total room nights available. In the timeshare industry, resort occupancy can be misleadingly high since it includes owned inventory. To remedy this, timeshare operators also monitor rental occupancy which is calculated as units rented/total units available for rent. It is not uncommon for a timeshare resort to have very high year round resort occupancy rates, but when considered on a daily, weekly, monthly, or seasonal basis, rental occupancies may be more in line with typical occupancies experienced by hotels and resorts.

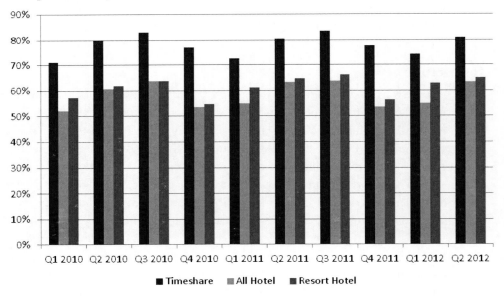

Figure 17.2: A comparison of occupancy levels in the United States. Source: Forecasting

Inventory allocation

Inventory managers at timeshare resorts, much like other lodging properties, must be able to forecast owner usage across the various options. Each owner usage option has its own implication for the inventory management team as well as the onsite operation team. Owners who choose to occupy or exchange directly impact room blocking and operations. Anticipating available rental inventory in advance allows the inventory management team to establish solid sales strategies. Finally, because the ultimate goal is to sell, rather than rent the timeshare resort inventory, some percentage of unowned inventory may be allocated to marketing in order to allow prospective buyers to experience the product before purchase.

Figure 17.3 depicts the typical usage of timeshare resort inventory on an annual basis. Because this is an annual view, the effects of seasonality are at play. Nonetheless, the comparison of timeshare resort occupancies of 79% annually to hotel resort occupancies of 60% annually is an impressive statistic for the time-share segment.

The largest percentage of inventory usage is attributed to owner occupancy. In fact, one could combine the 19% of exchange guest inventory with the 45% of owner/owner guest inventory and classify all of this as owner inventory if the management company was not interested in segmenting out owners of their particular timeshare resort. Vacant inventory can be the result of owners who are not current with their fees and therefore not eligible to occupy their inventory, and/or inventory that had no demand due to seasonality, or was out of service intentionally for maintenance or other purposes.

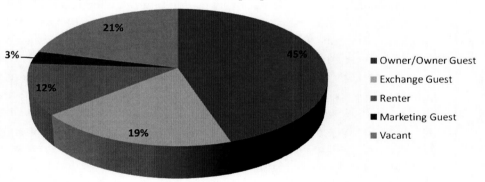

Figure 17.3: Timeshare ownership

Inventory variations

Because the product is owned by the individual buyer, it is important that they have access to, i.e., can occupy, what it is that they have purchased. For example, if the timeshare resort has undergone a rooms renovation and a portion of the units have been refurbished using funding from the homeowners' association, the returning owner will expect to be able to stay in a refurbished unit which may mean that rental inventory may be of lesser quality (if it is not refurbished) and therefore, it may not command a premium price in the market if the furnishings are outdated. Often, however, the size of the timeshare units in comparison to traditional hotel lodging commands a premium if for no other reason than because of the square footage and features of the condominium or villa style unit.

17

Timeshare management companies may attempt to allocate unfurbished inventory to those guests exchanging into the property, but this strategy may backfire as well. Exchange companies use guests comments from departure surveys to gauge the quality and service levels of resorts affiliated with their companies. Negative ratings due to unit quality may jeopardize the timeshare resort's quality rating and/or affiliation with the exchange company.

Inventory optimisation

Appropriate allocation of inventory according to customer segment is critical in achieving and/or maintaining owner/guest satisfaction ratings. In its simplest form, guest satisfaction is the result of the actual experience meeting or exceeding expectations. It has been suggested that higher guest satisfaction ratings may be associated with retention, referral and repeat purchase. Since the objective of the timeshare industry is to sell the inventory to individual consumers, it is imperative that inventory managers in the timeshare industry understand how the inventory is allocated across customer segments and where misalignments in value or satisfaction may occur.

Timeshare resorts that are actively selling timeshare interests are interested in reaching every guest staying on property in order to attempt to sell them more products. This guest contact is measured by a penetration rate – a calculation that considers the number of guests contacted divided by the total number of guests on property. Once contacted, a response rate is calculated. This is the number of guests who responded to the initial contact divided by all of the guests that were contacted. If the sales person then has an opportunity to make a sales presentation to the responding guest, this is calculated in the show rate – a calculation that considers the number of guests that showed up for a presentation divided by the total number that responded. After the presentation, if the guest decided to purchase, this is considered in the conversion rate – a calculation that considers the number of guests that purchased divided by the number of guests that showed up for a presentation. Finally, to determine the overall efficiency of the timeshare sales presentations over a period of time, the volume per guest (VPG) is calculated by dividing the total sales volume over a stated period of time by the total number of guests seen over that same period of time. Volume per guest (VPG) is calculated and monitored on various periods of time (morning/afternoon/daily/weekly/monthly/seasonally), at the individual level (customer segment, salesperson, sales manager), at the resort level, at the distribution channel level, and at the program level based on the product sold. Because the focus of timeshare developers and management companies is to get unsold inventory sold, VPG and the various positive and negative impacts to achieving high VPGs must be understood and focused on at all levels of the resort operations. The overall effective optimisation of inventory through informed inventory management should yield high guest satisfaction resulting in positive referrals and repurchases.

■ Timeshare terminology

Deeded ownership: a form of timeshare ownership that provides for ownership without end and is comparable to home ownership

Exchange companies: independent companies that coordinate the use of inventory among multiple timeshare resorts allowing an owner from one company to give their up their usage in their resort in exchange for the use of another owner's usage in another resort.

Maintenance fees: the annual dues that are paid by the timeshare owners to cover the regular operations and general upkeep of the timeshare resort and any other related programs or services, i.e., reservation call center.

Points-based: a popular ownership and/or usage form of timeshare that designated a point equivalent for timeshare weeks/days/unit types/locations/seasons. Rather than being confined to a single week/season/unit type or location, timeshare owners would receive an amount of points that could be used in varying increments for their timeshare vacations.

Rental occupancy: the result of dividing total units rented by total units available for rent. In timeshare resorts, rental occupancy is a subset of resort occupancy and is dictated by the number of units the management company has responsibility to rent as a result of the inventory being owned by the developer or relinquished by the owner for use by the management company.

Resort occupancy: the result of dividing total units occupied by total units available. In timeshare resorts, resort occupancy can be misleading since it presumes owners will occupy their units unless they have otherwise advised the management company of their intention to relinquish their use rights.

Right to use ownership: a timeshare ownership form that provides a purchaser the right to occupy a timeshare unit (or units or program) for a designated period of time. Disney Vacation Club sells a right to use form of ownership for a term of approximately 40 years because it is interested in retaining ownership of the real estate on and/or adjacent to its theme parks.

■ Summary

- The timeshare industry represents a fertile ground for the application of revenue management techniques in search for revenue maximization.
- Clear distinction needs to be made between resort occupancy (which has much in common with traditional revenue management calculations) and rental occupancy.

17

References

ARDA International Foundation. (2012a). *Analysis of the Global Shared Vacation Ownership Industry*. Washington, D.C.: Oxford Economics and The Research Intelligence Group.

ARDA International Foundation (2012b). *State of the Timeshare Industry*. Washington, D.C.: Ernst & Young.

Cross, R., Higbie, J. & Cross, D. (2009). Revenue management's renaissance: a rebirth of the art and science of profitable revenue generation. *Cornell Hospitality Quarterly,* **50**(1), 56-81.

Gregory, A. & Weinland, J. (2012). Applying the right marketing mix: improve HOA revenues and resort satisfaction. *Developments Magazine,* September, 60-62.

Kimes, S. (2009). Hotel revenue management in an economic downturn: results of an international study. *Cornell Hospitality Report,* **8**(14): Cornell University Center for Hospitality.

Timeshare Industry Resource Manual. (2010). Washington, DC: American Resort Development Association.

Conclusion

In a context of open markets, many service firms emerge and develop by integrating an approach based on revenue management. This innovative managerial method is aimed at optimizing revenue through two drivers: joint management of a fixed capacity and differential pricing of the firm in a dynamic framework. Considered nowadays as a strategic position, the expertise of the revenue manager is critical in leveraging maximum benefit from the optimization of revenue, the contribution of discriminant analysis, and the design of strategic and working recommendations. The function of revenue management is transversal and mobilises corporate players through educational and training systems. It is also based on tools and practices of revenue management in a context of customer relationship management.

This book has presented an overview of a range of firms and organisations that have adopted and adapted the foundations of revenue management to the specificities of their business sector. Numerous examples enable the reader to see revenue management as it is implemented today across the full spectrum of the hospitality and tourism industries.

Revenue Management is applied in many different sectors, and continues to grow both through a more dynamic and globalised approach (total revenue management) and an innovative adaptation to new sectors (culture, logistics). Current contributions are provided by academics and practitioners all with experience in the field of revenue management. This book gathers testimonies, stories and inventive ideas. It is intended for students and future practitioners interested in this innovative managerial approach.

Index